Implementing
Quality Assurance

Practical Laboratory Management Series

Implementing Quality Assurance

Paul Bozzo, MD, FCAP
Medical Director
Tucson Medical Center
Tucson, AZ

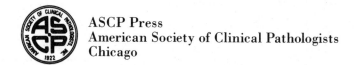

ASCP Press
American Society of Clinical Pathologists
Chicago

Acquisition & Development: Joshua Weikersheimer
Editor: Philip Rogers
Production Manager: Lisa Pollak
Production Coordinator: Jennifer Sabella

Printed on Recycled Paper ♻

Library of Congress Cataloging-in-Publication Data

Bozzo, Paul, 1938–
    Implementing quality assurance / Paul Bozzo.
        p.   cm.
    Includes bibliographical references and index.
    ISBN 0-89189-290-7
    1. Pathological laboratories — Quality control.   I. Title.
    RB36.3.Q34B69   1991
    616.07′5′0685 — dc20   90-42512
                                                                                     CIP

Printed in the United States of America.

95   94   93   92   5   4   3   2

This book is dedicated to my children, Andrea and John, and to all the personnel at both Tucson Medical Center Laboratory and TMCHE Laboratory without whose help this book would not have been possible.

Contents

Preface

Even today, with the "writing on the wall" so to speak, there remains resistance to quality assurance. Many laboratorians feel that it is complicated and difficult and merely represents paperwork designed to satisfy other groups, such as the Joint Commission on Accreditation of Healthcare Organizations, the College of American Pathologists (enforcing Clinical Laboratory Improvement Act of 1988), hospital administrators, third-party payers (ie, government, self-insured companies, and HMOs), the public, and the media. Despite these feelings, laboratorians should not forget that the patient is the ultimate customer.

Quality assurance need not be a tremendous burden; on the contrary, it can offer insights that will improve the performance of your laboratory. The resulting improvements are not just for the regulatory agency: "Quality is for I not only for they." The "I" in this case is the entire laboratory; the "they" is the customers, the third-party payers (including the government), and the media. Quality should involve everyone. We should remember that there is always room for the good to become the best.

Quality assurance is here to stay—we may not want it, we may resist it, but we will not get rid of it. Regulatory agencies will develop quality assurance guidelines without our input unless we have adequately documented programs. The current emphasis on quality assurance with multiple inspections by regulatory bodies forces us to deal with a rapid evolution of quality management: how do you argue against programs seeking improved patient care? On the other hand, quality is no stranger to the lab; the medical laboratory has always been involved with extensive quality control, including proficiency testing and strict quality control inspection. It has always been *good for business* when we are able to measure performance and improve our knowledge so that the information can be converted to improved performance. Development of standards and measurement are key features in all business plans that seek ongoing improvement. There is one caveat to bear in mind though: medicine does not deal with inanimate objects, such as automobiles or shoes, but with people. Thus, practicing medicine has never been totally objective; while it is a science and is therefore measurable in some degree, it is also an art.

Review any time management course and you will find that the imperatives will include the following: devise a plan, prioritize, then do it. Quality assurance is no different from time management. We must have a plan that includes periodic assessment, prioritization of problems, and effective follow-up action when indicated.

Not everyone recognizes the need for quality assurance in the laboratory. Historically it has not been an issue that laboratories have welcomed with open arms, and like quality assurance of other areas in the hospital, it was initially entered into superficially, a mere completing of paperwork to satisfy the regulatory agents. Since then laboratory quality management has evolved on a parallel course with hospital quality assurance programs.

Not only are government regulatory agencies demanding quality assurance but also consumers. However, consumers are forcing a different consideration, for although they want the best quality in medical care, a significant portion of their concern is related to cost. As the percent of the gross national product related to health care has increased over the last two decades from 6.8% to slightly under 11%, the consumer has become deeply concerned about paying for quality health care. The December 1988 issue of *Financier* magazine (published by the Bank Administration Institute) predicted that by the end of 1990 Americans will spend more on health care than they do on food—only housing will take more out of family budgets.[1] In 1988 the cost of medical care in the United States was $540 billion; in 1990 it escalated to $600 billion. Although inflation has a significant role in this increased health care spending, it is not the only large factor. Gibson and Mueller estimate that 52% of the increase can be attributed to inflation, but 48% can be attributed to increased utilization.[2] The Health Care Financing Administration has predicted that America will spend about 14% to 15% of its gross national product on health care in the year 2000.[3] It is estimated that approximately 20% of the nation's 1989 health care dollars was spent for diagnostic procedures, roughly half of which, according to some observers, may not have been indicated.[4] Whether we agree or disagree with this report, we cannot argue that there is no need for concern about cost-effectiveness. The consumer wants the best medical care at the lowest reasonable cost.

Because the consumer is concerned, the media have become concerned, and their even closer scrutiny should keep us concerned. Consumers, especially third-party payers and the government, are shaping the way laboratories will be compensated and controlled. They want documented proof of quality in health care. Lack of documentation of quality could prove costly in dealing not only with third-party payers but also with a society of litigious consumers who are heavily influenced by media reports, such as the following from Joseph Califano, Jr (Secretary of Health, Education, and Welfare from 1977 to 1979), in the *New York Times*[5]: "A former editor of the Journal of the American Medical Association is convinced that more than half of the 40 million medical tests performed each day 'do not really contribute to a patient's diagnosis or therapy.'" Appropriateness of testing was discussed at a College of American Pathologists meeting in March 1989, and it was agreed that some portion of the testing may be medically unnecessary. The United States spends 50% more than the next highest spending nation and triple what is spent in Britain, yet it does not buy us greater longevity.[5] Doesn't it behoove us to respond to our potential critics with real data that document quality of patient care?

> "To succeed in the competitive marketplace of the 1990s, hospital managers must understand as never before how their key constituents (customers) . . . physicians, patients and payers define quality and values in health care. They want to know how their institutions compare with the competition."[6]

Quality, in part then, will be defined as that level of care that meets or exceeds the customer's needs.

We must also be careful that this cost control is not carried to excess. Some recently published data suggest that cost-cutting could affect the hospital mortality rate in highly regulated competitive areas.[7] While the validity of this study is questionable, the issues it raises are sobering. High hospital mortality rates could reflect a sicker patient population, poor quality of care, or a preponderance of patients from nursing homes and hospices. Thus, we must be careful not to relate mortality or morbidity rates directly to cost savings measures in the hospital.[7]

We must not let the quality of care suffer, yet we must document for the consumer that we are mindful of both patient outcomes and cost. This is the challenge and opportunity of quality assurance. If we err and become more concerned with costs than quality, consumers may feel, quite reasonably, that their health has become a low-value commodity. Furthermore, poor quality care is ultimately expensive — an ounce of prevention is always less costly than a pound of cure — thus the need for precise, accurate studies on quality that may eventually be made available to the public is clear. Since cost containment is a real issue, it is just a matter of time before the media and the public will want to know the results of quality assurance evaluations.

The Joint Commission on Accreditation of Healthcare Organizations initiated the Agenda for Change pilot program in 1988. It hopes to eventually establish a national database for self-monitoring. The laboratory appears to be a low-priority base in this scheme because it is not even listed in the first pilot program.[8]

We must ride this horse in the direction it's going. The demand is for effective quality assurance, not merely paperwork. We must avoid having the frenetic and increasingly expensive paper and computer chase keep us from doing our job, yet *we must have effective programs that show improvement, that relate to the quality of patient care, and that deal with cost containment.* It will not happen automatically.

It requires planning and execution. It requires measurement. We will only show real improvement if we select relevant problem areas and resolve them.

Programs dealing with cost containment are going to focus on the behavior of the physician. They will need to incorporate education, computer and personal feedback, peer pressure, and other innovative methods. Occasional or one-time attendance seminars are not going to answer the need for ongoing programs, because when the educative programs are withdrawn, performance frequently returns to the preeducation level.

I have 11 years of background in hospital quality assurance, 4 of those as chairman of a hospital-wide quality assurance program. My conclusions come largely from first-hand experience and observations drawn from within the hospital and, more specifically, the laboratories at the Tucson Medical Center and TMCHE (a private commercial laboratory) rather than from books. As a College of American Pathologists laboratory inspector, I have found that laboratory personnel sometimes operate without a prepared plan and without a goal; they try to fulfill regulatory requirements with only the vaguest sense of direction. Quality assurance plans must be thought through and *written* with your institution in mind. Review the mission statement of your institution. The statement's goals should dovetail with your overall goals for quality assurance. If you take the time to prepare a well-written plan, it will guide you toward continual improved quality in your laboratory. With that in mind I have written this book.

REFERENCES

1. *Arizona Daily Star*. June 25, 1989:1.
2. Gibson R, Mueller M. National health expenditures: fiscal year 1976. *Soc Secur Bull*. 1977;40:3–22.
3. *American Medical News*. January 12, 1990:25.
4. Tune L. Insurers seek savings on testing. *Clin Chem News*. 1989;15:1.
5. *Arizona Daily Star*. April 16, 1989:1.
6. *Health Week Hospitals Outlook*. July 31, 1989:40.
7. Sager M, Easterling DV, Kindig DA, Anderson OW. Changes in the location of death after passage of Medicare's prospective payment system. *N Engl J Med*. 1989;320:433–439.
8. Sisk FA. Trends in regulation and reimbursement. *MLO*. 1989;21:49–55.

Acknowledgements

A special vote of thanks goes to Joshua Weikersheimer, Director, ASCP Press, without whose encouragement this book would not have been written. I also thank Philip Rogers whose careful editing made many contributions.

Additional special thanks go to my fellow pathologists, Richard Armstrong, Ronald Sparks, David Goldman, Ralph Rohr, and Robert Ramsey, who continually contributed through our many discussions on quality assurance. Carl Lo, who was the Quality Assurance Chairperson of the Laboratory at Tucson Medical Center, Nancy Martin, Quality Assurance Coordinator at Tucson Medical Center, Kathy Mercer, and Art Palmer also gave me helpful suggestions. Arlene Hilberg reviewed the chapter on computer analysis as did Jim Pebbles, president, MIDS Inc, Tucson, AZ, and Dr Noel Lawson, Department of Pathology, St John's Hospital, Detroit, MI. Dr Henry Travers, Physician's Laboratory, Sioux Falls, SD, kindly reviewed the chapter on anatomic pathology and made several useful suggestions. Pat Scully, Esq, and Jeffrey Minker, Esq, were helpful in reviewing the chapter on risk management. Fred Bayer also reviewed several chapters, made suggestions, and provided references. Gail Straka provided the criteria for phlebotomy observation. Joni Condit made several suggestions for the chapter on commercial laboratories. Key individuals in the development of the questionnaire for commercial laboratories included Jane Miller, Carla Kregel, and Joy LaCombe.

Special thanks is also due to all those who have taken the courses I have given on quality assurance and unknowingly made contributions to the book through their comments. Some of the insight I have gained has been in my role as CAP inspector, and I am grateful to all the personnel at the hospitals I have reviewed.

And finally, thanks for secretarial help in typing the book goes to Heather Surplus, Laurel Thorpe and Teresa Annett, but a special vote of thanks goes to Doreen Hagerman who not only typed the major portion of the book but also fine-tuned many areas for me, including communicating with the editors and last-minute typing at inconvenient times.

Introduction

THE DEFINITION OF QUALITY ASSURANCE

The Joint Commission on Accreditation of Healthcare Organizations (JCAHO) requires that clinical laboratories participate in hospital-wide quality assurance programs to monitor and evaluate the appropriateness of medical laboratory
services in order to correct problems and to recognize clinical situations that require improvement.[1] Quality assurance
is best defined as a problem-finding, problem-solving activity.

The meaning of *quality* is dynamic and changes as
knowledge, values, and resources change. In general,
professional societies set their standards of quality based
on consumer needs and demands and the capabilities of
the provider, which may be limited by knowledge and
resources such as manpower or equipment. If quality is
defined as meeting or exceeding consumer needs, then we
must be aware of the standards by which the consumer
defines those needs.

Most people have a sense of what quality is. In a
restaurant it is attentive service and good food in a
pleasant environment. In a car it is appearance, performance, and a good service record. Quality in the laboratory could be defined as accurate test results and acceptable service, for example, quick turnaround times for tests
and effective communication of results. However, *the
standards by which we judge quality for the medical
profession are, for the most part, not readily available.*
Some articles have outlined standards for specific areas of
medicine and sometimes local standards are developed,
but there are no real national standards.[2,3]

Quality is effective health care for the individual but
should be differentiated from the *efficiency* of medical

care; quality is concerned with outcome and efficiency is related to process. But despite their separate meanings, they are related: the process affects the outcome. William G. Anderson, DO, trustee of the American Osteopathic Association, said:

> "Employers define quality in terms of value obtained for their health care dollars. For the patients, quality means . . . feeling better. To hospitals, quality is achieved when the patient goes home . . . before he exceeds the D.R.G. (diagnosis related group) limit."[4]

The challenge today is to contain costs without lowering the quality of care.[5]

Quality, according to *Webster's*,[6] is a peculiar and essential character; it is further defined as a degree of excellence, which implies superiority and that there is a preference or standard being set against which good, better, or excellent can be measured. Steffen[5] defines quality as the capacity to achieve a goal, which is even a more vague definition because both capacity and goals then need to be defined.

Quality assurance guidelines cannot be set in stone because each situation is unique. For example, turnaround times for tests are a reflection of equipment speed, the capability of the laboratory information system, the distance a phlebotomist must go to draw blood from a patient, the availability of the patient, and the amount of manpower available. Thus, it makes sense to set local and regional standards for quality assurance that are in line with the laboratory's abilities.

The goals of laboratory quality assurance should be the same as hospital-wide quality assurance. A 1986 report from the hosue of delegates of the American Medical Association (AMA) emphasized eight elements regarding quality care.[7] Quality care should:

1. Produce optimal improvement in patient health.
2. Emphasize health promotion and disease prevention.
3. Provide care in a timely manner.
4. Include informed consent.
5. Base care on accepted medical principles.
6. Provide care with empathy.
7. Use technology efficiently.
8. Document care to allow peer review.[8]

From this list it is obvious that a significant part of quality assurance is the setting of standards related to these elements. It is also apparent that laboratory quality assurance is part of hospital-wide quality assurance and should take its cues from the same source. The emphasis should be on translating the quality assurance program's findings into improved patient care. We need to look at process and outcome and relate them to laboratory-related services. Outcome includes improved health as reflected by fewer complications, shorter length of hospital stay, lower morbidity and mortality, more patient satisfaction, fewer follow-up office visits, and a quicker return to the patient's previous functional capacity. Any process that improves accuracy or service will contribute to all of the above.

Ideally, quality in the laboratory will contribute to the quality of care, which will contribute to the quality of life.

The best results can be achieved only in an environment that strides for perfection without creating so much tension that it interferes with performance. That tension may be related to overemphasis on the individual rather than the process. No matter how defined, once quality standards are instituted solutions to problems should study the process before the individual.

The task before us is not only to define *quality* but also to define the *scope* of a program necessary to maintain a level of excellence that exceeds the terms of these definitions. Rome was not built in a day; likewise, a quality assurance program cannot measure everything at once but must prioritize and focus on potential or perceived problems. Quality assurance leads to improvements that will invoke greater confidence in patients that their needs are being met. Follow-up studies will document that the action taken as a result of the quality assurance program was effective and improved patient care. If your quality assurance program finds no problems you do not necessarily have a great laboratory; however, you will find problems if you have a great quality assurance program.

An effective quality assurance program in the view of the regulatory bodies and the public at large, as well as in the view of the medical community, means documentation of improvement in the quality of care. Audits are a good method for documentation. A perceived improvement without documentation is not acceptable quality assurance. We will examine the requirements of the JCAHO in more detail, but we must be aware that the emphasis is on *an appropriate, comprehensive, hospital-wide program.* Thus, all the services in the laboratory must contribute to quality assurance; and many of the quality assurance indicators involve disciplines outside of the laboratory, requiring multidisciplinary quality assurance studies. For example, many service issues involve the nursing unit, thus fitting into the category of multidisciplinary or interdepartmental monitors. It is not necessary for every section to be always working on a quality assurance study, but rather each laboratory section should conduct a study at least once a year.

The appropriateness of testing will be addressed in Chapter 7, but suffice it to say that quality assurance will not only ask "Was the test necessary?" but also "Were there an adequate number of tests ordered, and were the results appropriately used?" Within the hospital's overall quality assurance program, the director of the medical laboratory assures that the department participates in the monitoring and evaluation of the quality and the appropriateness of services provided.[1] We should not limit our programs to technical quality assurance but should also consider equally important and valid issues such as "Was there a caring attitude?" and "Was the patient treated with dignity?"

There is no general consensus of what a definition for *quality patient care* or for *quality* would be without using vague terms such as "excellence" or "effectiveness." There is also no consensus of the scope of a comprehensive quality assurance program. Both issues will be addressed in more depth.

Knowing that quality will vary from institution to institution provided the following definition: *quality is a level of excellence that will contribute to the care of a patient within the abilities of an organization.* The degree of quality is a measure of the balance of risks and benefits in patient care.[9]

THE HISTORY OF QUALITY ASSURANCE

1910: The Flexner report on the quality of medical schools is published.

1913: The American College of Surgeons forms an accrediting organization for medical education.

1952: The Joint Commission on Accreditation of Hospitals is organized by the American College of Physicians, the American Hospital Association, the AMA, the Canadian Medical Association, and the American College of Surgeons. The Canadian Medical Association withdrew in 1959. The American Dental Association joined in 1980. There are now 21 members of the board of the JCAHO from the above groups and 3 consumer advocates.[10] (Note: The JCAHO has no direct sanctioning authority but indirectly, because of its prestige, affects the remuneration from organizations such as Medicare.)

1966: The Darling case—hospitals and medical staff are held responsible for the quality of care. Medicare and utilization review mechanisms, such as tissue committee and medical records review, have their roots in this era.

1967: Congress passes the Clinical Laboratories Improvement Act. This act mandates the equivalency for the College of American Pathologists (CAP) inspection and accreditation program.[11]

1972: Professional Standards Review Organization. Services for payment under the Social Security Act review standards for health care in the form of audits. The JCAHO publishes its manual on accreditation.

1979: The Standard for JCAHO states that "There should be evidence with a well-defined organized program designed to enhance patient care through ongoing objective assessment of important aspects of patient care and the correction of identified problems." The JCAHO drops its numerical requirements and asks hospitals to establish an effective quality assurance program, with the ultimate goal of improving the quality of health care. (A specific number of audit studies are to be completed each year based on the number of hospital beds in that institution.) An effective program adequately measures quality of performance and takes corrective action when necessary, so even though the numerical requirements are dropped they are incorporated into the definition of "adequate."

1981: The JCAHO shifts emphasis from measurement and assessment techniques to organizational behavior and relationship between cost and quality. Quality assurance could induce changes in health care trends. Implied is that quality care results in cost reduction.

1982: The JCAHO revises the Standard, emphasizing an ongoing and systematic program for evaluating patient care.

1990:   The JCAHO expects hospitals to demonstrate improvement in deficient areas through a clinical outcome assessment program.

Thus, to summarize the evolvement of quality assurance, we have the following list:

1. Do studies.
2. Do x number of studies.
3. Emphasis should be on criteria matching the objective and on follow-up action.
4. Numerical requirements for audits were dropped and the requirement was added that hospitals establish *effective* programs in quality assurance.
5. Emphasis should be on improved patient care through clinical outcome assessment.

THE FUTURE OF QUALITY ASSURANCE

The phase of quality assurance during which the motivator is the regulatory agencies is now; however, in the next phase the driving force will indirectly be the payers (insurance companies, self-insured corporations, government, and self-payers). More directly, the driving force will be competition between organizations, resulting in a need for self-regulation as opposed to governmental restrictions. In this competitive environment, organizations will have to show consumers that they are receiving a quality product.

THE FOUNDATION FOR QUALITY ASSURANCE

The following are key to quality assurance:

1. The establishment of goals. For example:
   a) Improve patient care.
   b) Provide excellent service to the consumer in a competitive atmosphere.
   c) Pass the inspections of regulatory agents.
2. The design of quality indicators related to potential or perceived problems.
3. The evaluation of study results to decide if objectives are being achieved.
4. The proposal for action to achieve these goals if they are not being achieved, including a date of reassessment.

The emphasis is on finding and defining problems with effective follow-up action.

COST-EFFECTIVENESS

Poor quality is expensive: consider the cost of repeated testing, unnecessary testing, and potential litigation. Basically, cost-effectiveness is getting "the most bang for your buck," that is, providing quality care without spending an excess of money. Cost-effectiveness, however, is not synonymous with cost reduction when it results in lower quality care. In the same vein, increased costs with no change in quality of care is also not cost-effective.

It would be a mistake to expect every laboratory quality assurance study to show where costs can be reduced. Furthermore, the cost savings for the patient are in decreased length of stay, the prescription of fewer drugs, the administration of fewer diagnostic tests, and decreased morbidity, none of which may be reflected in the laboratory budget. Most often laboratory cost-effectiveness involves the appropriateness of testing and the efficiency of the services. Are the tests done in-house done as inexpensively and with the same quality as when they are sent to a reference laboratory? If not, is it necessary to do these tests in-house because of turnaround time? Is the turnaround time for work sent to reference laboratories delaying patient results to such an extent that it adversely affects patient care? A periodic review of tests available in-house as well as outside would be a worthwhile quality assurance effort.

How much time and effort are we spending on quality assurance? Is it excessive or not? Quality assurance is effective if you find and resolve problems, resulting in improved laboratory service, which affects patient care. Whether your quality assurance program is cost-effective is difficult to judge, except, perhaps, in comparison with other similar institutions. This book should make the time you spend on laboratory quality assurance more efficient.

QUALITY CONTROL

Quality control is an integral component of quality assurance and is the aggregate of processes and techniques devised to detect, reduce, and correct deficiencies in an analytical process. Quality control strives for accuracy. If we describe accuracy as the inherent quality of the information being provided, then the definition also includes proper and timely collection of the specimen and distribution of the resulting information. This definition of accuracy is more valid and is included under the more universal term quality assurance.[12]

While quality control is essential to good patient care, how it relates to the accuracy of the testing process is not emphasized in this book; however, there is one facet that should be looked at because of its cost-effectiveness. The question is rightfully asked, "Are control ranges excessive?" One should not only ask if they are too broad, which is a common complaint with quality control parameters, but also if they are more narrow than clinical application would demand. If they are too narrow, would a broader range of standard deviations for controls mean less duplication of controls and be more cost-efficient? Since I started examining proficiency testing and quality control in the early 1960s, the range of acceptable results has narrowed and is now sometimes more strict than clinically necessary. A quality assurance plan should consider the relationship between quality control and cost in designing procedures to meet patient needs. It should include an effective interlaboratory program of proficiency testing aimed at minimizing the bias of the analytic process.[13]

CONSUMER ROLE

A consumer, according to *Webster's*,[6] is one who uses. Consumers of laboratory services include physicians and nurses, as well as other hospital staff, the self-payer, self-insured companies, large insurance companies, the government, and, most significantly, the patient. Given the competitive atmosphere of hospitals, we must be aware of the important role of the consumers.

"Health care providers took longer to crack in the face of consumerism because health care is harder for the consumer to understand," claims George Lundberg, MD. "Also the motivation to critique is less strong because taking care of the sick is good—who wants to challenge that?"[14] Large companies that are self-insured are now looking at quality issues in the hospitals they are paying. They are discovering geographical differences in incidence of diagnoses such as low back pain and the frequency of procedures such as hysterectomies. They are also finding significant variations in charges from institutions. They are aware that complications result in more costly bills, thus they are interested in mortality and morbidity. Prudential recently decided to pay for heart transplants at only 13 hospitals in the United States because they had the lowest frequency of complications.

Consumers are interested in quality issues because they know that poor quality care increases costs. They are willing to pay for medical care, but they sometimes question the necessity of procedures, such as diagnostic testing. We know that there is a difference in the number of laboratory tests performed at different hospitals. Volunteer Hospital Association studies showed significant differences in the number of tests performed for similar cases at multiple hospitals of the same size and type, for example, nonteaching vs teaching hospitals. If these data are available, how long before it will be used by the consumer in health care-related decisions?

A good quality assurance model will identify problems, assess them, and solve them. The solution must include communication of results to involved parties. Programs that identify relevant quality assurance issues and mechanisms to monitor, evaluate, resolve, and document these issues in a manner that is understandable to the consumer are needed. When problems are found, the changes sought should be achievable and result in improvement that can relate directly to patient care. The public should be aware that we are striving to give the highest quality care.

Summary

Quality is a common theme for businesses. Quality assurance has had success in businesses such as IBM and Toyota for a long time. Tom Peters defines 12 objectives of revolution in his book *Thriving on Chaos*[15] that could apply to quality assurance in the medical field. The comments in parentheses are mine.

1. Management is obsessed with quality (administrative support).
2. There is a guiding system or ideology (quality assurance plan).
3. Quality is measured (you cannot assume, you must measure).
4. Quality is rewarded (tied in with support from top management).
5. Everyone is trained in technology for assessing quality (everyone in the laboratory should be involved in quality assurance and understand it).

6. Teams involved in multiple functions/systems are used (multidisciplinary audits).
7. Small is very beautiful (every section should be able to operate independently as well as have the ability to integrate).
8. There is constant stimulation (you need a champion for quality assurance).
9. There is parallel organization structure devoted to quality improvement (the hospital quality assurance committee).
10. Everyone plays: suppliers play for the distributors and customers participate in the organization's quality process (similar to No. 5).
11. When quality goes up, costs go down (agree).
12. Quality improvements is a never-ending journey (agree, agree).

You cannot overemphasize that quality assurance is everyone's job, is ongoing, and contributes to the success of the institution involved. A word of caution, however: I am not encouraging quality assurance to be out of proportion to patient care. Quality assurance must be implemented in such a way that the paperwork is not overwhelming and its implementation does not merely result in resentment among the laboratory staff. Quality assurance must be well accepted or we will not achieve our goal of improved patient care.

REFERENCES

1. *Accreditation Manual for Hospitals, 1988*. Chicago, Ill: Joint Commission on Accreditation of Hospitals: 1987:172.
2. Hilborne LH, Oye RK, McArdle JE, Repinski JA, Rodgerson DO. Evaluation of STAT and routine turnaround times as a component of laboratory quality. *Am J Clin Pathol*. 1989;91:331–335.
3. Siegel DL, Edelstein PH, Nachamkin I. Inappropriate testing for diarrheal disease in the hospital. *JAMA*. 1990;263:979–982.
4. *American Medical News*. December 12, 1986:24.
5. Steffen GE. Quality medical care. *JAMA*. 1988;260:56–61.
6. *Webster's New Collegiate Dictionary*. Springfield, Mass: G&C Merriam Inc; 1976.
7. Council on Medical Service. Quality of care. *JAMA*. 1986;256:1032–1034.
8. Rutstein, DD, Berenberg W, Chalmers TC, Child CG, Fishman AP, Perrin BP. Measuring the quality of medical care. *N Engl J Med*. 1976;294:582–583.
9. Donabedian A. Exploration in quality assessment and monitoring. In: *The Definition of Quality and Approaches to Its Assessment*. Ann Arbor, Mich: Health Administrative Press; 1980;1:5.
10. Couch JB. The Joint Commission on Accreditation of Healthcare Organizations. In: Goldfield N, Nash D, eds. *Providing Quality Care: The Challenge to Physicians*. Philadelphia, Pa: The American College of Physicians; 1989:201–224.

11. Dorsey DB. Evolving concept of quality in laboratory practice. *Arch Pathol Lab Med*. 1989;113:1329–1334.

12. Zweig MH. Evaluation of clinical accuracy of laboratory tests. *Arch Pathol Lab Med*. 1988;112:383–386.

13. deVerdier CH, Haabrekke O, Leskinen E, Uldall A. Quality assurance in clinical chemistry: time to go from theory into action. *Scand J Clin Lab Invest*. 1986;46:393–396.

14. Freedman E. What's eroding the hospitals? *Hospitals*. 1985;59:76–80.

15. Peters T. *Thriving on Chaos*. New York, NY: Harper & Row Publishers Inc; 1987:85–100.

1. The Medical Director's Role in Quality Assurance

CLEARLY, THE MEDICAL director is responsible for developing and implementing a quality assurance program that covers all services that provide laboratory data. The medical director or an associate pathologist should be closely tied to the part of the program that determines the appropriateness of testing, since this part involves establishing guidelines using a consensus of physician opinion and (sometimes) managing physician behavior patterns. The medical director must also ensure that the quality assurance program is problem oriented, with evidence that any corrective action taken is effective. In addition, the medical director should ensure that corrective action involving an individual is educative not disciplinary (except as a last resort). Finally, unless the medical director can afford to devote a good deal of time to quality assurance, responsibilities should be delegated to other personnel, which in turn helps educate additional individuals in the quality assurance process.

MONITOR ACTIVITY CALENDAR

Once a year the medical director, the quality assurance chairperson (see Chapter 2), and the laboratory manager should meet with the supervisor and any pathologist assigned responsibility for a section. Their discussion should focus on known problems or they should attempt to unearth other problems. If there appear to be no problems, then they should consider discussing service issues, such as frequency of testing and turnaround time for test results. *Any focus on user satisfaction activities will tend to generate an issue for a quality assurance study.* To find issues for a quality assurance program, sometimes they only need to

1

talk to the primary users, who include physicians and anyone in the nursing service, on a one-on-one basis. Such a conversation should start off on a positive note; for example, "How is the laboratory doing? We are trying to fine-tune our operation." The conversation should avoid beginning with "Are there problems with the laboratory service?"

Questions to be asked about monitor activities:

1. Do these monitors focus on problem areas?
2. Are there any complaints or incident reports related to your section?
3. Are the studies fairly simple, that is, do they pick out a single focus and deal with a reasonable number of simple objectives?
4. Are the studies dealing with high-volume tests?
5. If the studies involve other departments, do you invite them to participate, resulting in a multidisciplinary, hospital-wide, quality assurance activity?

In addition, previous quality assurance studies should be reviewed to make sure that all loops have been closed. A copy of the summary reports and monitor activity calendars from the past 2 years should be available for these sessions. See Chapter 3 on quality assurance plans for an illustration of a summary report.

The section supervisor and, when applicable, the pathologist assigned to that section may want to meet with the quality assurance chairperson to focus in on problems prior to meeting with the medical director. The medical director should make sure that all pathologists assigned to a section that is the focus of a quality assurance study are involved and present for any review sessions. Several quality assurance topics should be addressed each quarter in the laboratory, although they need not apply to each section.

When choosing a topic for a quality assurance study, make sure the topic is significant to improved patient care. What if all the quality indicators show no problems? **Continued monitoring of activities that finds no problems is merely a whitewash.** An ongoing study that finds no problems should be discontinued unless periodic or continual monitoring of an area improves the quality of operations; for example, monitoring the phlebotomist's accuracy in identifying patients or the turnaround time of key tests in the intensive care area.

The following are areas of concern for the medical director of a laboratory:

1. Criteria for study of quality indicators: Development of criteria may require review of the literature. Frequently, development requires the input of clinicians, especially in the area of appropriateness of testing, since you want the criteria to be reached by consensus.
2. Communication: See Figure 1.1.

In addition, newsletters and general physician staff meetings may sometimes be appropriate for presentation of quality assurance studies.

The medical director should be responsible for effective communication during all phases of quality assurance. Solutions to problems in the laboratory should have a strong emphasis on communication, not only from management to staff but vice versa. Communication should be frequent, continuing throughout problem identification, the study itself, the summary of data, follow-up action,

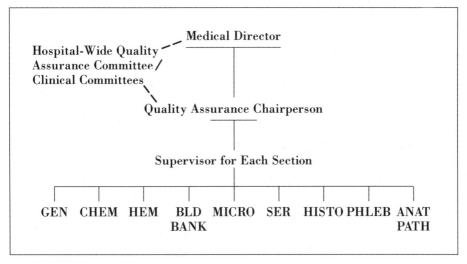

Figure 1.1   The general flow of information.

and repeated studies. In particular, communication is an important part of the follow-up action.

As demonstrated in Figure 1.1 the quality assurance chairperson's role is delegated by the medical director. The most important part of this scheme is effective communication to the contact person (generally the supervisor) in each section. The medical director should be confident that there has been effective communication to all people involved in the studies. If the medical director does not emphasize communication, it often becomes the weak link in the quality assurance process.

PERIODIC REVIEW

The medical director's review should verify that monitoring activity covers existing or potential problems, that criteria used for evaluating the monitor are valid, and that a completion date is established.

A periodic review of completed studies and progress of the monitor activities calendar should occur quarterly or semiannually. A periodic review could be the needed stimulus to complete the work. A deadline is frequently not met without the prodding of some sort of follow-up review to assure that the studies are being completed.

Questions the medical director should specifically ask about quality assurance studies include the following:

1. Should the studies be ongoing?
2. Were changes made as a result of the studies effective? If follow-up action was taken outside the laboratory, how do we confirm that it was effective?
3. Were the results of the studies shared with all involved departments and sections?

4. If there were educational efforts, did all involved personnel participate?

As was said earlier, all pathologists should be involved with the appropriateness of testing, which they should be prepared to discuss (along with other problems in the laboratory) with other groups connected with the quality assurance study, such as medical chart review committees. Participation should be encouraged by the medical director and clearly outlined in the quality assurance plan.

At these review meetings keep in mind some of the concerns of the JCAHO. I would include the following:

1. In-service education for laboratory personnel
2. Monitoring of laboratory requests
3. Receipt of test results ordered on a stat basis
4. Monitoring of data—are you looking at the results before they go out of the laboratory?
5. Turnaround time
6. Continuing education tied into the laboratory quality assurance program

TIMING

A quality assurance study is more significant when it uses recent and current data, for example, a study of response to therapeutic drug levels should focus on recent patients because the results more closely reflect current trends in the laboratory. If questions are asked about patient treatment a year ago, it is likely that no one will remember individual patients and that the approach to therapeutic drug levels has changed during that time. Once the study has been initiated, it should be completed in a short period of time.

SUMMARY

The following are published guidelines from the Council on Medical Service.[1] In summary form they represent elements the medical director should be acutely aware of when reviewing quality assurance activities. Pertinent CAP and JCAHO standards are listed in the appendix; these standards represent the minimum requirements against which laboratories are evaluated.

1. The general policies and processes to be utilized in any quality assurance activity should be developed and concurred with by the professionals whose performance will be scrutinized, and should be objectively and impartially administered.
2. Any remedial quality assurance activity related to an individual practitioner should be triggered by concern for that individual's overall practice patterns, rather than by deviation from specified criteria in single cases.
3. The institution of any remedial activity should be preceded by discussion with the practitioner involved.

4. Emphasis should be placed on education and modification of unacceptable practice patterns rather than on sanctions.
5. The quality assurance system should make available the appropriate educational resources needed to effect desired practice modifications.
6. Feedback mechanisms should be established to monitor and document needed changes in practice patterns.
7. Restrictions or disciplinary actions should be imposed on those practitioners not responsive to remedial activities whenever the appropriate professional peers deem such action necessary to protect the public.
8. The imposition of restrictions or discipline should be timely and consistent with due process.
9. Quality assurance systems should be structured and carried out in a manner that ensures immunity for practitioners applying such systems, so long as they act in good faith.
10. To the degree possible, quality assurance systems should be structured to recognize high-quality practice, as well as correct deficiencies.

REFERENCE

1. Council on Medical Service. Guidelines for quality assurance. *JAMA*. 1988; 259:2572-2573.

2. The Quality Assurance Chairperson's Role

A GOOD QUALITY ASSURANCE program contributes to the quality of the laboratory. Thus, it seems reasonable to designate a quality assurance chairperson who will allot a portion of time to management of quality. Ideally, the position should not merely be an additional responsibility for someone who already has too much work, although this "ideal" may only be possible in a larger laboratory. Obviously, if the laboratory has a small number of personnel it is difficult to assign separate time for this position; nonetheless, the position should be assigned where possible, and if it becomes extra work it must be rewarded appropriately. Whatever the organizational structure, someone has to assume responsibility for quality assurance.

Having an excellent quality assurance chairperson can be the key to a successful program. The chairperson may have varying levels of responsibilities depending on the division of labor with the medical director, but the two positions should share responsibility for the direction, design, and completion of the program. The laboratory manager may also share some of the same responsibilities.

The quality assurance chairperson needs to be the champion, the prime mover of your program. After all, laboratory personnel do not usually knock down walls in a rush to implement quality assurance. You need someone with a positive attitude and high energy who can convince the entire laboratory staff that quality assurance is not only necessary but also worthwhile.

Leadership styles are different and should be flexible. A consensus mode is excellent for setting criteria for the quality assurance monitor; however, an autocratic mode may be necessary at times to assure that follow-up action corrects any deficiencies. Persistence and tactfulness are leadership skills necessary to fulfill this role. The quality assurance chairperson must also be respected by staff as well as be administratively supported.

The role of the quality assurance chairperson is to *handle specifics* of the program design, namely, the who, what, when, where, and how regarding the studies (see Chapter 4). The chairperson is also involved in the implementation and review of the quality assurance plan. To *implement* the program, the quality assurance chairperson needs to make sure that quality assurance studies are ongoing and valid (the bottom line for a *valid* quality assurance study will always be improved patient care). The *design of individual audits* is also a responsibility of the chairperson. Additionally, a significant part of the quality assurance chairperson's responsibility is to make sure that educational efforts are ongoing and that some continuing education efforts in the laboratory appear to be directed by the results of quality assurance studies.

The quality assurance chairperson will preferably have a background in quality assurance, but could profit from books, journals, meetings, and participation in the overall hospital quality assurance program. A person with more than a passing interest in the job is necessary for the program's success.

The quality assurance chairperson maintains documentation for the quality assurance study, including the summary files, and is responsible, along with personnel in the study's area of focus, for the follow-through on *corrective action*. A tickler file with the dates for corrective action should be maintained. The tickler file should be easily identifiable in the summary files, as well as in the monitor activity calendar, and should be discussed at the periodic reviews organized by the medical director. The chairperson communicates with other departments on multidisciplinary studies and is responsible for sending the studies through committees and assuring that satisfactory communication of results occurs. Any official communication such as newsletters or committee presentations should be dated and recorded in the summary files. It is the responsibility of the medical director to conduct a periodic evaluation of the annual quality assurance plan, ensuring that monitors are being completed as scheduled; however, it can be a shared responsibility. Thus, we see there is a significant role for the quality assurance chairperson. A hospital laboratory with an outstanding quality assurance chairperson will have an outstanding program.

A statement of support for this position from the chief executive officer is often a good start to a quality assurance program. Because the position should not just be an add-on to an existing job, there should be real compensation for its performance, though not necessarily monetary. Instead, gratification could come from the added status of having a leadership role in the laboratory and hospital, the enhancement to a resume (the job should be a titled position), and a closer working relationship with the medical director. The chairperson should receive ample praise from both the medical director and administrative figures.

It is best to have one person serve as quality assurance chairperson for a sustained period, say, 4 years. This is a job that could easily cause "burnout," so during the last part of the time allotment, the succeeding chairperson should begin to work closely with the present chairperson to learn the position and ease the transition. Having another person closely involved with the position creates additional support for and understanding of quality assurance in the laboratory. Once again, having a capable, energetic person who is excited about the position and communicates that excitement, or better yet, exudes it, as opposed to one who is not genuinely interested in this position, can really make a quality assurance program work well, which will contribute to quality in your laboratory.

3. Quality Assurance Plan

UALITY ASSURANCE PLANS help to focus quality assurance
activities and aid in evaluation of organizational guide-
lines. Review the mission statement of the hospital and the
goals of the hospital-wide quality assurance plan. These
should be parallel to the goals of the laboratory quality
assurance plan. You need a plan that will identify quality
assurance issues, along with the mechanisms and people
necessary to evaluate and report these issues.

Features of a quality assurance plan vary for each
laboratory, but certain central parameters should be identical. The general features of a plan include goals, objectives, sources of authority, definition of scope of services,
selection of topics, a monitoring activity calendar, corrective action, periodic evaluation, and methods of communication (which should be a detailed part of every quality
assurance plan). I recommend including in your plan both
the minutes of goal-setting meetings and the official
minutes of quarterly or semiannual reviews of these goals.
I also recommend placing the quality assurance plan in a
notebook or files (a notebook is more convenient for regulatory agency inspections) followed by audit summary outlines, and followed by the more detailed data from each
study (detailed data from large laboratories may be bulky
and could be kept separate). (Continuing education devoted to quality assurance could also be documented in
this notebook.) The medical director should initial these
summary outlines as they are presented. Inspectors will
look over the plan, browse through the summary outlines,
and ask for selected details, but it is not realistic to think
that they will examine every study in detail. Nonetheless,
the actual data must be easily available on request.

THE PARTS OF A QUALITY ASSURANCE PLAN: WHO, WHAT, WHEN, WHERE, AND HOW

The authority and direction for quality assurance in a hospital derive ultimately from the board of trustees to whom results of all efforts are communicated. The medical director is responsible for the program, working closely with a quality assurance chairperson, the laboratory manager, and the department supervisors. All important positions of authority should be specifically identified in your plan by name. The ultimate authority in a private enterprise (independent laboratory) varies, but generally it is whoever assumes financial responsibility.

Goals and Objectives

The *goal* of laboratory quality assurance is to verify that the quality of services contributes to the overall delivery of excellent medical care. This goal should meet the needs of the laboratory's customers, who include not only the personnel taking care of the patients and individual patients, but also self-insured organizations, insurance companies, HMOs, the government, and the media. Goals tend not to change or change minimally from year to year.

Given the explicit goal of excellence in medical care, each laboratory should look at all aspects of care from the ordering of tests to the use of test results, which will include but not be limited to the appropriateness of testing, accuracy of specimen collection and testing, timeliness of response to the results, and appropriateness of response to results. These can be listed as part of your *overall objective* for the laboratory. Related to the appropriateness of testing and underlying all these studies is cost-effectiveness (which implies no adverse effects on the quality of patient care). All of these objectives should be flexible so they can be in line with the mission of the institution and reflect changes in the regulatory guidelines.

Problem identification, problem correction, and verification of follow-up action resulting in improved patient care are the *primary objectives*. These objectives, when focused, are unique to the institution and can be listed as part of the monitoring and evaluation schedule. Study topics should be selected and given priority according to potential impact on patient care (see Chapter 8). The key to a good quality assurance program is a strong focus on high-frequency problems, which can be achieved by listening to the needs and complaints of your customers: patients, physicians, and staff on the units. Viewed in this light, quality assurance can improve your laboratory's service rather than hinder it.

Goals are universal and should rarely change. Objectives, on the other hand, are more specific, should be reviewed annually, and will change often. Generally, specific quality assurance studies are included under the objectives for the year. Supervisors and pathologists along with every other laboratory employee should have an opportunity for input; it is important to share the goals and objectives of the quality assurance plan with the entire laboratory, because everyone in the laboratory contributes to quality service in some way.

Scope of Service and Responsibility

The program must be comprehensive, including all sections and shifts of the laboratory; effective quality assurance involves everyone. The supervisor or key contact person of each section should be responsible for setting specific problem-oriented goals for the year and performing ongoing quality assurance studies. Where studies involve multiple departments within the laboratory or are multidisciplinary within the hospital, the quality assurance chairperson can assist in design, organization, and communication. Documented in a prescribed fashion, the studies will be turned over to the quality assurance chairperson who, with the party responsible for that particular monitor, will present them to the medical director and laboratory manager. Once finalized, the quality assurance studies should be presented to an executive committee in the laboratory, which generally includes all the supervisors, and thereafter to the specific sections involved.

Involving people at all levels in a quality assurance plan occurs most easily by giving them responsibility for a monitor; this also encourages a more widespread awareness of quality assurance by the laboratory personnel and makes quality assurance seem more like a team effort. As surprising as it may seem, good ideas for monitors come from all levels of laboratory employees.

Quality assurance should be ongoing, which means that there should be evidence of continual quality assurance activity. Studies should be summarized and documented at least quarterly, with data generated throughout the year. Obviously, it is nearly impossible to collect data from every section every month; thus, the notion of ongoing studies applies to the laboratory as a whole, not necessarily to each section. It also applies to studies, such as identification of patient wristbands before phlebotomy, which some hospital laboratories do every day of the year.

Selection of Topics

Topics are selected and given priority based on their ultimate effect on patient care. Sources for the selection include, but are not limited to, physician/nurse complaints, incident reports, patient surveys, and problem identification by department employees. Topics to be avoided are so-called safe topics, that is, those in which no problems are anticipated. Once sectional meetings have been held and topics have been selected, they can be displayed as shown in Figure 3.1, which allows for easy tracking of activity.

Data collection is the responsibility of the department supervisor or designee. Sources of objective data include, but are not limited to, laboratory records, patient records, questionnaires, and observations (eg, observing the quality of the blood-drawing technique). Data should be simple and focused. Criteria should be reviewed with the quality assurance chairperson before data collection or after an initial small trial sample; for example, measuring 10 units initially enables you to look at a cross section of problems with data collection and analysis. If there is a problem with the data collection, it will frequently be detected in an initial trial sample.

Indicator topics	Jan	Feb	Mar	Apr	May	Jun	Jul	Aug	Sep	Oct	Nov	Dec
Body substance precaution		DC	X					DC	X			
Lab results charted before AM admittance for surgery				DC	X							
Incident reports	DC	DC	X	DC	DC	X	DC	DC	X	DC	DC	X
Patient satisfaction with phlebotomy procedure				DC	DC	DC	X		DC	DC	DC	X
Front office phone		DC	X				DC	X				

X = due; C = complete; DC = data collection in process.

Figure 3.1 Monitoring activity calendar.

When selecting topics for laboratory quality assurance studies, consider the following:

1. Is a particular test important in clinical decision-making?
2. Is there a significant problem that is affecting patient care?
3. Does this problem involve high-volume tests?
4. Does this problem affect other areas of the laboratory?

Corrective Action

JCAHO inspections now emphasize corrective action and evidence of improvement. These inspections force us to turn what might have merely been paperwork into concrete action.

When problems are identified, corrective action should be taken and a specific follow-up date determined to verify that the corrective action was effective. Corrective action may be aimed at individuals, groups, or administration. Corrective action in administration touches on areas such as man-hours, policy, or equipment. Corrective action should be educational not punitive, except when life-threatening negligence is repeated and the perpetrator is unresponsive to educational efforts. When educational efforts fail, corrective action could include reassignment and limitation of duties.

Intralaboratory Evaluation

Quality assurance studies should be evaluated quarterly or semiannually by the medical director, the quality assurance chairperson, and the laboratory manager. Discussion groups, including the section supervisor and pathologist, should be formed to evaluate the quality assurance studies. The medical director will preferably initial and date the studies and append comments where useful. Whenever no potential problems are found in studies, positive feedback should be widely dispensed; however, if no problems are identified over a period, that section should be scrutinized to guard against the selection of safe topics. Most section reviews should take no more than 15 to 20 minutes; the initial meeting where objectives are discussed in more detail may take longer.

Interdepartmental Communication

When quality assurance studies are completed, the communication process should include informing the technical and clerical personnel in the section of the result. Quality assurance involves everyone and the results should be communicated to everyone. When necessary, confidential matters can be coded. Communication outside the laboratory should be through the hospital-wide quality assurance committee or directed to specific clinical departmental meetings.

SAMPLE PLAN

The following is an example of a quality assurance plan for a laboratory:

Quality Assurance Plan Laboratory, Any Name Hospital

Goal: Quality service involving analysis of body fluids and tissues contributing to excellence in patient care.

Overall Objective of the Quality Assurance Program:
   Problem identification and correction
   Appropriateness of testing
   Accuracy of testing
   Timeliness of results
   Appropriate response to results
   Cost-effectiveness

Authority and Responsibility for Quality Assurance:
   Medical Director: James Bond, MD
   Department Head: Katherine Shakespeare
   Quality Assurance Chairperson: Herbert Hoover
   Laboratory Administrator: George Washington

Scope of Services:
   Orders
   Collection of specimens
   Performance of tests
      Hematology

Chemistry
Microbiology
Serology
Cytology
Histology
Transmission of test results
Response to test results

Provider of Services:
Physicians
Nurses
Clerks
Phlebotomists
Medical technologists
Histotechnicians
Cytologists
Cytotechnologists
Pathologists
Microbiologists

Note: The program will be comprehensive and will include all sections and all shifts.

Indicators of Quality: Criteria to judge the quality should be specific and as objective as possible.

Improved Patient Care:
User satisfaction surveys
Mortality, morbidity
Length of stay
Lack of readmission for the same problem
Quicker return to work
Cost-effectiveness
Utilization of resources
Hospital bill
JCAHO Standards
CAP Standards
Hospital or departmental standards
National or state standards (eg, Medicare regulations, state health care surveys.)
Comparison of present surveys to results of previous regulatory surveys

Monitoring: This will be done by assigned laboratory staff. A multidisciplinary audit involving areas outside the laboratory will include a combination of personnel from all the areas involved (Figure 3.2). You may want to code individual studies as high risk (HR), high volume (HV), or problem prone (PP). Obviously, multiple codes could apply to each study.

Data Analysis: This will be done by those involved with the audits as well as the supervisors, pathologists, and administrators of the laboratory. Completed data will then be further analyzed at departmental meetings.

Medical Quality Assurance
Summary Report

Indicator of Quality Category/ Topic	Reason/ Purpose of Monitoring Activity	Criteria and/or Standards	Summary of Findings	Conclusions	Follow-up Action/ Reappraisal Date	Opportunity to Improve Care

Committee Presentations and Dates:
Intralaboratory Meeting
Laboratory Meeting (Intrahospital)
Diagnostic Committee
Quality Assurance Committee

Figure 3.2   Medical quality assurance summary report used at the Tucson Medical Center.

Corrective Action: This may be individual, group, or administrative. Individual and group actions include but are not limited to improved orientation, counseling, and educational efforts. Individual actions are primarily educational but if unsuccessful include reassignment as well as scaled-back duties. Administrative action includes modifying policies, changing procedures, acquiring equipment, and hiring personnel. The success of the corrective action is judged by follow-up studies documenting improvement in the area of focus. Follow-up studies, when indicated, include projected dates of completion.

Communication: The primary communication is to those who are involved with the monitor's topic. If the quality assurance studies involve physicians, then the conclusions need to be disseminated to medical committees. Once the studies have been reported to the hospital-wide quality assurance committee, the committee can disseminate the information to various departments as necessary, to the executive committee, and from there to the board of trustees. Obviously, the board of trustees cannot read each and every audit in detail, but the chairperson of the hospital-wide quality assurance committee can selectively give particulars on studies he considers more significant.

Communication to:
    Individual involved
    Laboratory section
    Executive committee of the laboratory (ie, management, supervisors, and
        pathologists)
    Other departments in the hospital
    Clinical committees
    Hospital quality assurance committee

Means of Communication:
    Person-to-person
    Telephone
    Memos
    Minutes
    Newsletters
    Presentations

Evaluation:
    Done annually and findings shared with department staff, the hospital
        quality assurance committee, and the administration.

Location of Data:
    Laboratory director's office
    Quality assurance chairperson's files
    Files of individual sections

CONCLUSION

As a final check on your quality assurance plan, review it with the JCAHO 10-step monitoring process in mind (Figure 3.3).[1]

    Time spent writing a quality assurance plan is worthwhile because it focuses your activities. Although realistically the plan should be written and reviewed by a few people selected for this task, input should be sought from the entire laboratory because quality assurance involves everyone. It should be reviewed and rewritten annually since objectives and the monitoring activity calendar will change. Once written, it should be your guideline for the year, although as problems arise there may be alterations or additions. A key issue in the quarterly or semiannual review of quality assurance will be the status of the monitoring activity calendar. In my experience, having this guideline with dates for completion of quality assurance activities results in increased activity as the time for the quality assurance review approaches. Furthermore, the review gives you an overview of the problems in your laboratory. The corrections are the fine-tuning

1. Assign responsibility for quality assurance plan.
2. Define scope of patient care.
3. Identify important aspects of care.
4. Construct indicators.
5. Define thresholds for evaluation.
6. Collect and organize data.
7. Evaluate data.
8. Develop corrective action plan.
9. Assess actions; document improvement.
10. Communicate relevant information.

Figure 3.3 JCAHO 10-step monitoring process.

that can change a laboratory from one that provides average service to one that provides outstanding service. Most of the activity should center around accuracy, service issues, appropriateness of testing, and response to test results.

REFERENCE

1. *Medical Staff Monitoring and Evaluation: Department Review.* Chicago, Ill: Joint Commission on Accreditation of Healthcare Organizations; 1987.

4. Methodology

UDITS ARE FORMALIZED inquiries carried out and documented in a prescribed manner. A good audit should be simple, timely, inexpensive, not disruptive, consistent, objective, and acceptable to the medical community.

SIMPLE

Ideally, an audit will analyze one variable and be limited to 20 to 30 units of whatever has been defined as the study focus (eg, turnaround time for results or pathologic diagnosis), which should be a sufficient number to answer most questions and allow you to see any trends. If a problem exists but the trend or the effective corrective action is not apparent, you may have to enlarge the study. Some audits will be more complex, requiring a simultaneous study of multiple variables. For the most part, an audit is not designed to be statistically significant and scientifically accurate but rather is simply designed to let you know if you have any problems. If you already know of problems, attempt to correct them, then do a monitor to see if the corrective action was effective.

TIMELY

The more recent the data the more relevant. Obviously, concurrent or prospective audits have more relevance, but only if the results are communicated promptly. If retrospective audits are done, they should involve recent data: if too much time elapses after data collection, personnel or procedural changes may make the ensuing findings irrelevant. Timeliness is especially important when you seek to change behavior patterns.

INEXPENSIVE

The cost of the audit is generally going to be in direct proportion to the complexity and size of the study, because technical time, clerical time, physician time, etc, all have a price tag. This underscores the importance of a well-designed audit and the need for a plan that selects topics according to their relevance to patient care.

NOT DISRUPTIVE

Quality assurance practices should avoid interference with normal work flow (unfortunately not always possible) because otherwise the data collected will not reflect the true everyday patterns of the laboratory. One solution would be to redefine and possibly simplify the quality indicator to facilitate the process. Other solutions would include collecting data during off-peak working times or implementing software programs that allow you to track a particular problem automatically.

Real or perceived problems that tend to focus responsibility on an individual can be extremely disruptive, destructive, and unfair, especially if based on rumors rather than objective data. All individuals targeted in an audit should be included in any data collection. Often, what seems to be a particular individual's problem is not as limited as initially perceived. **The initial focus should always be on the process.**

CONSISTENT AND OBJECTIVE

The criteria used to establish your data base need to be applied the same way every time, and they need to be objective. While some studies may be subjective by their nature, even these should have guidelines whose aim is to limit that subjectivity as much as possible. For example, have observers grade phlebotomy technique according to approved, detailed written guidelines rather than subjective criteria; this should remove a lot of the personal bias that may cause inconsistent ratings between observers. Development of objective criteria for procedures such as phlebotomy will also fine-tune any related procedure manual, which should be of value to the phlebotomists.

Criteria that ask questions that are answerable by a simple yes or no are objective criteria. For example, if you ask whether a turnaround time was within an acceptable limit, the answer is simply yes or no.

ACCEPTABLE TO THE MEDICAL COMMUNITY

For an audit to be acceptable to the medical community, it should be logical and medically sound. Some proponents argue that audits should be designed by professionals who are outside the medical arena because those inside will create audits conforming to their pattern of practice. However, outside professionals are not always familiar with valid idiosyncrasies of the local medical practice, making them ill-suited to produce realistic designs. One might argue that outcome audits would remove local prejudice; however, quality indicators in laboratory quality assurance have a vague and indirect relationship to outcome. Ideally, you want the conclusions from your audit to have specific positive effects on the quality of care.

It is frequently difficult to relate the result of an individual test, the service related to that test, or the diagnosis to a specific patient outcome. Furthermore, patient outcome is connected to multiple variables, many of which relate simultaneously to laboratory issues; indirectly, all things done in the laboratory will contribute to this outcome. The difficulty lies in determining the causal relationship between outcome and any one laboratory activity.

If we overlook perceived or actual problem areas and ignore valid guidelines, then we support the argument against involving local medical personnel in making quality assurance decisions. Valid guidelines will support the quality of care and, if sound, should lead to improvement in care. Quality indicators that result in improved performance add credibility to a program.

TYPES OF AUDITS

Concurrent vs Prospective vs Retrospective

Concurrent audits look at data as they are generated and are based on real time observation. Two common problems with a concurrent audit are that individuals may alter behavior at various times during the study, and finding time for data collection on an ongoing basis is difficult. Audits based on observation are concurrent. Prospective audits are structured in advance and patient data are gathered on an ongoing basis. Prospective audits examine records at the end of the day when they are easily retrievable. One might argue that prospective audits are really just retrospective audits that cover the immediate past rather than the remote past. Retrospective audits look strictly at past data and frequently examine laboratory and/or clinical records after the patient has been discharged.

All retrospective audits include examination of records, either clinical charts or data kept in the laboratory, such as work logs. When examining the clinical records, do not focus on one specific area, for example, progress notes, since so many other parts of the clinical record dovetail, including nurses' notes, physician orders, discharge notes, etc. The response to a therapeutic drug level might only be found by examining a physician order rather than a progress note, for example, an order to lower or discontinue digoxin therapy in response to toxic serum levels of digoxin. In addition, whenever we do retrospective audits, we have an opportunity to see that the laboratory charting is correct, that is, complete and in order.

I have found prospective and concurrent audits easier to do than retrospective audits because when the records are available, you have an opportunity to talk to people and acquire that information while the topic is current and can be freshly remembered by individuals involved. In concurrent and prospective audits, the educational impact, if done on an ongoing basis, is more effective because it is immediate and affects future outcome.

Structure vs Process vs Outcome

Different approaches to monitoring quality include reviewing structure, process, and outcome, which are independent of each other yet interrelated. Structure affects process and process affects outcome. It can be difficult to relate specifics in the structure of a process to the outcome; it is also frequently difficult to show that a certain outcome is the result of a particular process since so many variables contribute to medical outcome. Furthermore, the type of outcome must be defined: is it physical, psychological, or social? Structure is the more predictable element to monitor and includes mechanisms for monitoring quality; for example, monitoring the precision of a chemistry analyzer would be an audit of structure.

There is tremendous pressure from the JCAHO and the media to conduct *outcome* audits that relate to improved patient care, even though many of the quality indicators in the laboratory are *process* audits that already show improvement in that aspect of care. If process audits truly affect care they automatically relate to patient outcome. Unfortunately, an outcome can be difficult to pinpoint. For example, one desired outcome is a lower morbidity rate; however, improved laboratory services, even when significant, might not affect morbidity. If we improve the accuracy of cytologic testing by 5%, a significant amount, we still cannot show the impact on morbidity unless we look at long-term follow-up in thousands of cases. Donabedian[1] hits the nail on the head in the following assessment:

"When the causal relationship between process and outcome is established, either can be used to make inferences about quality. . . . When outcome is used to make inferences about the quality of care it is necessary to first establish that the outcome can, in fact, be attributed to that care."

As we determine what types of audits should be done, you will see that many of them are process audits that examine our methods. An example of a process audit could be as simple as measuring the legibility of orders: several people read the orders and determine which ones are illegible. On the other hand, if you examine a quality indicator related to legibility, namely, how many orders are transcribed incorrectly because of legibility, then you are studying a result related to legibility that affects patient outcomes. Illegibility is so common it has become a joke: "Your writing is so bad you could be a doctor." Don't laugh: it is a worthwhile quality indicator in most hospitals.

Observations

Criteria that include observation frequently introduce subjectivity into the audit process; nonetheless, observation is an excellent, underused form of monitoring. Observation studies should be done using guidelines that are specific and as objective as possible. The following considerations apply to observation:

1. Presence of observer should not influence the event (this may be difficult to avoid).
2. Observer may not participate in the event.

3. Attitude and expectations of the observer may result in bias.
   Severity bias — observer is too negative.
   Leniency bias — observer is too positive.

One way to eliminate some observer bias would be to have multiple observers (either simultaneously observing or at different times) whose data could then be compared. Contrasting results between observers would highlight prejudices.

It is extremely important to spend time developing guidelines for observation. For the most part, this should require only a careful look at your procedural manuals. For example, phlebotomy methods should be detailed in a procedural manual. On the other hand, if you want to gauge telephone etiquette, you probably will not find guidelines for it in a manual. Observation studies, then, become secondarily an excellent opportunity to review and update procedural manuals. My experience with customer service in a commercial laboratory suggests that standardized answers to frequently asked questions could be useful.

Questionnaires

Questionnaires are also an effective tool. Restaurants, hotels, and major businesses serving the public use them for feedback on problems. Answers to questionnaires are an easy indicator of problems to audit or, in the case of service-related functions such as phlebotomy, may actually be part of the data.

Problems with questionnaires include the respondent's level of knowledge, attitudes and feelings, wording of the questions, and ease of returning the questionnaire. For example, a patient that has a bad experience in care not related to the laboratory could carry over negative feelings in response to a laboratory questionnaire. To avoid these problems, it helps to keep the following rules in mind:

1. Keep the questionnaire short and simple; focus on a few select issues.
2. Whenever possible, let respondents complete the questionnaire when they are removed from the event being studied.
3. Facilitate return of the questionnaire.
4. Respond to identified problems as soon as possible.

A carefully developed questionnaire that deals with a few select issues will produce more response than the questionnaire that has multiple issues. The higher the number of responses and the greater the percent of respondents the more valid the study. Sometimes it may be worthwhile to send a second questionnaire to those who do not respond on the initial request.[2]

Patients and physicians are customers of the laboratory. Quality management must meet their needs. Questionnaires are helpful in uncovering these needs. If addressed to physicians, an attached personalized note from the medical director could improve the response rate.

I prefer questionnaires over personal interviews, because it avoids the problem of induced bias; the voice and manner of the interviewer sometimes communicate the desired response. Furthermore, interviewing requires training personnel to conduct the interviews, which is a luxury most laboratories cannot afford. However, if personal interviews are conducted, some training must be done. Many hospitals have volunteers that conduct patient surveys, calling patients or their families after their discharge; of course, one drawback is that these volunteers, too, must be trained. One of the advantages of telephone interviews is that the response percentage is frequently higher.

Many of these surveys contain laboratory-related questions that could be incorporated into your quality assurance program. You should have the opportunity to review these questions (including those asked in telephone interviews) and see the data generated by the responses.

An important part of the effective use of questionnaires is rapid and effective response. Questionnaires allow you to see how customers define quality. Once defined, you must take timely action that will meet or exceed customers' needs so they can see that their responses led to fruitful changes. There is one caveat, however: be sure that the needs of the customers are practical and achievable. Sometimes customers have a different view of health care and may expect too little or too much. Patients often focus on amenities and how staff relate to them personally. In interviews with 51 patients discharged from a hospital, fewer than half the patients discussed a physician's scientific and professional competence[3]; we could probably expect the same focus by patients answering surveys related to laboratory service. Even if patients apparently focus on "superficial" issues in surveys, assessment of quality should include patient satisfaction at all levels. To measure customer satisfaction with the laboratory, physician surveys are generally a good source of information, because physicians tend to place more emphasis on technical components of the laboratory.

Random vs Consecutive vs Systematic

Random sampling has no imposed order; it is the equivalent of pulling samples out of a hat. Consecutive sampling is often used if the perceived problem is a low-volume item. In a consecutive study, you would look at each example as it occurs. A systematic audit might be conducted on the fourth Tuesday of each month or might look at the orders from a different unit in the hospital each month on one particular day. I use systematic sampling for anatomic peer review at a small hospital. Each month I select a number between zero and nine and review every surgical report ending with that number.

SIZE OF AUDIT

Thirty is a useful number of units (samples) to study. Since there are roughly 30 days in a month, something you measure once a day would result in a sample size of 30. Thirty is generally a manageable number with which to work; however, it is impossible to predict whether 30 is sufficient for each study. For example, there may be times when you perceive a problem yet 30 samples does not reveal any problems, thus you need to study more samples. On the other hand, there are times when 10 samples are sufficient for you to identify the problem. My experience with most service-related issues has shown that 30 samples generally allows you to see a trend. The standard error of the estimate is inversely proportional to the square root of the sample size, thus doubling the sample size from 30 to 60 increases your precision by approximately 40% (Scott Emerson, MD, PhD, Department of Biostatistics, University of Arizona Health Science Center, oral communication, August 1990). Therefore, you must weigh the need for accuracy against size and cost.[4,5]

Obviously, the larger the number of samples the more valid the conclusion, though a common mistake in the design phase is to call for such large numbers that data collection becomes burdensome, expensive, and, at times, an insurmountable obstacle to completion of the audit. Study size makes up a substantial portion of the cost of quality assurance. It is better to review your data after you collect 5 to 10 units of information, allowing you to test your hypothesis, that is, you can see if there are any problems in the data collection or if there is obviously a trend. Say that the objective is to measure the turnaround time for hemoglobin and hematocrit test results from the intensive care unit. After gathering 10 units of information, you might decide to complete the data gathering, move on to corrective action, or redesign the audit. If the majority of units show too slow a turnaround time, then, if possible, move immediately to choose an appropriate corrective action. If there is slow turnaround time but you cannot identify the reason, then you need to redesign the audit. The problem could be with any one or more of the following:

1. Communication of orders
2. The phlebotomist
3. Transportation
4. Logging the specimen into the laboratory
5. Performance of the test
6. Communication of the result

Once you have isolated the problem, you may want to redesign your study so that you can focus on that area.

Another possibility would be that after reviewing the data from 10 turnaround times you find no problems, in which case you might decide 30 is a sufficient number to complete the audit. You might ask yourself other questions: are you interested in all shifts, one test, one location, etc?

Audits are not scientific studies designed for publication. They merely look for problems and trends; 5 to 10 cases or 30 cases may give you enough information to meet your needs. On the other hand, if the problem is perceived but not found after 30 samples, you should decide if the frequency and impact of the problem warrants a larger, possibly ongoing, study.

Frequency of Audit

You should have ongoing audits, which does not mean that you are doing a daily monitor in each section, but that there should be some audit activity each month. Regulatory agencies have stopped placing emphasis on numbers, so most ongoing audits are periodic audits done on a regular basis. Periodic audits are systematic or random but are also done on a regular basis; a systematic audit might choose every Tuesday for study, whereas a random audit would select 1 random day each week.

A good example of an ongoing audit would be assessing the turnaround times for frozen sections. You look at 10 each month on a regular basis. If after a time you do not find any unacceptable results, it hardly seems necessary to continue the audit; however, it cannot hurt to continue monitoring areas of importance. Sometimes the simple knowledge that something is being audited is sufficient to ensure continued improved performance.

Ongoing audits can be more easily conducted with the aid of a computer that can give you monthly reports and identify outliers at variance with defined guidelines. Some studies are ongoing by nature; for example, you might want to follow up every incident report or you may feel that armband identification of patients before obtaining a blood sample is important enough to require an ongoing consistent monitor. The impact of the problem on patient care will dictate the frequency of the audit.

METHODOLOGY OF AUDITS

General vs Specific Objectives

One might want to look at response time of phlebotomy for the entire hospital or a specific unit, for the entire day or a specific shift or period. A specific audit might study complaints about phlebotomy turnaround time between 5 and 7 PM from the coronary care unit. It is more cost-effective to do specific audits. Even if the problem is a general one involving the entire hospital, it is sometimes more effective to do a sample audit of one section of the hospital, analyze the data, determine the nature of the problem, correct the problem, and do a study involving the entire hospital as a follow-up. It is easier to study the problem in a focused area where the problem may be reflective of a more universal problem.

Technical vs "Artistic" Objectives

This objective can best be illustrated by example. In phlebotomy, the technical aspect might be the technique of drawing the correct specimen or a sufficient amount of blood. The "artistic" aspect might be in an observer's grading of the interaction between phlebotomists and patients: Is their approach to patients professional? Do they introduce themselves to patients properly? How is their attitude? Are they courteous? Do they answer all of the patients' questions? Although these studies are subjective, they often are very informative and can help you determine if a patient has been satisfied.

Patient Focus: Individual vs Group vs General

For the most part, the only time an audit focuses on an individual patient is in the resolution of specific complaints. Most of the time patients are separated by location, for example, pediatric ward or labor and delivery ward, so the audit can focus on a specific area. When conducting a quality assurance study in the emergency department, however, you may want to separate the trauma patients or those with cardiac arrests from other patients since there is a particular reason for faster laboratory test turnaround times for these patients. The problem you investigate should help you determine which type of patient focus you select. As was stated earlier, some problems apply to the whole hospital.

Consensus Criteria

Include a cross section of people when reviewing and establishing criteria. I have always used a consensus approach but frequently will develop a set of criteria that can be used as a nidus for the discussion. These criteria are sometimes accepted as presented and at other times totally rejected; in any case, having a preliminary set of criteria generally speeds up the process of selection. If your audit involves a specific service, then make sure that all departments that utilize the service help establish the criteria. For example, when setting criteria for a service that is used by the emergency department, you might want the head nurse for the emergency department and the physicians in that department to review your criteria ahead of time. Do not limit involvement to physicians: if the study is unacceptable to other users, you will end up with a poorly received result. If the users have helped formulate the criteria, they are less likely to reject the conclusions.

Specific Criteria

When you look at turnaround time, focus on a limited area; you may want to focus on a specific test. Avoid generalizations such as "good technique." If you review the quality of slides, catalog specific features (negative or positive) that clearly mark preparations, for example, thickness of tissue, absence of folds, presence of knife artifacts. If your objective is to review turnaround time for services to the emergency department, you must define an acceptable turnaround time and how it will be measured. Will you use a stopwatch or simply examine records? Keep the objective before you as you formulate the criteria. Occasionally, I come across an audit whose criteria have nothing to do with the objective. For example, if the objective of a cytology audit is to assess the quality of the interpretation of the Pap smear but the criteria are the date of the last menstrual period and whether the patient is undergoing hormone therapy, you have criteria that are not important to the objective. You may want the information the criteria will provide in this case, but the criteria do not specifically relate to the accuracy of the cytologist's interpretation of the slide. Unfortunately, the relationship between the objective and the criteria is sometimes forgotten, even in a well-developed quality assurance program. The most common problem is setting criteria that go far beyond the objective. In the example above, the criteria for accuracy of interpretation of the slide could be consensus agreement from two cytologists. However, the criteria also included the clinical information received, which contributes to the accuracy of the reading but goes beyond the initial objective. On the other hand, sometimes an interest in information not related to the objective will develop, and if you have two separate quality indicators that you can study simultaneously, it would be more cost-efficient to do so.

Simple Criteria

Whenever possible, develop criteria in the form of questions that can be answered objectively with a yes or no answer. Again, if measuring the turnaround time for laboratory services to the emergency department, record the time; it either meets the criteria (yes) or it does not (no). At first, simply measure the turnaround time without analyzing individual components that contribute to the turnaround time. If everything is in order you have completed the study; if not, you may want to simplify the study further, for example, look specifically at the turnaround time in the laboratory or emergency department by itself. Unfortunately, the political thing to do in all cases is first to look in your own backyard, namely, the laboratory. You should also look at your data after collecting about 10 units to see if there are problems with the criteria that were not anticipated. For example, you collect 10 samples and discover that the time between the physician's ordering laboratory work and the clerk's actually ordering the test is not recorded. Thus, you may have discovered a data collection problem. If the total turnaround time is satisfactory, then you need not correct this problem; however, if the total turnaround time is unsatisfactory, the collection process has to be well documented so you can examine each facet and pinpoint where the problem lies.

Realistic Criteria

The criteria should have achievable goals. Our goal is to have 100% compliance with most laboratory quality indicators, but there are very few things in life that are perfect. For example, while we aim for a set turnaround time for a test, we may not achieve it each time, and sometimes for valid reasons: if four of five phlebotomists call in sick on a shift, you cannot expect the usual turnaround time.

On the other hand, even without extenuating circumstances you may not achieve your goal every time. It depends on the objective. If you want all critical results telephoned to the clinician rapidly, then you should have 100% of the criteria fulfilled. If you want diagnostic accuracy in surgical pathology, you should meet your goal the majority of the time. Stepping away from 100% compliance is not aiming for mediocrity; you simply cannot realistically fulfill your criteria 100% of the time. In any case, the threshold remains 100%.

Realistic criteria are often difficult to establish. The literature may offer ideas, but frequently you will have to rely on common sense or trial and error. Say that you want to know the turnaround time for a simple crossmatch without atypical antibodies. The results of your initial study show that a specific turnaround time figure for this type of crossmatch is achieved in 80% of cases. You discover that the variant times occur during a particular shift. After counseling the workers on that shift and observing how they do their work, the acceptable turnaround time is achieved in 95% of all cases. You repeat the study with similar results. This appears to be the acceptable and achievable turnaround time for your hospital.

Suppose that you then research the literature and find that turnaround time, on the whole, is faster elsewhere. If your observations fail to generate ideas for improvement and various follow-up actions fail to improve turnaround time, it is likely that the faster turnaround time in the literature is not realistic for your personnel. You might consider contacting the authors of articles that report shorter turnaround times to see if they can offer any insights. An additional source of information could be the results of a study conducted in an institution similar to yours. If the crucial factor is equipment, that can be changed; but frequently it relates to personnel. Obviously, simply requiring personnel to work more quickly may not be conducive to error-free work. If you have gone through these steps, you can probably conclude that the shorter turnaround time is not realistic for your laboratory. Be honest about your ability to achieve goals.

Summary Report

The summary report (see Figure 3-2, p 15) should include the total number of units studied and what percentage of these were acceptable according to criteria that reflect the objective. Any of the unacceptable results that were due to unavoidable occurrences should be explained, for example, if turnaround time was poor because of equipment failure. However, if there was repeated equipment failure, you have an administrative problem, namely, the need for major equipment overhaul or replacement. In addition to determining the number at variance, percent of total, and whether the objective (goal) was achieved and why it was not, our summary report includes a category, "Summary of Findings: Opportunities to Improve Care, Services, and Patient Outcomes." This section includes a short statement relating the effects of the study to patient care and how patient care can be improved. For example, in a cytology monitor we found that accurate clinical information regarding the date of the last menstrual period made our comments on cell maturation more valuable in evaluation of a patient's hormonal status; thus, we made note of it in this section.

Relationship to Patient Care

The JCAHO is now focusing on outcomes of quality assurance monitors that relate to patient care. Everything in the laboratory relates to patient outcome: service, accuracy, and appropriateness of testing can improve patient care. By eliminating inappropriate testing, you could help prevent the time and cost wasted in obtaining a specimen from the patient, doing and interpreting a test, doing excessive workup related to a potentially false-positive result, and potentially increasing length of hospital stay for the patient. Eliminating inaccurate results has the same effect. Additionally, any improvement in turnaround time can theoretically shorten the length of stay necessary and, at times, can affect timeliness of critical decisions that have an immediate impact on patient care.

The media and politicians are concentrating on outcome as related to reduced health expenditures. If the quality of care is not improved, however, reduced costs will not necessarily be more cost-effective; they could in fact be more costly in the long run. It is difficult to measure patient outcome to laboratory costs except as part of the entire hospital bill, which relates to a number of issues including physician behavior (test ordering patterns, response to test results) and severity of disease. For individual patient costs related to outcome we can look at type of disease, severity of disease, length of stay, mortality, morbidity, readmission to the hospital, psychological and social function, and return to work. Anything that reduces laboratory costs in the short run but adversely affects patient care is neither cost-effective nor desirable for the patient or third-party payers.

Each quality indicator can indirectly be related to quality of care but frequently only in an individual sense and without a special causal relationship. Outcome in the true sense of the word relates to the patient and in the truest sense of the word needs to be determined on a case-to-case basis. The desired outcome is for the patient to return to society functioning at a level that is comparable to or better than before the illness. Anything that improves laboratory services should improve patient care outcomes in some way.

Follow-up Action

If no problem is found, state that the audit results indicate no additional follow-up is needed. If corrective action is indicated, be specific and find out why. Look at the process first, the individual second, and then decide where the follow-up action should be directed. Individual action includes counseling and education; in situations where these are not effective, reassignment or removal from duties in the laboratory might be necessary. Group action includes individual counseling of members of the group, group education, or rescheduling to change a group. Be specific about required changes. Quality assurance is a tool for educating the provider and consumers about the strengths and weaknesses of the system, but it is also a tool for change when change is necessary.

The follow-up action must be effective for it to be meaningful. There are many examples where the follow-up educational process was only effective as long as the education was ongoing or for a short time thereafter.[6,7] Many of these studies are at university medical centers and involve residents, which is a far cry from a study that involves staff physicians in the private sector with long-standing behavioral patterns. In my own experience I have found that sometimes the positive results continue only as long as the educational stimulus is present.

Communication

Effective communication is essential for improvement in a quality assurance study; it is the medical director's role to emphasize and document effective communication. Information should be disseminated without breaching confidentiality. Regardless of who assumes responsibility for passing on information, the medical director must oversee the process and is ultimately responsible (Figure 4.1).

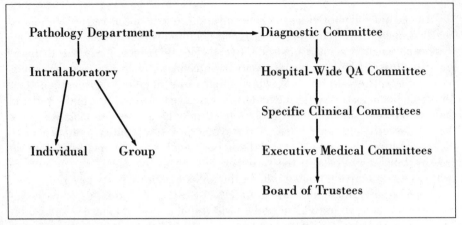

Figure 4.1 Possible scheme of communication.

Communication to an individual is accomplished by telephone, in person, or personal letter. Personal communication, if done in a nonthreatening manner, is most effective since it allows for a dialogue. Unfortunately, scheduling multiple meetings of this nature may be quite tedious and unpractical, especially if busy clinicians are involved. Communication to a specific group, for example, cardiologists or nursing and ward clerks, is best at meetings specifically arranged for quality assurance or departmental and sectional meetings. In my experience, the most effective communication is directed specifically to an individual or group involved in the study. In the event communication with larger groups is necessary, it is most easily accomplished through newsletters and presentations, although the response at general meetings can be of value. Nonetheless, each form of communication makes some contribution to spreading information, and should be done in a clear, precise, brief, and nonaccusatory manner. It's hard to gain support with a long and convoluted message. A message related to improved medical care for the patient will more readily enlist the cooperation of the staff.

When communicating on a one-to-one basis, it is important not to be *too* diplomatic; if at first the listener does not understand the message, some bluntness may be required. After I talk to people, I sometimes ask them to humor me and summarize the discussion because the subject matter is very important to me. I have been amazed at some of their responses, which frequently reveal a definite lack of communication, whether due to my failure or that of the listener. To remedy this, you must alter your message, emphasizing the areas (as bluntly as needed) where the communication was ineffective.

If the quality assurance program is comprehensive, there may be follow-up action directed at management, frequently pertaining to equipment or staff. This is where some quality assurance programs may come to a screeching halt because of budget constraints, hospital policy, fear of unions, and fear of the effect on business. Input from the medical director to administration is very valuable; when changes require management decisions, the medical director needs to emphasize the effect of the changes on the quality of patient care.

Eventually, information must be communicated to the executive committee and to the board of trustees. For this communication it is best to highlight those studies that are of particular significance since there generally are a large number of studies to review. Some hospitals place communication to the executive level in the hands of the chairman of the hospital-wide quality assurance committee, who will prioritize communication of the various quality assurance studies.

All personnel in studied sections should be informed of the results of quality assurance studies. Unfortunately, intralaboratory communication sometimes stops at the supervisory level. This can be avoided to some extent if you coordinate your intralaboratory continuing education program with your quality assurance program.

A spot check on communication effectiveness can be very informative. If you send letters to physicians that discuss quality assurance, you might call them later to gauge their familiarity with the contents of the letter. Such a follow-up may seem distasteful, but effective quality assurance communication *requires* that someone make sure the communication loop is complete and effective. That person may be the medical director, the quality assurance chairperson, or another designee; in any case, a champion is necessary for an outstanding quality assurance program.

Abbreviated Summary Report

An abbreviated summary report (see Figure 3-2, p 15) is useful for inspections and distribution to committees, because it provides a quick summary of the pertinent data. Keep in mind, however, that inspectors may select a few topics for which they will want to see more specific data. Also, as part of the summary report keep track of any action related to the audit that is initiated at committee level.

CONCLUSION

Quality indicators need not be complicated to be meaningful. A simple, focused study — with follow-up communication to the appropriate people and departments and corrective action when indicated — is sufficient for an efficient quality assurance program. The goal is to find areas of concern, preferably those related to high-volume items. Closing the monitor loop in a timely fashion to maintain the relevance of the quality indicator is important, as is finding a champion who understands quality assurance and who will make sure the program runs smoothly and as planned.

REFERENCES

1. Donabedian A. *Explorations in Quality Assessment and Monitoring, I: The Definition of Quality and Approaches to Its Assessment.* Ann Arbor, Mich: Health Administrative Press; 1980:81-82,103.

2. Ogram DM. Surveys: assessing the effectiveness of service. *Can J Technol.* 1987;49:59-60.

3. Coser RL. A home away from home. *Soc Probl.* 1956;4:3-17.

4. Matthews DE, Rarewell VT. *Using and Understanding Medical Statistics.* New York, NY: S Karger Press; 1988:204.

5. Roser B. *Fundamentals of Biostatistics.* Boston, Mass: Dunbury Press; 1982:189-205.

6. Rhyne RL, Gehlbach SH. Effects of educational feedback strategy on physician utilization of thryroid function panels. *J Fam Pract.* 1979;5: 1003-1007.

7. Eisenberg JM. An educational program to modify laboratory use by house staff. *J Med Educ.* 1977;52:278.

5. Quality Assurance in Anatomic Pathology: Frozen Sections, Surgical Reports, Autopsies

PATHOLOGISTS HAVE ALWAYS been concerned about quality control in anatomic pathology, although in the past they rarely documented it. That lack of documentation is rapidly changing. Historically, quality assurance in anatomic pathology can be traced to a 1929 article[1] that discusses the reliability of frozen sections. However, after that there is a hiatus in the literature with little discussion of quality assurance related to anatomic pathology until the 1970s.[2-4]

Resistance to quality assurance studies in anatomic pathology continues to exist in some institutions. In my role as a CAP inspector I have found that when the subject of quality assurance is brought up with pathologists, they mention consultations and sharing of information as proof of quality assurance. However, documentation is not readily available: consultation records may be found attached to a report and individual cases may be discussed with other pathologists, but it is often difficult to identify these consultations without the tedious task of going through the surgical reports page by page. In addition, intradepartmental consultations are frequently hidden in the content of the individual reports and are not documented separately.

These consultations are valid quality assurance activities but they need to be not only documented but also retrievable at the time of inspection. For example, copies of consultations can be initialed by the medical director with a note as to whether there was a disagreement and whether the department requested the consultation. These reports can be summarized semiannually with categorized disagreements by individual pathologists and a statement of whether the disagreement was major or minor. These reports can then be distributed, discussed, and recorded as a form of peer review, after which the number of disagreements and categories of disagreements can be recorded in an ongoing manner. Quality assurance in anatomic pathology requires continual documentation, a summary report with resultant group discussion, and the ability to take effective action when needed.

Most commonly, pathologists have focused on the accuracy of the diagnosis, which is interpretive and, to some degree, subjective. Thus, a diagnosis is made based on knowledge and opinion combined with a need for clinical data, and is affected by variations in terminology. There is a resistance to "Big Brother" looking over our shoulders. Criticism of or from one's peers is uncomfortable and time-consuming, frequently requiring more than the 48 hours generally allotted to routine surgical pathology turnaround. So why should this subject be pursued? First, quality assurance in anatomic pathology is necessary and demanded by the JCAHO and by the CAP. Second, it gauges the accuracy of diagnosis, which affects patient care. Third, it is an important part of the reputation of the laboratory among clinicians. Fourth, it includes service issues, which also affect how the laboratory is perceived by clinicians.

Service (turnaround time) dovetails with other areas in the hospital that are involved with surgical pathology and thus qualifies as a multidisciplinary audit. If the program is organized well, a multidisciplinary audit need not be a costly use of time. Obviously, you would have to spend all your time doing quality assurance if you were to do all the things discussed in this chapter, but an *adequate* anatomic pathology quality assurance program should be *ongoing* and approach problems that are generally high-volume procedures. By focusing on areas of the greatest concern, you will more likely generate results that will benefit patient care.

Documentation should be discussed quarterly (or at least semiannually) and should be followed up by effective corrective action, the results of which should be kept on file. The same principles discussed in the preceding chapter on methodology, including objectives, data collection, conclusions, and follow-up, are also applicable here. Anything that improves the quality of anatomic pathology will improve patient care. Remember that follow-up action should be educational, not punitive, and that the problem is not necessarily with the individual but may be with the system.

Dudley's[5] 1975 statement is still relevant to quality assurance:

"The morality of self-assessment is without question; indeed it is such an implicit part of professional conduct that when it is discussed we tend . . . to feel embarrassed. Nevertheless, technical skills are becoming much more complex, practical knowledge so much greater that it would be arrogant to feel that we are totally able to scrutinize ourselves or that alternatively a qualifying examination . . . gives once and for all the right to practice professionally without anything more than the most nugatory supervision. I take it as axiomatic, although others may disagree, that none of us should be adverse to some form of feedback of performance that permits an external critique."

The attitude toward quality assurance in anatomic pathology is rapidly changing. In a 1988 questionnaire sent out by the CAP to 500 medical directors of laboratories, approximately two thirds had a defined surgical pathology review program (L. Deppish, vice-chairman, CAP Surgical Pathology Committee, Western Reserve Care System, Youngstown, Ohio, personal communication, July 1990). There is now a program for quality assurance in anatomic pathology in place in most hospitals. There is no question that this is a marked improvement over earlier practice. If you already have a quality assurance program in place, this chapter will help to fine-tune it.

The following is a sample quality assurance program for anatomic pathology.

Anatomic Pathology Quality Assurance Program: An Overview

I.   Purpose

    A.   Insure the highest quality of anatomic pathology service to patients by the following:

        1.   Monitor and evaluate completeness, accuracy, and consistency of surgical, cytologic, and necropsy pathologic diagnoses (see Chapter 6 for further discussion of cytology).

        2.   Identify and resolve problems of misdiagnosis by looking not only at individual cases but also at summarized data for trends related to the process.

        3.   Maximize uniformity of diagnostic criteria and terminology among pathologists.

        4.   Insure optimal communication of clinical information by the attending physician to the pathologist. Review the adequacy of clinical information related to both surgery and cytology cases.

        5.   Insure optimal communication of pathologic findings to clinical physicians.

        6.   Monitor histologic testing, including turnaround time, quality of slides, and accuracy of labels.

    B.   Pathologist's continuing education.

II. Scope

    A.   All pathologists in the department will participate in the anatomic quality assurance program.

    B.   The quality assurance program in anatomic pathology includes, but is not limited to, the following:

        1.   Frozen section diagnoses.

        2.   Inpatient and outpatient surgical pathology.

        3.   Expert consultations.

        4.   Turnaround time for the above three items.

        5.   Review of previous surgical and cytologic materials in comparison with current material.

        6.   Consistency of cytologic and tissue diagnoses.

        7.   Review of gynecologic cytologic specimens that have normal findings, preferably cases judged to be high risk by review of the clinical data.

8. Cytopathologist peer review of suspicious or abnormal findings in cytologic specimens.
9. Review of adequacy of submitted cytologic specimens. Is there sufficient cellular material for diagnosis? Were endocervical cells identified? Does the amount of blood and inflammation prevent accurate interpretation?
10. Review of all autopsy reports by clinical review committees. Feedback from these committees to the pathologists highlight cases where diagnoses are significantly discordant and suggest areas where clinical intervention is useful. This assures there is some follow-up.
11. Guidelines for cases in which autopsy is desirable.
12. Peer review of a percentage of the autopsies by a second pathologist.
13. Proper labeling and identification of patient specimens.
14. Proficiency testing.
15. Adherence to body substance precaution program.
16. Review of procedure manual.

III. Participants: all pathologists; histology and cytology personnel.

IV. Communication

A. All quality assurance summary reports are reviewed in the laboratory, then submitted to the hospital diagnostic committee, and routed from there to the hospital quality assurance committee. If appropriate, these studies are distributed to the proper committees for review, for example, medicine, surgery, and emergency services; obstetrics and gynecology; or pediatrics.

B. Significant comments regarding anatomic quality assurance studies from the above committees will be evaluated by the pathology department.

V. Evaluation: Semiannually, the anatomic and cytologic quality assurance data will be evaluated for cause of variation, significant trends, and efficiency, and given priority according to clinical relevance.

GROUP VS SOLO PRACTICE

In a group practice, pathologists can review each other's work, generally in an ongoing fashion. However, the solo practitioner must rely on an outside consultant and is therefore limited to a retrospective audit. The solo practitioner could do a blind review of cases that are not unique, such as a group of cervical biopsy specimens, but there is a good chance many of the cases will be remembered. I strongly recommend that a solo practitioner use a consultant to do peer review for a percentage of cases.

SURGICAL PATHOLOGY

As the path of a specimen is traced through the laboratory focus on areas to evaluate for quality assurance. A few days each month or each quarter should be set aside for the pathologist doing the gross examination to focus on quality indicators, such as evaluating the time of arrival of the specimens, fixation of specimens, and labeling of specimens.

Timing

Are the specimens received in the histology section in a timely fashion so reports are not delayed? For example, are there an excess number of specimens removed on Monday but not processed until Tuesday? Is the gross surgical examination set up too early? Are the specimens left in the operating room area too long? Is there a special effort made to process diagnostic biopsy specimens on the day they are done even when they come in late? You should do a periodic spot check to answer these questions, preferably on a monthly basis. Some areas can easily be checked on a more regular basis. Before leaving the laboratory at the end of the day, check the gross examination room and the surgical suites for surgical specimens for which an earlier diagnosis could have an impact on patient care. For example, an earlier diagnosis of a biopsy could allow therapy to start or shorten the length of the patient's stay.

Spot checks can be done quickly and with little effort, yet when documented fulfill the criteria for a quality assurance study. You do not have to look at quality assurance indicators on a daily basis for an effective study. Timing is generally a multidisciplinary audit; it frequently involves a problem in the process and may involve surgery as well as pathology.

Fixation

Are specimens being crammed into a container with too little fixative? Are specimens placed into small containers because larger containers are not available? Are they available but no one knows their location? Are specimens received fresh when necessary? If they are received fresh is the pathologist available for consultation on a timely basis? You should set aside days to review the adequacy of fixation. Also, the histology section personnel should periodically document when the pathologist is available in relation to when specimens are received fresh.

Should uteri be opened in the operating room so the endometrium will not be autolyzed? The latter becomes a problem more frequently on weekends or when specimens arrive late in the evening. The Tucson Medical Center laboratory decided to give up cutting the undisturbed specimen in order to get better sections of the endometrium; the surgeons were asked to open the uteri at the time of surgery. It has made a difference in the quality of those sections.

Do you have instructions for users for special handling of specimens, for example, B5-fixed specimens? Importantly, are these instructions readily available to users and do they clearly communicate which specimens are to have special fixatives, the time that the specimen should be in the fixative, and if the specimen should be delivered to a specific place? More importantly, are the instructions followed?

Every laboratory will have some inadequately fixed specimens. The real question is how many laboratories note that a specimen is unacceptable due to poor fixation and initiate effective follow-up action? Why is there inadequate fixation? This is likely related to the process. Is it education of the operating room personnel, lack of availability of the proper size containers, inconvenience of the location of the container, etc? Perhaps the pathologists are processing the specimens before adequate time for fixation has passed. Unless you ask the question why and have answered it correctly, effective follow-up action is unlikely.

Labeling

Is the patient's name legible? Are the labels on the correct container? There may be some specimens that are obviously in error, for example, endometrial curettings that are labeled cervical biopsy. There may be significant errors that cannot be rectified by the microscopic examination and that are generally undetectable unless the clinical picture is obvious. For example, there might be a mix-up involving the left and right bronchial biopsy specimens, one of which shows a carcinoma in-situ; if this mix-up occurs frequently, it could be a sign of carelessness.

Accuracy in labeling should be monitored continually. If there are obvious mix-ups yet the containers are correctly labeled, send a form letter to surgical personnel describing the problem. A form letter brings a problem to their attention, making it easier to take action when a trend is noted. When data are collected related to a problem, you may be surprised to see how often the problem occurred over the course of, say, 1 month. By using a form letter you facilitate looking at a potentially serious problem on an ongoing basis.

Sometimes the mix-up is not always obvious. A clinically undiagnosed melanoma from the right arm labeled incorrectly as being from the left arm could have disastrous therapeutic implications if multiple specimens were submitted. When mislabeling is identified, bring it to the attention of the involved personnel. The potential damage from a careless attitude must be corrected.

Incident Reports

Incident reports may be generated against the laboratory or by the laboratory. In one 6-month period the Tucson Medical Center laboratory had 19 incident reports, the majority of which were directed against the operating room for inadequate fixation, no fixation, or mislabeling. Because of the recurrent nature of the problems, the laboratory instituted continuing education programs for surgery department personnel and contributed to the surgery department's orientation program for new employees. On the other hand, there were also incident reports generated against the laboratory regarding misplaced specimens or tardiness in processing the specimens. Incident reports may pinpoint problems that are worth focusing on for an ongoing study. Rapid response to problems is important, because personnel still remember details of the incident that may help clarify how or why the incident occurred. An immediate response shows that the laboratory cares about quality, as demonstrated by its immediate action to correct a problem and prevent future recurrence.

Clinical Information

Do you receive legible, accurate, and adequate information about each of the specimens? Do you have a preoperative and postoperative diagnosis? In many institutions the answer to these questions may be no, yet the pursuit of this information is frequently ignored because of frustration in attaining it. How often do you contact physicians and discuss a problem, yet the problem continues? This clinical information frequently affects the final diagnosis, yet specimens are often signed out without this information and without the appropriate physician being contacted to obtain this information. During a busy day, the specimen may be signed out based only on the information derived from the gross and microscopic patterns, disregarding the clinical information. The Tucson Medical Center laboratory had this problem with liver biopsy specimens: we found that we would have reached more consensus opinions on the diagnosis if we had had more clinical information.

Although they know that adequate clinical information is essential to diagnosing frozen sections, few pathology groups have pursued this goal with much energy or enthusiasm. Vogel's[2] article on neurosurgical specimens highlights this inadequacy, but the problem is not limited to any one subspecialty of surgical pathology: Rogers et al,[3] in their review of frozen section diagnoses, noted that 10% of errors in diagnoses related to lack of communication between pathologists and surgeons.

Figure 5.1 is an example of the form letter I send to clinicians who provide me with inadequate information. Copies of each letter are kept in a file, allowing me to compile data on the clinical information received and to look for trends that need correcting. If a trend is identified, I ask why. Sometimes a laboratory's procedures do not facilitate sharing clinical information, or a laboratory fails to stress the need for this information. If physicians receive an excessive number of letters related to the lack of clinical information, I call them and discuss the need for clinical information in more detail, illustrating the point with examples. A personal call is a more effective mode of communication than a letter; however, it is also more time-consuming and may at times be irritating to the involved physician.

FROZEN SECTIONS

Bruer[6] in 1938 commented that frozen section diagnosis "is about as accurate as tossing up a nickel and calling tails malignant." Today, however, it is accepted as

Dear Dr.

Your surgical specimen from *(surgical case No., patient's name)* was received without clinical information. The College of American Pathologists and the Joint Commission on Accreditation of Healthcare Organizations regulations require clinical information for each case. Furthermore, clinical information frequently contributes to a correct final diagnosis.

A letter is being sent out for each case as part of an ongoing quality assurance study that tracks the number of cases without adequate clinical information.

Thanking you in advance,

Paul Bozzo, MD
Department of Pathology
Tucson Medical Center

Figure 5.1 Letter regarding inadequate clinical information.

a highly accurate diagnostic tool. Because few diagnostic techniques have such a serious and immediate impact on the care of the patient, it is important to evaluate the diagnostic accuracy of frozen sections. The appropriateness of frozen sections (ie, was the frozen section indicated clinically) should also be evaluated, as should cases in which a frozen section was indicated but was not done. Such an evaluation should be made based on guidelines formed by clinician consensus.

Guidelines

Prioritize setting guidelines for evaluation according to clinical relevance and frequency, for example, guidelines for how you want to handle biopsy specimens with mammographic abnormalities should be established early because of their importance. Some pathologists feel that frozen sections should not be done on these specimens because they are small, making diagnoses difficult. If you find that biopsy specimens with mammographic abnormalities account for a significant number of discordant diagnoses of your frozen section data, then you have discovered a problem with the process of frozen sections of biopsy specimens with mammographic abnormalities. Remember, you cannot set guidelines for frozen sections of everything at once. Prioritize guidelines by clinical relevance and frequency.

When setting guidelines for frozen sections, also look at the contents of the frozen section diagnoses. Margins of tumors and similar information are used by oncologists and radiotherapists, thus it seems reasonable to ask them for their opinion on frozen sections. For example, our radiotherapist and oncologist not only need the lines of resection for lung tumors to be clear but clear by a good margin:

they feel that frozen section results should inform the surgeon of the proximity of the tumor to the margin.

Diagnosis

There are several methods for classifying variations in frozen section diagnoses and final surgical reports. The threshold for frozen sections is 100% concordance. You need to look at all cases that are discordant with that final surgical diagnosis. (Note: I assume throughout this discussion that the frozen section diagnosis is included in the final surgical report.) At the Tucson Medical Center we simply look at interpretive errors, where the correct diagnosis was possible on review of the initial frozen section. However, Rogers et al[3] point out the following potential errors to evaluate:

1. Microscopic sampling errors: The lesion was in the tissue sampled for frozen section but was not present in the sections studied.
2. Gross sampling errors: The lesion was in the tissue sent for frozen section but was not sampled at that time.
3. Histology problems: There are poor sections or inadequate stains.
4. Communication errors: There are times when information that the surgeon failed to pass on could have resulted in a correct diagnosis. For example, the neurosurgeon makes a diagnosis of meningioma but fails to communicate that to the laboratory, while the pathologist makes a diagnosis of low-grade astrocytoma based on a small amount of material.[2] Or if a surgeon knows that a patient with small cell tumor has a seminoma and fails to communicate that information, the pathologist will find it extremely difficult to interpret the frozen section accurately as a seminoma. Another example would be not knowing that a patient was irradiated, which changes the significance of a cytologic atypia diagnosis, possibly resulting in a different conclusion.

Interpretive frozen section errors are probably the easiest to evaluate and the chief concern of most pathologists. There are false positives and false negatives. False positives would generally be more significant, but false negatives can also be significant, for example, calling a line of resection negative when it is positive for tumor.

Monitoring Activity

You could monitor all of the above potential errors on an ongoing continuous or ongoing intermittent basis as part of your quality assurance study, but you might want to limit it to a specific category, for example, neurosurgical cases. There are numerous ways to monitor this activity. My success with ongoing quality assurance activities (ie, the individual fills out a form or an addendum report at the time of peer review, or turns in a copy of the surgical report with an attached note that details differences of opinion) is temporized by studies where I have reviewed every case during a specific time and found a number that were not included in the study. For example, the pathology group at the Tucson Medical

Center was going to have one person review all the neurosurgical cases when they were completed. At one point I pulled the cases for 1 year from the collection. There were a significant number of cases missing from the group, which had been compiled in an ongoing manner. The easiest way to track data is to have a note attached to the reports at variance and turn them in to one person for compilation.

Look at the summarized data and try to analyze why there is a problem. Do not immediately focus on the individual involved in the process. If there are particular diagnoses that are frequently in error, more sections should be reviewed or more than one pathologist should review the cases before they are reported. For example, if there is a problem in diagnosing atypia vs low-grade adenocarcinoma of the prostate on needle biopsy specimens, you may decide to have two pathologists review all cases in this category. Again, there needs to be agreement on guidelines.

The prospective approach to frozen section quality assurance would appear to be the easiest; however, you may want to do a combination of approaches. In a prospective approach, the pathologist doing the surgical report hands in a copy of the disagreement with an explanatory note or fills out a form documenting disagreements between the frozen section diagnosis and the final diagnosis whenever discrepancies arise.

What a discordant diagnosis is needs to be defined, since obviously there are different approaches to making a diagnosis. For example, one editorial[4] discusses diagnostic performance on frozen sections in the operating room and suggests that performance be judged on whether the lesion was correctly labeled malignant. I feel this is too liberal a definition: malignant melanoma and squamous cell carcinoma are both malignant but the therapeutic approach is different and it would be clinically meaningful if these were confused. Thus, you can see how differently guidelines can be set and how it might affect diagnoses.

Two ways to collect data for frozen section quality assurance studies are shown below. Keep in mind that it may be preferable to put this information on a computer and format it so you can track it according to topic, unit of time, and the individual involved. H. Travers, MD (Physician's Laboratory Ltd, Sioux Falls, SD, written communication, June 1990), has suggested (and I would agree) that breaking the data into specimen type (eg, liver biopsy specimens, gastric resections) could give you some insight into problems with the process or help you choose where to focus your attention. If there are a large number of errors involving neurosurgical cases you might automatically have two pathologists available for consultation. If there are a large number of errors involving skin biopsy specimens where the clinical diagnosis is melanoma, you might decide that it would be better to make the initial diagnosis on permanent not frozen sections. You then have to inform your clinicians not to do frozen sections for skin biopsy specimens with a differential of melanoma because of the error rate for frozen sections.

1. A copy of the surgical report categorizing the misdiagnosis is submitted by the reviewing pathologist, with an explanatory note added to the bottom of the

```
Pathologist:
Frozen Section Diagnosis:
Final Diagnosis:
Reviewer's Comments:
Category of Disagreements:
Comment:
```

Figure 5.2   Form evaluating disagreements in diagnosis.

original report. This report should be routed to a single pathologist, who tracks these variations. Quality assurance is more effective when data are reviewed on a regular basis, because ongoing reviews tend to result in consistent improvements in the quality of surgical pathology. Group discussions should include a consensus opinion on the categorization of errors, corrective action, and whether to continue the study in its present form. Again, it cannot be overemphasized that the aim of the quality assurance monitors should be educational and the data should be in summary form so they can be quickly scanned. Whenever possible, the number of errors for an individual should be related to work load, that is, as a percentage of the total work load. Decreasing the work load will not necessarily cut errors, but if someone's work load is out of proportion to a colleague's it may account for some problems.

2. A form is filled out incorporating the above information as agreed to at the group discussion (Figure 5.2). For a solo practitioner, an outside pathologist could perform the evaluation.

One way to use this form would be to categorize disagreements as minor or major: minor disagreements have no significant therapeutic implication, while major disagreements do. The comment section should explain why the correct diagnosis was missed. For example, "poor stain interfered with the interpretation" explains why there was an error, but it does not explain why the specimen was not restained. You may wish to include interpretive errors as well as other categories: microscopic (lesion was only present on deeper sectioning of the block) or gross sampling errors, histologic, or communication problems.

Collecting the data over a longer period allows you to see whether a trend is consistent or not. You might also compare your group and individual data with those published in the literature. What is an acceptable accuracy for frozen sections? Most studies require less than 2% disagreement between the final diagnosis and the frozen section diagnosis.[3,7-10] The expected false-positive error is well below 1%.[3,9,10] Q-Probes data on frozen sections showed a concordance of 96.5% on 1,952 frozen sections, with 3.9% deferred and 3.5% in discordance.[11] You want to keep track of deferred diagnoses, which occur in situations where at the time of the surgical consultation (frozen section) the pathologist tells the surgeon that no diagnosis will be rendered and that the surgeon will have to wait until permanent sections are available for diagnosis. In most of these series, deferred diagnoses are not included in the disagreements. Deferred diagnoses in the literature range from 1.3% to 10%.[3,9,10]

Turnaround Time

The laboratory should set a standard time frame within which the frozen section is finalized. Ten to 20 minutes should be sufficient; if a longer time is required, examine the protocol for frozen sections. Since the protocol will vary from institution to institution, establish a suitable time frame for your own needs by analyzing your present data. Suppose that 80% of the time a frozen section is diagnosed within 15 minutes of the time it is received. If you have included the time it takes for the section to arrive at the laboratory from the surgical suite, you have a complete turnaround time for frozen sections that is efficient relative to the effects on patient care. Analyze the other 20% and determine why there was a slower turnaround time. Were the frozen sections more difficult to diagnose, requiring an additional pathologist to review the case? Was the pathologist unavailable? Were they delayed because of a lack of clinical information? Were they difficult to section on the cryostat, which is the case with fatty tissues? Were special stains done on them? Were multiple sections rather than single sections required? How many diagnoses were deferred? The deferred cases should reflect a degree of difficulty.

If your turnaround time remains 15 minutes 80% of the time, and you cannot find problems to be corrected, then your threshold should be 80% for 15 minutes. However, anyone who looks critically should be able to fine-tune turnaround time for frozen sections.

The expectations of clinicians play an important part in determining the threshold for turnaround time. Many clinicians have trained or practiced at other hospitals, and any dissatisfaction on their behalf may come as a result of past expectations. Their dissatisfaction may force you to look even more carefully at those times that are beyond your threshold. Remember, expectations by the clinicians should be *reasonable* and *achievable*.

If results are expected to be delayed beyond your usual turnaround time because of some difficulty, the attending clinician should be informed. A surgeon who has been duly informed of a problem will probably prove to be more understanding of a delayed result and may even be able to provide additional significant information. For example, a surgeon may be able to obtain a biopsy specimen that proves to be more diagnostic from a different area of the tumor, or may have found an additional tumor in the lymph nodes, or may inform the laboratory that a previous biopsy specimen was diagnosed as malignant. All of this information may help you to reach a diagnosis faster.

Turnaround time is easily monitored on a periodic basis by noting the time of arrival in the department and time of the final diagnosis. A more accurate approach would include the time the biopsy was taken in the operating room, but that might not be easily available. You might find there is a very good turnaround time within the laboratory but that the frozen sections are delayed due to slow transportation from the surgical suite.

THE SURGICAL REPORT

Gross findings are no longer available once the specimen is described and sectioned, so it is important to have a complete and accurate gross description that is evaluated through review of the report. However, it is very easy to forget this and focus on the diagnosis. Thus, there should be protocols for doing surgical reports in every department. One quality assurance approach might be to see if the protocol is followed, but this may not be practical because a protocol is most often used by the laboratory as a reference. An intermittent review of *specific* protocols with associated group discussion would be an excellent quality assurance activity. You might choose to periodically select a specific specimen, such as mastectomy, and see in what way the protocol differs for gross description, number of sections, and requests for special stains. There will be variation, but it should be reasonable. The information in the gross description should consistently satisfy the need for an accurate microscopic diagnosis and also provide any information the submitting physician might need, such as the size of the lesion.

The following are quality indicators related to surgical reports:

1. Adequate clinical information to perform the gross examination. If this information is not available, then the specimen should be set aside until that information becomes available (see earlier discussion in this chapter under "Clinical Information").
2. Size of the specimen.
3. Size of recognizable lesion.
4. Lines of resection for malignant tumor.
5. Correlation with the clinical information received. If the clinician states that the appendix is perforated, there should be a statement in the pathology report about the presence or absence of perforation. If an extremity has been amputated or a bowel resection has been done for ischemia, there should be a statement about the viability of the lines of resection.
6. Descriptions should be objective and not draw unwarranted conclusions. For example, an objective description would state that a skin lesion is irregular in its shape and a pigmented area is centrally placed grossly not involving the apparent lines of resection Based on the gross description, it would be unacceptable to conclude that there is a central melanoma with clear margins. A papillary lesion should be described as such, not as a papillary carcinoma or a choroid plexus papilloma.
7. Descriptions should be concise and accurate, which are subjective indicators but usually obvious. They should also be in a logical sequence and grammatically correct, and use correct spelling. Careless descriptions can affect clinicians' response to the report because they may feel carelessness indicates a lack of importance. A mistake in the description can also result in a different

meaning, for example, "would favor malignancy" might be accidentally typed as "would not favor malignancy" as a comment on a difficult diagnosis.

8. The number of slides and pieces of tissue submitted for microscopic examination should be included. There should be a statement about the amount of tissue processed, which could be simply noted in code; for example, (1-X-N) means 1 block, multiple pieces, no tissue left, and (2-3-S) means 2 blocks, 3 sections, some tissue left. If slides are to be sent to consultants or are meant for peer review, such a code allows you to quickly check that an adequate number of slides were received and that the slides were returned. A coding system also tells the consultant whether the entire case is available or if there is some tissue left to be processed.

Obviously, there are other quality indicators you might choose for quality assurance studies. The best approach is to choose one that is relevant, that is, one that is a high-volume problem and will greatly affect the quality of patient care.

Microscopic Findings

Microscopic description should have the same criteria as gross findings, namely, that they be accurate, concise, and logical; and grammatically correct, using correct spelling. If the above criteria are not met, the results can be disastrous. For example, a melanoma mistakenly described as 2 cm instead of 2 mm in depth has a significant prognostic implication for the patient. There are times when the result is humorous, although it can still reflect a careless attitude in the department; for example, one time a 26-cm fetus was almost reported to the clinician as a 26-cm penis. Fortunately, this was detected beforehand, but it did underline the problems that exist with inappropriate wording of gross descriptions.

You may decide not to give a microscopic description of each case. Each laboratory will have its own criteria for when a microscopic description is necessary, which is okay as long as the criteria are uniform. Microscopic descriptions can often be omitted in cases where the diagnosis is sufficient; for example, microscopic descriptions do not add much to the diagnosis of chronic cholecystitis. Thus, a microscopic description is best used when the diagnosis is not sufficient to convey relevant information to the clinician, when the diagnosis is in doubt, or when a lesion is unusual.

Quality Control for Histopathology

Figure 5.3 is an example of a quality control sheet for histopathology, which could be filled out on a spot-check basis. Look at 10 to 30 random cases per month and fill out this evaluation. The pathology group at Tucson Medical Center does random cases but we also make sure that this number includes some needle biopsy specimens, such as liver and/or kidney, since these are cut thinner to see details more clearly.

Quality control is probably best accomplished with a team using a multi-headed microscope and the input of several pathologists as well as the histology

Sections:
   Knife marks:
   Thickness:
   Completeness:
   Fragmentation:
   Miscellaneous:
Stains:
   Acceptable:
   Unacceptable:
Comment on all unacceptable results: _____

_____

(*Note:* Completeness would require looking at the block of tissue as well as the slide to see that the sections adequately represent the material in the block.)

Figure 5.3   Quality control sheet for histopathology.

department supervisor. If you have more than one histotechnician, you might consider rotating the histotechnicians as well as the pathologists so that more personnel can feel they are contributing to this quality assurance indicator.

Diagnosis

The diagnosis should be accurate and terminology relating to it should be acceptable and uniform within the department.

First, accurate (or correct) needs to be defined. For most groups, this is based on a consensus opinion, the opinion of an outside expert, or, in some cases, the consensus of the opinions of outside experts. Biological behavior is generally an undisputed final judge of the diagnosis, unless one argues that the surgical material was not representative. It would be futile to argue that a lesion was benign when it metastasized. You could argue that it was not possible to diagnose the malignancy because it appeared benign histologically, for example, benign metastasizing leiomyoma. However, the presence of recurrences may still leave the original diagnosis in question since lesions not classified as malignant may recur locally (additional discussion of this appears below under "Expected Accuracy in Surgical Pathology").

The problems faced with this type of peer review are sometimes related to the subjectivity of the interpretive evaluation. Other problems with peer review occur when an institution has one person with a subspecialty interest that nobody in the group feels qualified to peer review, or someone is considered to make the best diagnoses, which are used as "gold standards." Outside consultation can alleviate this to some degree.

The following is an approach that has been used at Tucson Medical Center for a number of years when disagreements are shown to the pathologist who was responsible for the diagnosis.

1. If the pathologist agrees that another diagnosis is more accurate and has some therapeutic implication, an addendum (revised) report is submitted.
2. If the pathologist agrees that another diagnosis is possible but feels it has no significance, the pathologist may choose to ignore it but has at least been made aware of it. Also, the person doing the peer review may choose not to sign the report. If an addendum is produced for every little thing, it may reflect on the pathologist's credibility with the clinicians. The downside of this, however, is that minor problems can become significant if they are from the same individual. Generally, the group will be aware of this and may want to focus on it. Focusing on fairly insignificant issues can make the peer review process seem less tenable to the individual pathologist and can increase work load, but if you feel it has therapeutic implication it should not be ignored. You want to continue improving quality.
3. If the pathologist disagrees with an alternative diagnosis, you may want to have other members of the group review the diagnosis. If there is a consensus opinion, then the pathologist may then choose to submit an addendum report or seek outside consultation. However, if the pathologist seeks outside consultation when there is a consensus disagreeing with him, this action needs to be communicated to the responsible clinician immediately because of the delay associated with outside consultations and to avoid care being given based on the original diagnosis, which is in question. This is not a frequent occurrence and generally the outside consultant will agree with the majority opinion. However, there will be times when the outside consultant will support the pathologist who has persisted in his opinion.

Remember, the pathologist has signed the report and taken responsibility for it; therefore, unless the pathologist is acting irresponsibly and affecting patient care, do not change the report without the pathologist's consent. If available, the original pathologist will always handle the addendum. There are times when because of lack of availability (eg, vacation or illness) someone else may assume that obligation at least to the extent of talking to the involved clinician.

Many of the problems in diagnosis found by peer review are oversights by the pathologist who made the original diagnosis, for example, small but significant fragments of tissue on the slide were not noted. These findings are usually accepted by the pathologist with no argument (but sometimes with embarrassment). There is no doubt that anatomic pathology requires some compulsiveness. These oversights tend to occur less frequently with ongoing peer review.

Categorization of the Disagreements

At the Tucson Medical Center major and minor disagreements in diagnosis are separated according to therapeutic implication for the patient; thus, a major disagreement would have therapeutic implications, a minor one would not. Minor disagreements with no therapeutic implications could be identified or ignored, depending on the compulsiveness of the reviewer. Be aware that a large number of amended reports may reflect negatively on the group. The bottom line is that action taken should have clinical relevance, because the confidence of the attending physicians is significant and may be affected when they see a large number of minor amended reports, even if they have no therapeutic implications.

There are also missed diagnoses that might be classified as major but do not have any therapeutic implication, for example, a diagnosis of scar tissue vs neurofibroma or leiomyoma. If calcification is missed on a frozen section diagnosis of fibrocystic change of the breast, it has no therapeutic significance. However, the radiologist and surgeon may want to know if the calcification they saw on mammography was present in the tissue. Thus, this omission, even though minor, may have clinical relevance. If there are large numbers of minor missed diagnoses, you will probably turn up a more serious problem. Use common sense on how many addendum reports you submit. At the Tucson Medical Center we review the disagreements semiannually and reach a consensus on the type of disagreement, that is, major or minor. Other institutions have a more complicated scheme for categorization of discrepancies. The following is an example of a different approach[12]:

Category 1: This category includes minor disagreements with wording of diagnoses, undetected errors in spelling, or other such lapses that do not affect patient care.

Category 2: This category includes mistakes in diagnosis that have minimal effect on patient care, ambiguous diagnoses, failure to review relevant prior accessions, or the omission of diagnostically or prognostically important information.

Category 3: This category includes major discrepancies or omissions in diagnosis that would affect the treatment of the patient and, if confirmed, would require the issuing of a corrected report.

Category 4: This category includes major discrepancies in diagnosis of such a gross and profound nature that they call into serious question the competence of the reporting pathologist.

The advantage of this system is it makes you aware of all the features you should be looking for. Disadvantages include potential difficulties in separating category 3 from category 4 and reaching agreement regarding the categorization of each case.

Expected Accuracy in Surgical Pathology

What is an accurate diagnosis? In Penner's[13] work for the CAP Performance Improvement Program Study, the correct or accurate diagnosis was by consensus of a panel of pathologists. Consensus was defined as over 50% agreement (at a later date, the diagnosis was relegated to the opinion of a so-called expert). In the initial histopathology project, there was consensus in 77% of the slides; however, the disagreements might have been due to terminology and, therefore, would have been minor.

Feinstein and others[14] looked at disagreement in classifying lung cancers by experienced pathologists between their first and second readings. The range of disagreements was 2% to 20%. They also compared their diagnosis with the consensus diagnosis (the most common diagnosis). The disagreement ranged from 2% for well-differentiated adenocarcinoma to 42% for poorly differentiated adenocarcinoma. This study does not reflect the average surgical case load seen in daily practice, that is, it does not include surgery on fallopian tubes, hernia sacs, basal cell carcinoma, etc, nor does it include cases for which a gross description is given and the diagnosis is based on the gross findings.

Studies[15,16] at teaching institutions have suggested a good accuracy in diagnosis is approximately 98%. My experience has found that significant errors should be less than 1% for experienced pathologists. However, there is no absolute figure that is acceptable, because there are too many factors that contribute to accuracy, including the experience of the pathologist, the difficulty of the cases, the definition of the disagreements, and the compulsiveness of the reviewer.

A study from St Thomas Hospital and Medical School in London reviewed 300 cases originally diagnosed by both junior and senior pathologists (MRC Pathology Diplomas) and found a consensus (all the participants agreed) in 97.9% of the cases by the senior pathologists and 92% of the cases by the junior pathologists. This was done knowing age and sex of the patient and site of origin of the tissue.[15]

Whitehead and others[16] reviewed 3000 surgical pathology cases before completion of the final surgical report. There were 231 cases (7.8%) in which at least one reviewer disagreed, and in 67 (2.2%) of the cases the diagnosis was modified after the review. Changes were judged to be critical in 29 (0.96%) of the cases, that is, those cases in which discrepancies had a definite effect on patient care. Nonconcurrence rates among reviewers ranged from 3.2% to 5.3%. Half of the nonconsensus cases and two thirds of the cases with altered diagnoses were identified by a single reviewer, which shows that often the more compulsive pathologist will disagree on cases that others would either bypass or miss.

This study[16] was done for a limited time and was not ongoing. The average amount of time spent per case was 2.2 minutes; whether that time is sufficient is difficult to evaluate without knowing the exact type of cases. Many surgical case loads include cases that could be quickly reviewed, such as tonsils, hernia sacs, and nevi. The decision to modify the report in this study was left up to the individual pathologist.

Number of Cases to be Reviewed

How many cases should be reviewed? Ideally, every case should be read twice and the report reviewed; in many situations, however, this is unnecessary. At the Tucson Medical Center we initially found it valuable to review all cases, and some people continue to do so. Now, on the whole, all reports are reviewed and all diagnostic biopsy specimens are microscopically peer reviewed as well as the majority of the surgical cases. However, there are pathologists in the group who do not always microscopically review cases that involve fallopian tubes, gallbladders, products of conception, and simple appendixes, because the yield of substantial changes is so small compared with the time required for the review. At the Tucson Medical Center there are four pathologists who annually report and review approximately 13,000 surgical reports, and peer review all the cases. A fifth pathologist is responsible for approximately 14,000 outpatient surgical reports per year. For the outpatient surgical reports, the pathologist group reviews only 10% of skin cases and 100% of other cases, such as gynecologic and urologic specimens (primarily needle biopsy specimens of prostate), because of time. Almost all of the nonskin cases are diagnostic biopsy specimens (in our group, the person reading the skins is the only one with board certification in dermatopathology). Time is definitely the limiting factor; however, we feel we now have a review system that focuses on all significant cases. Furthermore, the pathologist doing the review may choose to microscopically review all cases on any given day. For example, even though products of conception are not reviewed, any specimen submitted as a product of conception in which fetal parts or definite placental parts are not identified may be carefully and completely reviewed.

If you cannot afford the time to review all cases, you should review a set number of cases. I do the peer review of 10% of the cases for a hospital that does not submit cases involving fallopian tubes, hernia sacs, or gross examination for review. However, 10% of the surgical load at this hospital is a small number. You must analyze your case load and make the decision according to the needs of the individual institution. One fairly popular approach is to review only the diagnoses that are malignant; unfortunately, this will identify false-positive but not false-negative diagnoses.[2]

In my experience there is an additional benefit to reviewing cases twice that is not reflected in the statistics on cases where significant misdiagnoses were found: the effect of knowing that someone will be reviewing the slides, which may knowingly or unconsciously make one more alert and contribute to greater uniformity in the group. In addition, it may also increase the number of consultations within the group before the surgical report is complete. A review can also help substantiate your diagnosis in the view of the clinicians. Again, you should ask yourself if it is cost-effective to review cases, particularly if you have disagreements with therapeutic implications in less than 1% of all cases. If there are 10,000 surgical reports of which 50 to 100 cases have therapeutic implications and only a small percent have major therapeutic implications, you should consider the time involved, the probability of a major therapeutic implication, and the other negative and positive effects of the peer review process (including personality conflicts between pathologists). You should try to walk the fine line between cost and actual improved patient care. If the quality of care improves, it is probably worth the cost. *Poor quality costs.* On top of all this, remember that you will never be 100% accurate, even when cases are reviewed twice. Figure 5.4 lists possible approaches to reviewing cases.

1. Review all cases.
2. Review a certain percentage of cases.
   a) x% each day by random selection
   b) x% each day by a set case number, for example, those case numbers ending in 4, or the case number could be changed arbitrarily each day
   c) x% each day, but exclude certain diagnoses, for example, cases involving gross examination, fallopian tubes, and hernia sacs
3. Review all malignant diagnoses.
4. Review all diagnostic biopsy specimens.
5. Select x% of cases at the discretion of the reviewer.
6. Review all cases on certain days. Reviewer selects the days unannounced.

Figure 5.4   Review options.

Timing of the Review

With the continued stress on patient length of stay in the hospital, clinicians are justifiably demanding a quick turnaround time for surgical pathology diagnoses, and with the small number of significant changes noted it is not practical to hold up the report distribution for the review. At the Tucson Medical Center the review is generally completed within 24 hours of the time a pathologist makes the original diagnosis, except on weekends. Other groups will perform reviews just before completed cases are distributed to the clinicians. If a review is done before the report is generated then it must be decided at that time if there are variations in the report or diagnosis or if these variations are actually interdepartmental consultations. If certain cases, for example, all of the biopsy specimens, are signed out together, it is difficult to use them for peer review unless some commitment to diagnosis is made prior to that review or you use outside consultations to do peer review on the group as a single unit. Ideally, the review is done after the surgical report is generated but before the report is distributed to the clinician. Peer review should not reduce consultations but should increase them.

Consultation

The ironic thing about consultations is that most of the time you already know you have a problem—that is the reason you call for a consultation in the first place. Nevertheless, consultations are sometimes initiated by patients, lawyers, or clinicians. Additionally, consultations are sometimes generated by the biological behavior of a lesion, which may be an undisputed judge of the "correct" diagnosis. For example, a lesion initially called benign might at a later date show evidence of associated metastatic tumor, prompting a review of the biopsy specimen from the primary site.

Discrepancies as a result of consultations should be graded as minor or major using one of the above-mentioned formats. Grading any discrepancies can most easily be accomplished by making a copy of the original diagnosis and the subsequent consultation and marking them as agreeing or not, then classifying the agreement (ie, major or minor). You should also keep track of whether the consultations were requested by the pathologist who originally reported the case. The cases in which the pathologist initiates the consultation have an anticipated problem. Consultations initiated by people other than the pathologist pertain to problems that were not anticipated, which are more important for that reason. I suggest filing and assembling the data semiannually.

In my role as medical director, original reports with attached consultations are brought to me on an ongoing basis. I mark the reports as agreeing or disagreeing. I mark disagreements as major or minor and note whether the consultation was requested by the original pathologist. This information is compiled on an ongoing basis on a word processor. You could also use a spreadsheet. Semiannually, I compile a summary and route it to each pathologist. The pathology group then meets and discusses the summary. This ongoing method involves very little time; on the other hand, if the data are only compiled a few times a year, the task becomes more onerous. Whereas it requires very little effort to look at three to four consultations per week and compute the data, it seems to be more of a task to look at, say, 100 at one time. It's also a lot easier to procrastinate when facing a larger task! The following data are collected for the summary:

1. Surgical number
2. Name of original pathologist
3. Name of consultant
4. Original diagnosis
5. Consultant diagnosis
6. Requested consultation or not
7. Agreeing or disagreeing diagnosis
8. Major or minor disagreement

Previous Biopsy Specimens

Previous biopsy specimens should be reviewed at the time of the most recent biopsy and incorporated in the report. For example, it is appropriate to review the first lung biopsy specimen when looking at a second lung biopsy specimen. It is also appropriate to review previous biopsy specimens if metastatic tumor is being considered, because they could show the source of metastases. Discordant diagnoses should be noted on an ongoing basis in a similar manner to that of the surgical peer review, namely, by attaching to the report a note completed by the reviewing pathologist or a form customarily filled out when there is a disagreement. There should be very few disagreements. Again, this documentation should be incorporated into a semiannual summary and presented for discussion.

Committee or Conference Presentations

Presentations are useful as a form of peer review: simply indicate that the case was presented at, for example, a conference (provide specific information related to the presentation, including dates). Note whether there was agreement or disagreement with the diagnosis in discussions following the presentation. As with surgical peer reviews, the original pathologist should be allowed to review any disagreements.

Communication of Results

Communication of the results to the appropriate clinician(s) involves a number of steps:

1. Determine if results are delivered in a timely fashion, that is, reports are completed quickly and given promptly to the appropriate people. See how long it takes if results are mailed. Spot checks are necessary to measure timeliness; you could occasionally contact a clinician to see how long it takes to receive results. Additionally, you could determine what percent of your surgical reports are completed in 24 hours by conducting a simple spot check once a month that counts how many were not completed that day. A regular collection of data will give you an average figure for a 24-hour period and allow you to assess whether corrective action is necessary. You may discover there is a problem. If so, look at whether it is an individual, a group, or an administrative problem. For example, an administrative problem would occur when there are too few people to complete the typing. Correct the problem and do a follow-up monitor if required. I most often find that problems with communication of results involve the process rather than the individual.
2. Verify that results are telephoned to the physician in critical situations where a written report may take too long to receive. For example, when a diagnosis indicates there may be an ectopic pregnancy, the Tucson Medical Center pathology group alerts the physician by telephone. Physicians are also called when unsuspected diagnoses such as melanomas and malignant neoplasms are found. Each institution must set its own uniform policy for when it is necessary to call a physician. In such instances, "physician called" is typed at the bottom of the report.
3. Find out if clinicians complain about the communication of results, then focus your studies on any areas of complaint. File and categorize complaints so you can spot trends and take swift and appropriate corrective action. Remember that quality improvement should be ongoing and that a cessation of complaints will be the true indicator of effective corrective action.
4. Make sure the diagnoses are easily understood. This study could be conducted through the ongoing peer review process, by charting complaints related to difficulties in understanding the report, or by doing a focused review when indicated. For example, if one pathologist's reports are frequently worded in a confusing manner, discuss the situation and focus the peer review process on this problem for this pathologist's cases until the problem is resolved. Correct the situation as it is reviewed.
5. Follow up biopsy diagnoses when warranted. For example, more tissue may be

requested in hedged diagnoses, or there may be diagnoses in which apparent margins are involved and additional tissue needs to be routinely removed.

Setting Guidelines

I know of no laboratory that has written guidelines for making diagnoses; such an endeavor would result in guidelines the length of a textbook. However, some guidelines will have to be set as you focus on particular diagnoses, so that you will have uniform standards for peer review. At the Tucson Medical Center, there were a large number of disagreements on the categorization and diagnosis of endometrial hyperplasia, so we spent time to develop guidelines for its diagnosis. To standardize criteria, have pathologists diagnose a group of cases individually and then try to mesh their results; this should help standardize the terminology and hopefully the approach to some diagnoses. If not, outside consultation may help set guidelines.

Guidelines should be set by not only the criteria for diagnosis but also the number of sections, the details of gross description and sectioning, the order of the wording of the diagnosis, for example, the site and the side (right or left), and the final diagnosis. For instance, will the diagnosis be worded cystic and adenomatous hyperplasia of the endometrium or endometrial hyperplasia complex vs simple, and with or without cytologic atypia? In addition, the diagnosis should be in line with that found in the literature. Focus your energy on setting guidelines for frequent and clinically relevant problem areas.

A CAP task force has set data guidelines for bladder cancer, breast cancer, and Hodgkin's disease. Although these guidelines are not for diagnosis, they demonstrate how guidelines can be developed by clinician consensus. The CAP guidelines provide data needed for quality patient care against which clinicians can compare their own data (L. Deppish, vice-chairman, CAP Surgical Pathology Committee, Western Reserve Care System, Youngstown, Ohio, personal communication, July 1990).

Proficiency Testing

Proficiency testing is a way of life in the laboratory. Proficiency testing is an excellent form of quality assurance in anatomic pathology; the results of the testing can be filed and included as a quality indicator. Proficiency testing provides slides with identical clinical information. It is significant if the diagnoses of one pathologist are consistently at odds with those of his or her peers. Consider proficiency testing as a monitor for anatomic pathology quality assurance.

Some people would argue that proficiency testing is not too useful. In the event slides are difficult to interpret, such as the ones proficiency testing sometimes provides, in your daily practice you can always call the physician, take additional sections, consult with a peer, and send slides off for outside consultation. Furthermore, everyone has some subspecial interest in which he or she feels more

Month:

Number of surgical reports:

Number of consultations:
    Major disagreements:
    Minor disagreements:

Number of surgical reports peer reviewed:
    Major disagreements:
    Minor disagreements:

Number of frozen sections:
    Major disagreements with final diagnosis:
    Minor disagreements with final diagnosis:

Figure 5.5   Periodic summary report.

qualified than in other areas, and proficiency testing may focus on an area of less confidence. These comments point out some of the weaknesses of proficiency testing, but I feel its contributions to quality assurance outweigh them.

Periodic Summary Report

You should compile a simple monthly, quarterly, or semiannual summary that records quality indicators and allows you to see at a glance where potential problem areas are. Include in a summary any results collected from studies. Figure 5.5 shows an example of a summary report. A summary should also include whether the number of disagreements is acceptable. If unacceptable, a plan of corrective action should be indicated. Keep in mind that corrective action should focus on improving quality care, and the process rather than the individual should be examined first whenever possible.

Appropriateness of Procedures

One problematic issue in anatomic pathology is the appropriateness of procedures. Some procedures are straightforward, but others are not so clear-cut. If a specimen, for example, a normal appendix, shows no disease, should it have been removed? In my experience, when the number of resected normal appendixes decreases the number of ruptured appendixes increases. Thus, removal of normal appendixes is not necessarily inappropriate, even when removal is not indicated by disease.

At the Tucson Medical Center we classify the specimens under the following four categories:

1. Pathologic diagnosis supports the clinical diagnosis.
2. Pathologic diagnosis differs significantly from the clinical diagnosis (includes removal of disease-free organs).
3. Discovery of unexpected neoplasms or inadequate surgical margins for a neoplasm.
4. Gross examination only.

The JCAHO has asked that pathologists verify that each surgical case is an appropriate surgical intervention. According to the categories above, every surgical case classified under category 1 would be looked at as appropriate, because the pathologic diagnosis in itself supports the surgery being done. For categories 2, 3, and 4 you may need more data to support the appropriateness of the surgery. At the Tucson Medical Center we send cases in categories 2 and 3 to committees for review.

Follow-up Action and Attitude

I cannot stress enough that the attitude toward corrective action should be educational not punitive. In a peer review, pathologists should not view themselves as police but rather as colleagues striving to improve the quality of their work. The setting of standards by a group is in itself educational, because the standards are often set during a review and solidified by the periodic review of results. Even if standards are not written, the discussions that take place during peer review can generate a more uniform approach to assigning diagnoses.

In your follow-up action, focus particularly on areas where there are **frequent** differences of opinion. The Tucson Medical Center group had a problem with classification of hyperplasia of the endometrium. To correct this problem, we looked at the classification scheme, read literature on it, debated the issue, and finally agreed on a scheme that we all now use. We then studied a group of previously diagnosed endometrial hyperplasia specimens and tested ourselves with the new classification scheme and knowledge gained from our discussions. The result was an increased knowledge of the subject, improved performance, and a more uniform approach. This exemplifies how focusing on the process — as opposed to the individual — is beneficial: the problem is discovered and corrected, the process is improved, and everyone learns from the experience.

Since interpretation is subjective and since even in the best of circumstances pathologists may not always agree, you should be aware of the sensitivity of an issue. Sometimes a person's ego is on the line. When there is disagreement over a case, do not start a discussion by saying "so-and-so made an error" or "you are wrong," but rather say "in my opinion this is such and such" or "could you show me how you arrived at the diagnosis?" or "let me show you what I saw on the slides." On the other hand, the original pathologist should expect some disagreements. The discussion is intended to inform, not impugn.

The right presentation and attitude are key to a smooth review process; otherwise, egos may suffer. A positive attitude goes a long way. The best thing to keep in mind is that people are human, thus you need to leave room for human error. Also keep in mind that every group of pathologists will have somone who is the best and someone who is the worst at making diagnoses, which does not necessarily mean that anyone's performance is unacceptable, but simply that there are always going to be differences in human abilities. The bottom line is that all pathologists, no matter their ability, should feel part of a team that is striving to do its best.

Unless there is a major problem that warrants not allowing a pathologist to practice anatomic pathology, pathologists should only be identified with code numbers when reports leave the department. Defining a major problem is subjective, but basically it refers to a situation where the number and seriousness of the problems are such that the person is considered incompetent. This judgment should follow a failed attempt to educate and counsel.

When it is questionable that a pathologist is meeting the group's standards, every attempt should be made to educate the person involved. The nature of the problem should be serious before that person is isolated for an educative approach. Be sure that the problem was viewed as objectively as possible and that personal differences do not play a role.

Aside from education, other action must be taken to ensure that problems in the laboratory are corrected, followed by a review that verifies the corrective action is effective. Even as you implement the corrective action, continue to monitor the problem area until you have satisfactory results. After the problem has been corrected, a periodic spot check is worthwhile to monitor the ongoing effectiveness of the corrective action. Remember that your goals should be realistic; there are few monitors that will generate 100% compliance, unless your standards are excessively lenient. Of course, your threshold or goal remains 100% accuracy.

Summary

As with all quality assurance you must develop a simple plan and follow it. For a plan to work you must have a leader (theoretically, the medical director) to champion it. Again, the bottom line is to find problems that affect patient care and to implement and enforce improvements.

THE AUTOPSY

Autopsies are an excellent form of peer review. They are the final diagnostic tool for solving clinical dilemmas and are excellent for teaching. They confirm, clarify, and correct antemortem diagnoses. Twenty years ago autopsies were performed on approximately 50% of hospital deaths. By 1980 the rate had dropped to 14% in community hospitals and 38% at teaching hospitals.[17] Goldman and others[18] did a study of autopsies and found that in cases of misdiagnosis, correct diagnosis would have theoretically prolonged survival in 8% of patients in 1960, 12% in 1970, and 11% in 1980. The authors concluded that advances in diagnostic testing have not reduced the value of autopsies.

Battle and others[19] gathered information on 2067 autopsies from 32 hospitals and found that discrepancies between antemortem and postmortem diagnosis were influenced by the hospital type. Community hospitals had more discrepancies than university hospitals, and small facilities had more discrepancies than large ones. They found that misdiagnosis adversely affected survival in 13% of the autopsies. Landefeld and others[20] reviewed 233 autopsies at both a university hospital and a community hospital and concluded that major, unsuspected findings would have resulted in a change in therapy and improved survival had they been diagnosed antemortem in 12% and 21% of the autopsies at the university hospital and the community hospital, respectively.

Autopsies are important for monitoring the quality of care. They contribute to our knowledge of disease and improve clinical acumen and accuracy of diagnosis. Furthermore, the findings are helpful to families with inheritable disorders. Despite their value, the number of autopsies continues to decline. A headline from the *New York Times* health section[21] stated: "Sharp Drop in Autopsies Stirs Fear That Quality of Care May Also Fall." The article quoted a 1984 survey of 1326 hospitals, which showed that 215 performed autopsies on less than 5% of their patients who died during hospitalization. There seems to be an attitude now that there is little to be learned from autopsies because of advanced diagnostic techniques. This attitude, combined with the current medical legal environment (a litigious public) and apathy on the part of some pathologists, has contributed to this decline. The pathologists' apathy may in part be a reflection of fear that the autopsy will reveal something important that was missed, which could result in a malpractice suit, and the view that the autopsy does not contribute significant new knowledge. Personally, I believe the well-performed autopsy continues to be a major source of medical education.

To further understand the importance of autopsies, you need only look at mortality statistics. In 1986 the Health Care Financing Administration published data from 5500 hospitals in which they formulated an expected death rate from variables such as age, gender, and diagnosis related groups (DRGs). These data identified outlier hospitals whose mortality statistics were below the expected value. Unfortunately the data used were not always valid: a hospital that was basically a hospice was included, and the fact that a hospital handling a lot of terminally ill patients would have a higher mortality rate was not taken into account.[22] The data were made available to the public, and some hospitals with good reports used this fact in their advertising.

The data for 1988 were published in late 1989 for the 6000 hospitals that treat Medicare patients. The 1988 data showed that 196 hospitals (3.4%) exceeded their predicted mortality among Medicare patients.[23] The Health Care Financing Administration suggested a correlation between high mortality rates and lower quality of care. Thomas Morford, the Health Care Financing Administration director of quality standards, tried to make clear that mortality rates are only one measure used in the evaluation of the quality of care; however, the data caused a general uproar, receiving comments such as "inaccurate" and "meaningless."[24] This apparent inaccuracy in mortality rates emphasizes the need to perform more autopsies[24]: it is generally difficult to draw valid conclusions on the quality of care from mortality rates, whereas the data from autopsies could contribute to more valid conclusions regarding unwarranted deaths.

Robert Dubois[22] lists the following as influences on death rates in outlier hospitals:

1. Statistical selection effects. Patients may choose to die at home; the availability of nursing homes or hospices needs to be considered.
2. Time frame. Mortality data should include a comparison of deaths in the hospital compared with deaths within 30 days after discharge. Included in the comparison should be any autopsy data and the availability of such data for the two groups.
3. Diagnosis coding errors.
4. Severity of illness.
5. Ethical decisions.
6. Quality of care. This influence is actually what may be foremost on the mind of the public when they read these data.

Obviously, accurate data from autopsies would contribute to influences 3 and 4 above. Thus, the clinical correlation portion of the autopsy as well as the diagnosis should be done with extreme care; conclusions should be based on objective data whenever possible.

Accurate diagnoses affect the DRGs and the comorbidities, which have financial implications. Increased scrutiny has been placed on physicians and hospitals for their quality of care; this same scrutiny will likely carry over to pathologists for the accuracy of data obtained from autopsies.

It is not surprising that the JCAHO has adopted policies that call for the use of autopsies by each hospital as a means of assessing quality of care. The JCAHO now requires hospitals to incorporate autopsy findings into an organization-wide quality assurance activity that assures autopsy reports are completed within 60 days unless exempted by medical staff bylaws. Discussed below are some of the new policies the JCAHO has adopted relating to autopsies.

MS.6.1.8.3: The medical staff, with other appropriate hospital staff, develops and uses criteria that identify clinical, legal, and other circumstances in which an autopsy is required or should otherwise be performed.[25]

The medical staff committees at the Tucson Medical Center established criteria for autopsies as follows:

1. Unanticipated deaths.
2. Deaths in which the exact cause of death is not known (cause is sufficiently obscured to delay completion of death certificate).
3. Deaths related to genetically inheritable condition (for purposes of genetic counseling).
4. Deaths in which the autopsy would meaningfully augment medical knowledge. This category is vague; however, unknown and unanticipated medical complications would be included. Also, diagnoses not made clinically have therapeutic implications.

5. Potentially iatrogenic deaths (within 48 hours of surgery or invasive diagnostic procedure).
6. Death incident to or within 7 days of obstetrical delivery.
7. Death occurring in patients receiving experimental therapy if autopsy results are considered helpful to evaluation of experimental regimen.
8. Intraoperative or intraprocedural deaths (usually Office of Medical Examiner cases).
9. Accidental deaths (also usually Office of Medical Examiner cases).

You might consider adding the following criteria to those above:

1. When there are concerns about the possible spread of a contagious disease (one could argue that this comes under criteria 4, above).
2. When death occurs suddenly, unexpectedly, or under mysterious circumstances from apparently natural causes but does not come under the jurisdiction of a medical examiner or coroner.
3. When the cause of death could affect insurance settlements, such as policies that cover cancer or that grant double indemnity for accidental death.
4. All neonatal deaths.
5. When the death occurs in a nursing home and the quality of care is questioned. Although it often does not, this should fall under the jurisdiction of the medical examiner. Of course, nursing home occupants often die in the hospital, where their deaths may be investigated by the hospital pathologist.

You should choose procedures for which you would like to perform a certain percent of autopsies according to the needs of your institution. For example, you may choose to perform autopsies of all patients (or 50%) under 40 years of age who underwent angioplasty.

MS.6.1.7.3.1: Findings from autopsies are used as a source of clinical information in the conduct of quality assurance activities.[25]

All autopsies at the Tucson Medical Center are reviewed by the appropriate committee, namely, medicine, surgery, pediatrics, family practice, or obstetrics and gynecology. These committees have separate subcommittees that evaluate clinical performance within those specialties; when this function was part of their general meetings, there was usually insufficient time to address the concerns raised about quality assurance, which is not related to a lack of concern but rather to the large amount of business that each committee has on its agenda. However, quality assurance is important enough to have a separate, dedicated meeting by each specialty on quality assurance issues. Obviously, it is not necessary to have specialty quality assurance committees at smaller hospitals where there may be only one to two physicians in each specialty. Each hospital must determine its own need for subcommittees devoted entirely to evaluating clinical performance.

These committees receive a copy of each autopsy protocol related to their service. Questions asked related to the quality of care pertain to therapy, diagnostic tests, appropriateness, and timeliness. Pathologists should be involved in these meetings, whether autopsies are discussed or not, just as they should be involved in discussing the appropriateness of testing. The meetings should definitely focus on comparing the clinical diagnosis with the discharge notes and the autopsy diagnosis, with a discussion on the reasons for any discrepancies and whether they affected the outcome. These meetings should be treated as quality assurance monitors and documented, listing the number of discrepancies, any trends in problems found, and action taken to correct them.

If autopsies are not reviewed by committee, the pathologist should take the initiative to specifically look for major discrepancies in diagnosis and refer such cases to a hospital committee. Although Tucson Medical Center guidelines require that all important discrepancies be presented at the specialty management meetings, I have found on my own a number of cases where there was no review by committee even though the discrepancies warranted it. These were sent to the appropriate committees. I routinely review 10% of our autopsies as a precaution against missed discrepancies, using a form shown later in this chapter. This review is a good opportunity to look at the clinical pathologic findings while at the same time comparing them with the clinician's discharge notes.

MR.2.2.15.9: When a necropsy is performed, provisional anatomic diagnoses are recorded in the medical records within 3 days, and the complete protocol is made part of the record within 60 days, unless exceptions for special studies are established by the medical staff.[25]

From a practical standpoint, an autopsy should be completed as soon as possible while details of a patient's condition are still fresh in the mind of the attending physician. Certainly, delaying the autopsy diagnosis will not kindle an interest in use of the autopsy service. Furthermore, the urgency of completing an autopsy is sometimes found in the need of families to discuss the autopsy findings with their physician to complete their grievance process. Generally, provisional diagnosis will be sufficient for the grievance process, but some families may want the finalized autopsy report.

The quality of an autopsy needs to be assured. Ask yourself the following questions about autopsy procedures:

1. Is the autopsy form standardized? Does it include acceptable diagnosis, gross and microscopic description, and a clinical summary in which the autopsy findings are correlated with the clinical findings (assuming the clinical history is known)?
2. Is the autopsy report organized and complete? Are all systems discussed in a manner that will answer the clinician's concerns?

In the autopsy review, discordant diagnoses should be treated the same as in the surgical pathology review. Where there are disagreements classify them as major or minor based on how the missed diagnosis affected the patient's care. Make sure the care was not merely supportive care of a terminal case. Figure 5.6 is an example of a summary autopsy form,[26] while Figure 5.7 is a revised version of Figure 5.6 that I have used.

To conclude, ask yourself the following about autopsies:

Mortality Review Report

Nursing Unit _____ Attending Physician _____

Admission Date _____ Date of Death _____ Length of Stay _____

Age _____ Sex _____ Autopsy Number _____ DRG _____

Clinical Diagnosis: _____

_____

_____

Autopsy Diagnosis: _____

_____

_____

Significant clinical conditions that were not addressed in the autopsy report: _____

_____

_____

	Yes	No	NA
1. On the basis of the patient's condition on admission, was death an anticipated possibility?	—	—	—
2. Were appropriate patient care measures provided?	—	—	—
a. Diagnostic?	—	—	—
b. Therapeutic?	—	—	—
c. Supportive?	—	—	—
3. Was appropriate consultation obtained?	—	—	—
4. Was surgery or an invasive diagnostic procedure performed? Specify: _____	—	—	—
5. Did death occur within 48 hours after surgery or an invasive diagnostic procedure?	—	—	—
6. Was CPR performed?	—	—	—
7. Was death explained by the primary autopsy diagnosis and/or secondary diagnosis?	—	—	—
8. In retrospect, was death preventable?	—	—	—
9. Section chairman review of record suggested?	—	—	—

Figure 5.6 Autopsy form.

1. Are the autopsies being used for clinical quality assurance and can that be documented easily?
2. Are the autopsies performed and completed in a timely fashion? This can be easily checked by periodically going through your files to see how many are outstanding.
3. Are the autopsies themselves evaluated for quality? A spot-check mechanism should be done to verify this.

Mortality Review Report

Patient Name: _____ Autopsy Number: _____

Clinical Diagnosis**: _____

_____

_____

Autopsy Diagnosis: See attached face sheet from autopsy.**

Autopsy diagnoses that were significant and not diagnosed clinically: __

_____

Significant clinical diagnoses that were not addressed in the autopsy: __

_____

	Yes	No	NA	Not Sure*
1. Was death unanticipated?	____	____	____	____
2. Was death explained by the primary autopsy diagnosis and/or secondary diagnoses?	____	____	____	____
3. Was the patient terminal and care merely supportive?	____	____	____	____
4. Were appropriate patient care measures provided?	____	____	____	____
a. Diagnostic?	____	____	____	____
b. Therapeutic?	____	____	____	____
5. Was appropriate consultation obtained?	____	____	____	____
6. Was surgery or an invasive diagnostic procedure performed? Specify: _____	____	____	____	____
7. Did death occur within 48 hours after surgery or an invasive diagnostic procedure?	____	____	____	____
8. Was CPR performed?	____	____	____	____
9. In retrospect, was death preventable?	____	____	____	____
10. Section chairman review of record suggested?	____	____	____	____

*Comment on all in this category.

**Note: You may want to attach a copy of the discharge summary and the final autopsy diagnosis and indicate "See Attached" on the form where applicable.

Clinical Pathology Correlation: _____ Acceptable _____ Not Acceptable*

(Continued following page.)

Figure 5.7 Revised autopsy form.

Quality of Slides: _____ Acceptable _____ Not Acceptable*

Gross Description: _____ Acceptable _____ Not Acceptable*

Microscopic Description: _____ Acceptable _____ Not Acceptable*
Are all diagnoses detailed in the gross and microscopic description included in the autopsy report?

Final Diagnosis: _____ Acceptable _____ Not Acceptable*
*Make specific comment when not acceptable.
Additional Comments: _____

Figure 5.7   Revised autopsy form (continued).

Autopsies are an important quality assurance tool, but only if they are done well. The quality of autopsies must be evaluated to verify that they are fulfilling their role in a hospital-wide quality assurance program. The criteria for a quality autopsy should be established by consensus opinion from the staff. The benefits of the autopsy include continuing medical education and improved patient care.

The diminishing role of the autopsy may be, in part, due to the attitude of pathologists and clinicians that autopsies are no longer necessary.[27,28] One way to increase the number of autopsies is to emphasize performing autopsies when there is a problem that is clinically relevant, such as deaths in patients under 40 years of age who have undergone angioplasty. Historically, autopsies have made a tremendous contribution to medicine; they should continue to do so.

TIME NECESSARY FOR QUALITY ASSURANCE IN ANATOMIC PATHOLOGY

Each pathology group must decide how much time it is willing to spend on quality assurance in anatomic pathology. The time must be factored into a program that is acceptable to the group but still within the framework of regulations. Quality assurance activities should be done on a regular basis so they become part of the daily routine and involve all pathologists. Each group should rotate the primary responsibility for peer review; one option is to assign certain days for peer review. At the Tucson Medical Center the pathologist on call does the peer review for the week.

Reading all slides twice can be time-consuming; the second reading takes a quarter to half as much time as the original reading, depending on how thorough you are. If reading all the slides twice proves to be too time-consuming, consider some form of selective review. Some groups have chosen to double-check malignant biopsy specimens only, although this does not catch false negatives that are really malignant. Another alternative is to spot-check all diagnostic biopsy specimens.

At the Tucson Medical Center we would be hard-pressed to justify reading all slides twice based on cost: we find major errors in approximately 0.05% of the cases. Is this cost-effective? If you were one of the patients benefitting from the review you would think so. Every major error has therapeutic implications but does not mean the outcome will be different each time. For example, if there is a false-negative result, the patient may have to undergo biopsy again; but even if the second biopsy findings are positive, the final outcome for the patient may be the same.

The time you spend on quality assurance in anatomic pathology is worthwhile because it improves the quality of your work. However, the amount of time need not be excessive to generate improvements. It's unlikely you could afford to spend the time on ongoing studies for all the quality indicators reviewed in this chapter; merely select and prioritize indicators that relate to problems in your laboratory. Once those problems are corrected, move on to others.

REFERENCES

1. McCarthy WC. The diagnostic reliability of frozen sections. *Am J Pathol.* 1929;5:377-380.

2. Vogel FS. The pathologist's intraoperative relationship with the neurosurgeon. *Surg Pathol.* 1988;1:173-175.

3. Rogers C, Klatt E, Chandrasoma P, et al. Accuracy of frozen section diagnosis in a teaching hospital. *Arch Pathol Lab Med.* 1987;111:514-517.

4. Penner DW. Quality assurance in diagnostic surgical pathology. *Arch Pathol Lab Med.* 1987;111:513.

5. Dudley HAF. Audit and the pathologist. *Proc R Soc Med.* 1975;68:634-637.

6. Bruer ML. Frozen section biopsy at operation. *Am J Clin Pathol.* 1938;8:153-169.

7. Fuller RH. Frozen sections. *Ariz Med.* 1957;14:657-659.

8. Nakazawa H, Rosen P, Lane N, Lattes R. Frozen section experience in 3000 cases. *Am J Clin Pathol.* 1968;49:41-51.

9. Dahlin DC. Seventy-five years' experience with frozen sections at the Mayo Clinic. *Mayo Clin Proc.* 1980;55:721-723.

10. Dankwa EK, Davies JD. Frozen section diagnosis: an audit. *J Clin Pathol.* 1985;38:1235-1240.

11. Howanitz PJ, Hoffman GG, Zarbo RJ. The accuracy of frozen-section diagnoses in 34 hospitals. *Arch Pathol Lab Med.* 1990;114:355-359.

12. Travers H. Quality assurance in anatomic pathology. Presented at the Arizona Pathology Society Meeting; May 14, 1988; Tucson, Ariz.

13. Penner DW. Quality assurance in anatomic pathology. In: Howanitz PJ,

Howanitz JH, eds. *Laboratory Quality Assurance.* New York, NY: McGraw-Hill Inc; 1987:296-316.

14. Feinstein AR, Gelfman A, Yesner R, Auerbach O, Hackel DB, Pratt C. Observer variability in the histopathologic diagnosis of lung cancer. *Am Rev Respir Dis.* 1970;101:671-684.

15. Owen DA, Tighe JR. Quality evaluation in histopathology. *Br Med J.* 1975;1:149-150.

16. Whitehead ME, Fitzwater JE, Lindley SK, Kern SB, Ulirish RC, Winecoll WF. Quality assurance of histopathologic diagnosis: a prospective audit of three thousand cases. *Am J Clin Pathol.* 1984;81:487-491.

17. *Hospital Peer Review.* March 1988:32.

18. Goldman L, Sayson R, Robbins S, Cohn LH, Bettman M, Weisberg M. The value of the autopsy in three medical areas. *N Engl J Med.* 1983;308:1000-1005.

19. Battle RM, Pathak D, Humble CG, et al. Factors influencing discrepancies between premortem and postmortem diagnosis. *JAMA.* 1987;258:339-344.

20. Landefeld CS, Curen MM, Meyers A, Geller R, Robbins S, Goldman L. Diagnostic yield of the autopsy in a university hospital and a community hospital. *N Engl J Med.* 1988;318:1249-1254.

21. *New York Times.* July 21, 1988:18.

22. Dubois R. Mortality and quality. In: Goldfield N, Nash D, eds. *Providing Quality Care: The Challenge to the Physicians.* Philadelphia, Pa: American College of Physicians; 1989.

23. *American Medical News.* January 12, 1990:3.

24. *Washington Report.* January 8, 1990:9.

25. *Accreditation Manual for Hospitals, 1988.* Chicago, Ill: Joint Commission on Accreditation of Hospitals; 1987:172.

26. Travers H. Quality assurance in anatomic pathology. *Lab Med.* February 1989:85-92.

27. Hill RB, Anderson RE. The autopsy and affairs of health. *Arch Pathol Lab Med.* 1989;113:1111-1113.

28. Cottreay C, McIntyre L, Favara BE. Professional attitude toward the autopsy. *Am J Clin Pathol.* 1989;92:673-676.

6. Quality Assurance in Cytology

CYTOLOGY IS PRESENTLY the focus of negative national attention. A headline from the *Wall Street Journal* read: "Lax Laboratories: Hurried Screening of Pap Smears Elevates Error Rate of the Test for Cervical Cancer."[1] Another headline in the *Arizona Daily Star* read: "Health Care's Misplaced Millions."[2] The article implied financial loss related to poor quality of cytology screenings. These headlines were followed by national television coverage and responses from the medical community, which agreed that there was room for improvements.[3-5] Thus, pathologists and cytotechnicians should be moved to implement programs that will assure quality, before strict government regulations do it for them. The best way to create a quality assurance program in cytology is to document it by reviewing specific quality indicators.

REQUEST SLIP

When you receive a request for a cytologic diagnosis, is it filled out with all the pertinent information needed to help make the diagnosis? If not, what steps are taken to obtain that information? As part of a quality assurance program, review some request slips to determine if the information is sufficient to make a diagnosis. If not, make some phone calls to obtain that information.

As medical director, copies of all request slips lacking necessary information are given to me. After 1 to 2 months of collecting data, I contact all offices that have submitted more than one request slip with insufficient information to remind them of the importance of the missing information. This reminder sometimes needs to be repeated because I have found that once it stops, the problems quickly return. This reminder is also a good public relations move on behalf of the laboratory, because it demonstrates the laboratory's commitment to quality.

Patient's Name

Slides must be labeled with the patient's name. Without a correct name, you cannot double-check an abnormal cytologic specimen when the colposcopic and/or histologic findings do not support the cytologic diagnosis. Initially, when a name was missing, I would call the office that sent the inadequately labeled slide. Consequently, there was a marked decrease in the number of unlabeled slides, occurring in less than 1% of cases submitted to the Tucson Medical Center laboratory. This quality assurance activity was ongoing also, because once people were no longer reminded, the situation generally reverted back to where it was before. In addition, I would add "slide received with this request was not identified with the patient's name" to the report in red ink as a reminder to the office staff as well as the physician who submitted the smear. This monitor has presently been discontinued, however, since now we return all inadequately labeled slides to the physician's office for identification.

Fixation

Ideally, all drying artifact is noted on the cytology report. A simple, prospective quality assurance study of drying artifact could focus on the 10% of slides rescreened. If the physician sprays fixative immediately and uniformly on the Pap smear, theoretically there should be no drying artifact; however, the physician has no way of knowing this unless there is feedback from the cytology department. A focused quality assurance study could have the cytologist and the cytopathologist specifically note how often drying artifact appears. Every slide may have a few cells with drying artifact, but the amount should not interfere with valid interpretation. You may discover you are not detecting all the drying artifact. At the Tucson Medical Center the percentage of slides on which we detected drying artifact increased when we compared the cytologic diagnosis with that of the biopsy specimen. We were forced to look at cytologic diagnoses that did not agree with the diagnoses of the biopsy specimens, and we realized that we may have undercalled or overcalled our cytologic diagnoses due to the drying artifact. Such a finding would support doing a prospective study. As with all monitors, any trends should be documented and communicated to the involved clinicians.

Adequate Amount of Diagnostic Material

Whether an adequate amount of material has been submitted for diagnosis is subjective. Again, I suggest you do a focused review, looking more specifically at the adequacy of material on the slide. There is a tendency to be more strict when doing a focused review of cytologic specimens related to abnormal biopsy specimens. Thus, in retrospect a normal Pap smear with an abnormal biopsy specimen is more likely to be viewed as inadequate or less than adequate for valid interpretation. If this is noted with any frequency, a focused study of this monitor is warranted.

There are several reasons a cytology report may not reflect an abnormality diagnosed on the biopsy specimen: the cytologic material may have been misdiagnosed because cells were present but not highlighted; abnormal cells were not present on a Pap smear with an adequate amount of material; drying artifact, excessive inflammation, or blood prevented diagnosis; or there was insufficient material for diagnosis, which if properly diagnosed, would result in a repeated Pap smear. To ensure that an adequate amount has been submitted, you need to establish guidelines against which to measure it. Obviously, no strict number of cells is required, but there should be a substantial number of well-preserved cells occupying several streaks on the slides. In addition, protein-aceous material, excessive inflammation, or red blood cells should not mask the view of these cells; if there is a problem, document it and notify the office of origin.

Slides found to be inadequate should be labeled *unsatisfactory*. A group of pathologists would likely agree that a slide with only a few cells is inadequate; however, their agreement on what is adequate beyond that would be unlikely. The interaction and discussion among pathologists and cytologists in a group should lead to a fairly uniform interpretation of inadequate cytologic material within that group.

ENDOCERVICAL CELLS

There is a better correlation of cervical biopsy diagnosis with cytology diagnosis when endocervical cells are present on the Pap smear. A laboratory information system that collects data on the overall percent of specimens that have endocervical cells as well as the percent from individual physicians would be useful as a quality assurance indicator. Cytologists should routinely note the presence or absence of endocervical cells. If a physician repeatedly submits more than 50% of his Pap smears without endocervical cells, we send a letter on the significance of the presence of endocervical cells on the Pap smear. If the pattern persists, we call the clinician. As a result of this review, there has been a significant increase in the percent of specimens submitted with endocervical cells. Physician feedback has been very positive.

RESCREENING

If specimens are picked randomly for rescreening, the number of normal diagnoses changed to abnormal diagnoses as a result will be small in most laboratories. However, specimens from patients in high-risk groups should be rescreened regularly because of the danger a missed diagnosis can pose to these patients. Rescreening specimens should involve not only looking for missed malignant or atypical cells but also documenting the above-mentioned quality indicators (sufficient information, adequate material, etc). At the Tucson Medical Center, we have designed forms (Figure 6.1) that can be used to determine

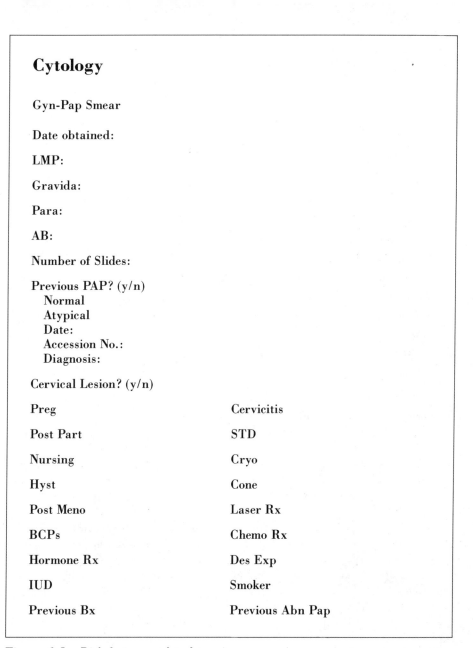

Cytology

Gyn-Pap Smear

Date obtained:

LMP:

Gravida:

Para:

AB:

Number of Slides:

Previous PAP? (y/n)
   Normal
   Atypical
   Date:
   Accession No.:
   Diagnosis:

Cervical Lesion? (y/n)

Preg	Cervicitis
Post Part	STD
Nursing	Cryo
Hyst	Cone
Post Meno	Laser Rx
BCPs	Chemo Rx
Hormone Rx	Des Exp
IUD	Smoker
Previous Bx	Previous Abn Pap

Figure 6.1   Risk factors used to determine rescreening.

rescreening. By assigning a number value to each risk factor, we come up with a total possible number. The 10% of the specimens with the highest numbers are rescreened. Although the selection is most easily done by computer, someone could be assigned to make the selection by looking at all the background information. Unfortunately, that information is not always available.

Cytology Quality Control

Negative Gyn-Random & High-Risk Rescreen

Date	Specimen #	Tech.	Initial DX	Final DX

Summary

Number of previous negative cases rescreened:

Number of previous negative cases found:

Number of cases reviewed:

Comments on the above: _____

Figure 6.2   Form for documenting rescreenings.

To maintain efficient use of the cytologists' time, clerical staff can be trained to select cases for rescreening; the cytologists should do the initial screening and, senior cytotechnologists or cytopathologists should do the rescreening. Any discrepancies should be referred to the original cytologist and to a pathologist for rescreening. These data should be summarized monthly, quarterly, or semiannually, and discussed at a quality assurance meeting. If corrective action is needed, initially it should be educational.

An alternative and less burdensome method for the rescreening selection would be to choose specimens from patients who have an abnormal history, such as previous abnormal biopsy, known malignancy, or abnormal cytologic findings, including the presence of inflammation, dysplasia, tumor, radiation effect, or infective agents. If this selection process does not total 10% of the gynecologic screenings that day, add some random specimens. The form depicted in Figure 6.2 was designed by cytologists at the Tucson Medical Center for documenting rescreenings.

Rescreen all previous normal cytologic findings when there are abnormal cytologic findings (moderate dysplasia or worse). Keep a log of these (Figure 6.3) and submit these for quality assurance study.

CORRELATION OF BIOPSY AND CYTOLOGIC SPECIMENS

Recreen all gynecologic cytologic specimens in which there are discrepancies with the biopsy findings. A variation of one grade is an acceptable discrepancy:

Summary

Number of cases reviewed:

Number of cases still thought to be negative:

Number of cases with discrepancies:

Comments on the above: _____

_____

Figure 6.3 Log for reviewing previous normal cytologic findings.

Surgical Number: Cytology Number:

Categories for lack of
cytology/histology correlation:

   Sampling Problem (Cytology):

   Interpretation (Cytology):

   Screening Oversight:

   Sampling Problem (Biopsy):

   Interpretation (Biopsy):

   Technical Problems—Specify: _____

   _____

Other: _____

_____

Comments: _____

_____

Initials: Pathologist _____ Cytologist _____

Figure 6.4 Cytology/Histology review.

for example, if the cytologic diagnosis is mild dysplasia (low-grade SIL) and the biopsy diagnosis is moderate dysplasia (high-grade SIL). All discrepancies should be documented and summarized periodically to find problem areas.

When the gynecologic biopsy specimens are diagnosed, the cytologic findings should be available for comparison; the cytologic results are recorded on the clinical information portion of the surgical report and the correlation is done immediately. Since this correlation is a daily, ongoing process, it only adds approximately 5 minutes to the pathologist's work load. If there is a discrepancy of over one grade between the cytologic and biopsy diagnoses, the cytologic and biopsy specimens should be reviewed again by the involved cytologist and pathologist. The review ideally should be without knowledge of the original diagnosis. The pathologists and cytologists at the Tucson Medical Center are asked to use the form shown in Figure 6.4 for the correlation. The same system of

Consensus DX		% Negative	% Suspicious	% Positive
Negative	Submitters	93.7	5.9	0.4
	Participants	93.2	3.5	3.7
Suspicious	Submitters	6.2	84.2	9.6
	Participants	19.4	65.9	14.7
Positive	Submitters	1.0	40.0	59.0
	Participants	2.8	16.0	80.0

Figure 6.5 Differences of opinion in diagnosis of cervical cytopathologic specimens.

rescreening can be done for nongynecologic specimens that have corresponding cytologic features.

After a specimen has been screened (and rescreened, if necessary), pathologists and cytologists should note whether the data were acceptable or unacceptable. If unacceptable, a specific course of follow-up action should be detailed. Again, there are egos on the line, so corrective action should be handled delicately, that is, the initial focus should be educative not punitive. It is rare that a problem cannot be solved by education.

ACCEPTABLE CONSENSUS

Penner[6] found no consensus on 5% of 1,575 cervical cytopathologic specimens, which meant there was less than 50% agreement on 5% of the cases. However, a 50% consensus may not be a good definition of a correct diagnosis. Figure 6.5, taken from Penner's data, illustrates the differences of opinion. Submitters were the group of pathologists that originally had responsibility for the cases, while participants were those who took part in the survey.

The cytopathology data had a consensus of diagnosis among 85% of the submitting pathologists.[6] Obviously, there is room for disagreement; the criteria for consensus at one institution may not be the same at another. Thus, expect some disagreement when diagnosing specimens. Again, background information contributes to the diagnosis: if it is known that the biopsy findings are abnormal, then that information may help or prejudice cytologists' detection of abnormal cells on the cytologic examination and their reaching an agreement in diagnosis.

ALTERNATIVE APPROACH

One method has apparently improved the detection rate of cervical lesions by intentionally introducing one known abnormal slide disguised as a routine specimen into each day's case load.[7] It is hard to prove that such a method actually does improve detection rates, since there is really no way of knowing how many specimens would be found to be abnormal on any given day with or without the added quality control slide. However, the observation that there was an increased detection rate of abnormal cytologic results after this approach was instituted might prove to be significant if correlated with corresponding biopsy specimen findings for those patients.

NUMBER OF SLIDES

Each cytologist works at a different pace, thus you cannot expect equal production levels across the board. You have to set your own guidelines as to what is an acceptable rate of work for your laboratory. The new Health Care Financing Administration standards[8] state that cytologists may not screen more than 80 new slides per day: some cytologists may not be able to comfortably screen that many cases while others may be very capable of screening an even larger number. The ability of the cytologist is not the only variable. The degree of difficulty of the slides can make the screening progress slower. Cytologic specimens that show a great deal of inflammation and dysplasia are more difficult to screen. When few abnormalities are missed, an acceptable rate of work for cytologists has likely been found.

SUMMARY

Quality assurance in cytology will most likely increase costs if implemented correctly; however, the cost is worth the improved accuracy of the screenings. The proposed proficiency testing for cytology should also contribute to more uniform interpretation of cytologic specimens, as should all educational efforts in this field (in theory — the proof of this hypothesis is difficult if not impossible). As usual, all testing measurements should be monitored to pinpoint trends that specifically need improvement. Cytologic diagnosis will never be perfect, but we should continue to perform quality assurance monitors that will fine-tune our diagnostic ability.

REFERENCES

1. *Wall Street Journal.* November 2, 1987:1.
2. *Arizona Daily Star.* April 16, 1989:C1.
3. Koss LG. The Papanicolaou test for cervical cancer detection: a triumph and a tragedy. *JAMA.* 1989;261:737-743.
4. Replies to quality assurance measures in cytopathology. *Acta Cytol.* 1988; 32:913-939. Letters to the Editor.
5. Council on Scientific Affairs. Quality assurance in cervical cytology: the Papanicolaou smear. *JAMA.* 1982;262:1672-1679.
6. Penner DW. Quality control and quality evaluation in histopathology and cytology. In: *Pathology Annual.* New York, NY: Appleton-Century Crofts;

1973;8:1-19.

7. Hindman WM. An Approach to the problem of false negatives in gynecologic cytologic screening. *Acta Cytol*. 1989;33:814-818.

8. *Summary Medicare, Medicaid and CLIA Programs: Regulations Implementing the Clinical Laboratory Improvement Amendments of 1988 (CLIA '88)*. Chicago, Ill: American Society of Clinical Pathologists; 1990:14.

7. Appropriateness of Testing

THE US PUBLIC is concerned about the appropriateness of testing because of its effects on both cost and quality of medical care; it is also of great interest to physicians, medical staff, hospitals, governments, third-party payers, and professional review organizations who provide and pay for care. Physicians are always deciding if care is necessary or not; laboratory testing is a big part of that decision. Determining the appropriateness of testing can be controversial and difficult, but it is also unavoidable.

The JCAHO requires hospitals to monitor the appropriateness of medical laboratory services as part of their quality assurance program. This requirement is controversial because it expects measurement of somewhat subjective judgments, which are influenced by (1) physician proficiency, values, and medical knowledge; (2) patient characteristics; and (3) medical technology and hospital resources.

It is this subjectivity in our applied science that makes appropriateness of testing so difficult to determine. A physician bases the decision to order a test on a number of considerations, including the outcome of a procedure, personal approach, the threat of malpractice, and pressure from the patient and family.[1] The patient's wishes play an important part in the physician's decision. For instance, a patient may need the test psychologically as a reassurance, which fact exemplifies the "art" of medicine[2]: although the patient does not need the test *physiologically*, the physician must consider it for the patient's *psychological* needs. Physicians' fear of malpractice is highlighted in a Gallup Poll commissioned by the AMA, which found that 78% of over 1000 physicians said they ordered extra tests for defensive purposes; on the other side of the coin, the poll found that 61% of the public said physicians ordered too many tests because of the fear of malpractice.[3] Since there is minimal harm in performing most laboratory tests, physicians must weigh the health outcome against the costs.

A Massachusetts study measured how many patients received a red blood cell transfusion for anemia, even though they were not adequately tested for anemia.[4] The local professional review organization speculated that a 40% reduction in blood transfusions could be achieved over 2 years. However, the first author of this article, William Dunham, MBA (Assistant Vice President of Utilization Management, Leominster Hospital, Leominster, Mass; personal communication, December 9, 1990), said that the study was never completed, despite its potential to show significant cost savings.

Defining appropriate testing is straightforward. An appropriate test is one in which the health benefits of the procedure exceed its health risks by a sufficiently wide margin to make the procedure worth doing. Defining the guidelines by which you judge the procedure worthwhile is much more difficult.

The literature on appropriateness of testing is sparse. What little there is generally points to overuse of services but contains little information on underuse. Most studies of overuse have found at least double-digit percentages of testing procedures were unnecessary. The Rand study extrapolated figures from the literature to speculate that approximately one quarter of these procedures (coronary angiography, upper gastrointestinal endoscopy) were done unnecessarily.[5] In a recent review by Blue Cross/Blue Shield in Minnesota, 6% of the test procedures were found to be unwarranted compared with 12% to 15% by systems users nationally.[6] Geographic variants are difficult to identify because of the multiple variables involved, including average age of population, increased financial pressure, insurance coverage, validity of data collection, and physician attitude. At this time, variations in statistics are not completely understood and will require additional research.

A University of Miami study looked at intensive care unit laboratory use.[7] By eliminating standard orders, repeated testing within certain time frames, and verbal orders (except in true emergencies) and by establishing guidelines and improving communication combined with personal feedback, they were able to reduce the number of tests by 42%. This reduction came without a difference in the severity of illness, length of stay, or mortality. They concluded that charges were eliminated without affecting quality of care. They emphasized that thinking, not widespread screening, discovers rare abnormalities.

Appropriateness of testing is particularly important because the US public is demanding value for its investment, at a time when the medical portion of the gross national product has increased to over 11% in 1989 from 6% in 1966. Furthermore, the HCFA recently predicted that the United States will spend 14% to 15% of its gross national product on health care in the year 2000.[8] Approximately $27 billion per year is spent on laboratory tests. The Blue Cross/Blue Shield Association reported that 20% to 60% of these tests are unnecessary. At a conference sponsored by the CAP most health experts agreed that some portion of the testing may be unnecessary.[9] If the assumption by Blue Cross/Blue Shield is correct, this would result in a savings of $5 to $16 billion per year.[10] The question is, are we getting the most value for the money spent.

The health care industry is strongly influenced by the purchaser, whether private or governmental; it is also influenced by the growing glut of providers that want more cost-effective systems because they are market driven. Cost containment, then, is one of the driving forces behind the quality assurance efforts directed at the appropriateness of testing. One of the problems with cost containment in the laboratory is that it affects the pocketbook of the pathologists who are on a percentage contract. Some people argue that the savings generated from a reduction in laboratory testing may not be as cost-effective as reducing high-cost procedures, such as image testing in radiology.[11] Nonetheless, either the laboratories will take steps to contain costs or others will do it for them, in which case the public might view laboratories as a group that was forced into being cost-conscious. This is not a desirable position for health care–related groups.

Can costs be reduced by reducing the number of laboratory tests—without loss of quality of care? We know that ordering more tests may not give you more significant information: additional testing does not replace a good history and physical examination. Sometimes additional testing leads to false-positive results, causing unnecessary follow-up. Other times, additional tests may provide incidental information that is minimally useful. For example, a slightly elevated lactate dehydrogenase level may be related to exercise but could result in expensive unnecessary follow-up testing. We cannot maintain that unnecessary testing is cost-efficient or always clinically relevant.

Laboratories must look at cost identification, cost benefits, and cost-effectiveness from the point of view of society, the patient, the payer, and the provider. The bottom line is that laboratory testing that does not clearly contribute additional health benefits to the patient is not cost-effective and is inappropriate,[12] which does not mean that testing that effectively contributes to *preventing* disease should be eliminated. It isn't just "the buck" that matters, but rather "the bang for the buck."

Consumers will pay more for quality if they believe it is the best, especially when it is related to health. To the orthopedic surgeon, quality may mean a reduction in nerve palsies; to the administrator, a savings on the number of laboratory tests ordered; and to the patient, less waiting time or having blood drawn in a more professional environment by a well-mannered phlebotomist. Thus, quality means something different to each person involved, which makes judging the appropriateness of a particular procedure difficult.

Laboratory test ordering can vary greatly. Faculty physicians at a major medical school had annual laboratory costs that differed by as much as 2000% among themselves for outpatient care of their hypertensive patients.[13] Medicare payments to independent clinical laboratories increased nearly 30% from 1985 to 1986, more than triple the rate of growth of payments to physician offices.[14] *Common Diagnostic Tests Use and Interpretation*,[15] published by the American College of Physicians, lists criteria for ordering tests. The prologue states that the book is a guideline designed to help the physician make a decision whether a diagnostic test will make a desirable difference in the care of the patient. The book is written with the expressed purpose of controlling costs that do not contribute to good medical care. The book is the product of a long-standing working relationship between the American College of Physicians and the Blue Cross/Blue Shield Association. It is part of their medical necessity project. The guidelines should be reviewed by clinicians and pathologists.

The CAP has published comments that take exception to guidelines from *Common Diagnostic Tests Use and Interpretation.*[15] These comments include the fact that the $30 billion spent in medical testing is a small amount compared with the $520 billion spent on health care. It is also difficult to match guidelines with every clinical situation. Furthermore, these guidelines were written without input from pathologists and other laboratorians.[9] One major problem is that no studies, to my knowledge, have established a relationship between test use and patient outcome. Thus, it is hard to say whether increased laboratory use results in a better outcome. At the Tucson Medical Center we have cut back on laboratory testing and have not seen any obvious deterioration in the quality of care.

It would be difficult to justify an additional chemistry profile if the first set of results was normal. It would be hard to argue that having the second set of normal results would contribute even remotely to improved quality of patient care. The government could reimburse providers based on the number or the type of tests ordered for a given health care condition,[14] since this is similar to reimbursement for the DRGs. If other insurance companies follow suit, then the laboratory could be a cost center (the hospital would receive a set amount of money for a particular disease). Thus, the laboratory would do as few tests as inexpensively as possible, and the only profit would come from the difference between the reimbursement and the total costs to the hospital.

When looking at rates of laboratory testing keep in mind that variations may result from differences in severity of illness, disease rates, and availability of services. Teaching hospitals are known to have higher testing rates than non-teaching hospitals, because students and residents may order tests to see what the results might be in different clinical situations for academic satisfaction rather than for practical reasons. Thus, teaching hospitals may come up short in reimbursement by third-party payers if reimbursement is set according to across-the-board standards.

John Kelly, MD,[16] who represented the AMA at a meeting for the CAP in 1990, emphasizes the need for quality assurance studies related to appropriateness.

"During the past few years, various studies have identified unexplained variations in the utilization of health services; other studies have indicated that some medical care may be inappropriate or marginally beneficial. From these studies, a general perception has arisen that a significant percentage—as much as 10%, 20%, or more—of all medical care is unnecessary. We believe that these generalizations are based on inadequate information to support such statements and, therefore, are unjustified. The presence of variations in the utilization of services is, in itself, not proof of inappropriate services. Also, generalizations from a few studies to all of medical care are unjustified. The AMA's efforts to develop practice parameters are designed to reduce unnecessary care, regardless of the amount, and to assure the appropriateness of patient care."

Volunteer Hospitals of America keeps statistics on the number of tests per patient discharged, which can be correlated with the severity of disease. The data show there can be variations of up to 100%, even between comparably sized hospitals. There are other comparative studies by which you can analyze cost. Data can be obtained from the American Hospital Association's Monitrends and the CAP Q-Probe program. These programs provide laboratory managers and hospital administrators the information they need to know about how their testing compares with other hospitals. These programs do not provide automatic conclusions about your testing procedures, but they do provide a data base sufficient to point out a trend worth pursuing.

If you decide your hospital has a high rate of testing, find the cause for it. Does your institution have sicker patients? Are physicians placing unnecessary orders? Is the 25th to 75th percentile a normative range of acceptable practice?[17] (If you are outside that range you may want to investigate further.) There are no standard answers to these difficult questions. Clinicians should be involved in answering these questions since cost containment without loss of quality care for the patient should be your goal. Laboratory personnel should know how much an individual test costs and should help decide its diagnostic value in various clinical settings. Clinicians have typically been resistant to this sort of input from the laboratory, but that resistance should be minimal now with the increased pressure from hospital administrators, HMOs, other third-party payers, and the public to evaluate medical costs.

Some of the factors that affect decisions on test selection are listed below.

Physician proficiency and values: These include the individual physician's knowledge, the degree of certainty demanded, and how well the case is managed. Frequently the more complicated the case, the more likely the physician is to order more tests. In most studies the biggest variable that determined how much testing was done was not patient characteristics but the opinion of the physician. In a study of tests ordered for hypertensive patients, physicians categorized their test ordering patterns as being high volume or low volume.[18] Accordingly, they ordered tests in order of importance, thereby establishing a baseline, assessing prognosis, reassuring the patient, and helping with treatment decisions. Many third-party payers feel that the test ordering pattern should be supported by a patient's symptoms; however, when the symptoms do not make the diagnosis clear, testing may be necessary to reach the diagnosis even though the symptoms do not clearly warrant it.

Medical knowledge: You probably expect that leading experts agree, for the most part, on the correct surgical procedure for a patient, yet in a cooperative study sponsored by the Rand Corporation conducted at UCLA on surgical procedures that included coronary angiography, coronary artery bypass surgery, colonostomy, cholecystectomy, and carotid endarterectomy, there was 30% to 81% disagreement on whether to do the procedure.[19] In another study from the Center for Health Policy Research and Education at Duke University, a panel of physicians constructed a mathematical model for strategies of action to counter colorectal cancer, which included effectiveness of various screening techniques.[20] A panel in 1981 studied the impact of fecal occult blood and 60-cm flexible sigmoidoscopy on the annual mortality rate; disagreement among members of the panel varied up to 100% for some decisions.[20] They found significant disagreement on issues, such as the time for development of cancer of the colon from adenomatous polyps and the number of early cancers that bleed and thus can be detected by looking for occult blood in the stool. The resolution of these issues impact on decisions such as the frequency and validity of testing the stool for occult blood as well as the frequency of performing colonoscopy.

The decision to order diagnostic tests is as difficult to make as the decision to do other procedures. Since the rationale for doing procedures is not supported by agreement on basic disease patterns, as mentioned above, the room for debate on frequency or even choice of procedures or tests to follow-up patients is great. Medical knowledge dovetails with physician proficiency and values; once again, you have to expect disagreement.

Patient characteristics: Patient characteristics are important in determining whether to order a test. Simply stated, "How sick is the patient?" This question cannot be answered by simply knowing the diagnosis. What standards should be set for appropriate testing based on patient diagnosis? Should the standards depend on the admitting diagnosis, the discharge diagnosis, or the patient's chief complaint. Patients that are hospitalized for palliative treatment for a terminal illness should require fewer diagnostic tests. If testing is done according to the patient's chief complaint, should the severity of the patient's condition be graded? Medisgroups, a software program for medical care quality control (Mediqual Systems Inc, Westboro, Mass), considers the patient's chief complaint and the severity of illness when it tries to assess the optimal amount of testing for patients who do well at different levels of sickness. It appears the chief complaint may be more useful and as accurate as the admitting diagnosis in determining the appropriate amount of testing. In my experience, the admitting diagnosis is not the same as the discharge diagnosis approximately 50% of the time, which would support this concept.

Medical technology and hospital resources: Medical technology and hospital resources affect which laboratory orders can be completed without the help of a reference laboratory; they also affect the quality of the service. Are the services available in a timely fashion: is there the necessary technology to perform an appropriate array of tests in-house to satisfy the physician's needs, and is the testing done in a cost-effective manner? If appropriateness of testing is studied for cost containment, then the cost-effectiveness of doing the testing in-house should be compared with sending it to a reference laboratory. Of course, the decision to send a test out rather than do it in-house includes issues aside from cost, such as service, quality, and accurate results. Obviously, cost-effective testing is not synonymous with cost reduction if it extends length of stay and adversely affects patient outcomes.

Appropriate testing has a positive impact on patient care, accomplishing efficiently what is achievable and practical. However, *achievable* and *practical* are difficult terms to apply to patient care. Still, these terms, along with what has the greatest positive impact on care, have to be defined to establish standards on which improvements can be made to satisfy the consumer's need for optimal medical care. Setting local standards is a big challenge to determining the appropriateness of testing because of the propensity for people to disagree. At the same time, physicians should not set standards that protect them from strict guidelines. The people most qualified to develop these standards are pathologists because of their extensive knowledge of clinical laboratory medicine. These standards should be *guidelines* for diagnostic testing. They should be achievable and practical, delicately balancing benefits and risks to the patient.

The following AMA guidelines for ordering tests are helpful and should be stressed in laboratory educational efforts[21]:

Will the test provide information not already available?
Will the test results alter treatment or clinical outcome?
Will a less expensive test give the same information?
Can the interval between tests be extended?

At the Tucson Medical Center we participated in a Travenol-related VIP program that examined disease categories, such as those relating to uncomplicated myocardial infarction, cholecystectomy, normal newborns, and triple bypass surgery, to establish testing standards for each category. One group of physicians recommended standardized testing for each disease. By consensus, standard laboratory orders for select disease categories were published. The resulting savings were significant.

The VIP study was a strong incentive to standardize our volume of laboratory tests for particular diseases, because our data were compared with other Volunteer Hospitals of America hospitals of similar size. These guidelines·are more readily accepted when they pertain to uncomplicated diseases, for example, an uncomplicated myocardial infarction. The more complicated cases have too many variables that resist the use of standard guidelines.

Peer review plays an important role in the acceptance of standardization of testing. For one disease category at the Tucson Medical Center we reviewed the standard postoperative test orders of two physician groups in the same subspecialty. Once they were made aware of differences in their standard orders they were willing to redefine their standard test orders, and we saved close to $40,000 in 1 year. For example, we did electrolyte testing once a day instead of three times a day the first postoperative day. We also replaced the daily electrolyte test orders with daily potassium testing.

Another institution did not set any real standards for testing, but charts were periodically examined by an outside consultant for the quality of admission and follow-up notes, the method of investigation, and the appropriateness of tests performed and drugs prescribed.[22] During the period of auditing there was improved documentation of the patients' clinical status in the progress notes and a decrease in both the number of tests performed and the amount of drugs prescribed, despite the lack of any standards. The method was not important, since there were no set guidelines followed, but the mere knowledge that these items were being reviewed resulted in desired behavioral changes.

Some guidelines for testing are already being applied. Concurrent Review Technology, a health care management firm in Shingle Springs, Calif, had physicians develop computerized guidelines for laboratory orders. The computer automatically flags questionable orders. The program looks at appropriateness of the individual test order as well as frequency. In one study, approximately 5% of the orders were flagged. These were reviewed by physicians who canceled about 50% of these orders. The company claims that for every dollar spent on the program four dollars are saved. The program is used for claims and physician education. Some of the larger insurers, including Prudential, Metropolitan Life, and Mutual of Omaha, are now using the program.[11]

QUALITY INDICATORS

Leukocyte Differential Count

A study on the leukocyte differential count was done at the Tucson Medical Center by Ralph Rohr, MD, and Florence Rivers, MT(ASCP) (unpublished data, 1987). It noted that almost one third of all Tucson Medical Center inpatients had a daily differential cell count done. Generous criteria were established for doing differential cell counts (see below). On review, the study concluded that three of every four differential cell counts were unnecessary. A newsletter was distributed and the information was presented at a general staff meeting.

One year later the situation was restudied; basically no difference in use was noted. At that point it was decided to change the order form so that a conscious effort is necessary to request a differential cell count; an order for a complete blood cell count provided an automated result without a manual differential cell count. We require an order to ask for a "CBC with differential" before a manual differential cell count is done.

As differential cell counts become more automated so that five-part differential cell counts are done automatically, this quality indicator may become less important. Still, many institutions still do not have an automated differential cell count capacity. Even with automation, the blood count without a manual differential cell count is more cost-effective simply because technical time is saved.

After an initial trial we found it is more practical to do differential cell counts for emergency department patients. In general, the physicians in that department felt they needed a differential cell count frequently enough that waiting for the results of an automated blood count and then ordering a differential cell count would be a disservice to the emergency department patient, for whom rapid turnaround time is often necessary.

The result of our changes in ordering differential cell counts was a 50% reduction hospital-wide in the number of manual differential cell counts performed. Several physicians objected strongly to the setting of guidelines for differential testing; they said they needed the differential cell count each time and wanted it done automatically. They were a small minority and were not supported by their peers, thus the guidelines were put in place. This is an excellent example of a consensus at work. The cost savings won over the vast majority of the staff and are shown in Figure 7.1. The study was done for 13 days, with 257 unnecessary differential cell counts discovered. 1323 hours is a two-thirds equivalent of a full-time employee.

$$\text{Unnecessary diffs} = 347 - 90 = 257$$

$$\text{Cost savings} = 257 \times \$10/\text{diff} - \$2{,}570 \text{ in 13 days}$$

$$\text{Annual cost savings} = \frac{365}{13} \times \$2{,}570 = \$72{,}158$$

$$\text{Annual time savings} = \frac{365}{13} \times 257 \times \frac{11 \text{ min/diff}}{60 \text{ min/hr}} = 1323 \text{ hr}$$

Figure 7.1 Cost savings as a result of changes in ordering differential cell counts.

As you can see, cost savings for the year were estimated at $72,000. This amount does not take into account the fixed costs that do not change as much, such as equipment and space. James Winkelman, MD, estimates from studies he has done that a 10% cut in test volume results in a 4% cut in laboratory costs.[15]

The following criteria serve as guidelines to performing a diiferential cell count at the Tucson Medical Center:

1. One differential cell count at the time of admission or for screening purposes.
2. Change of white blood cell count from normal to abnormal range (eg, $4.5 \times 10^9/\text{L}$ to $10.5 \times 10^9/\text{L}$) or vice versa.
3. Greater than 50% change in white blood cell value between consecutive results.
4. Change in white blood cell count from one tens range to another (eg, $12 \times 10^9/\text{L}$ to $21 \times 10^9/\text{L}$).
5. Three or more consecutive rising white blood cell counts.
6. Seven consecutive days of white blood cell counts (one differential cell count).

Below are the Blue Cross/Blue Shield guidelines for leukocyte differential count (LDC), which are much stricter but are useful for comparison with the ones above.[23]

1. Outpatient Screening/Case-finding
   1.1 The LDC is not routinely indicated in ambulatory asymptomatic patients.
2. Hospital Admission Screening/Case-finding
   2.1 The LDC is not indicated in patients in whom there is no reason to expect an abnormality.
   2.2 The LDC may be useful at hospital admission to confirm a suspected infection or to detect patients at risk of infection due to granulocytopenia caused by treatment or known disease.
   2.3 The LDC is not routinely indicated in patients admitted for elective surgery.
3. Diagnosis of Suspected Abnormality
   3.1 The LDC may be useful, regardless of the total leukocyte count, in the diagnostic evaluation of the following:

3.1.1   Newly suspected infection

3.1.2   New fever

3.1.3   Suspicion of primary hematologic disorder (eg, anemia and leukemia)

3.1.4   Suspicion of disease associated with secondary abnormalities of LDCs (eg, lymphoma and lymphocytopenia)

3.2   The LDC may be indicated in the diagnostic evaluation of patients with an abnormal leukocyte count if there is uncertainty about the cause of abnormality or when management may be affected (eg, isolation of leukopenic patients).

    3.2.1   The LDC is generally not indicated when bacterial infection is known and when leukocytosis is present.

4. Monitoring

  4.1   The leukocyte count is useful in patients at risk of leukopenia due to chemotherapy or bone marrow disease.

    4.1.1   If the leukocyte count is greater than 4.5×10^9/L, repeated LDC is not necessary to screen for granulocytopenia.

  4.2   Repeated leukocyte count and LDC may be useful in patients in whom it is unclear if treatment is effective or in whom the course of disease is difficult to discern.

  4.3   The appropriate interval for repeated LDC testing needs further study but is unlikely to be less then every 2 days in 7 in leukopenic patients.

  4.4   The LDC may be indicated in monitoring the following:

    4.4.1   Patients with infection not improving clinically

    4.4.2   Patients with new symptoms to suggest infection or hematologic disorder

    4.4.3   Patients with leukopenia

    4.4.4   Patients undergoing cytotoxic therapy if leukopenia is developing

    4.4.5   Patients whose current illness is associated with previous abnormalities, to assure their resolution

  4.5   An LDC is not indicated in patients who are improving clinically.

The guidelines do not clearly state what the appropriate recommended interval for repeated leukocyte differential count is. They do state that even mildly leukopenic patients may not need a repeated leukocyte differential count for several days or weeks. The leukocyte differential count may be helpful when it is unclear if treatment is effective. The leukocyte differential count is not indicated in patients with known bacterial infection when there is known leukocytosis or in patients who are improving clinically.[23]

Emphasis should be placed on ordering laboratory tests that will lead to therapeutic decisions. Again, the guidelines set by a university hospital may need to be more flexible for educational purposes. At the Tucson Medical Center, which is a teaching hospital, the published guidelines resulted in considerable discussion; a number of physicians said they had decided to stop ordering leukocyte differential counts on a routine basis, only ordering them when specific symptoms or history warranted it.

Prothrombin and Partial Thromboplastin Times

The best way to establish the appropriateness of orders for prothrombin and partial thromboplastin times is to utilize consensus opinion of clinicians, including hematologists schooled in coagulation. We did this at the Tucson Medical Center, basically using criteria published by the American College of Physicians and Blue Cross/Blue Shield.[15] Criteria used included monitoring anticoagulation therapy and clinical bleeding diathesis, and following up patients who underwent open heart surgery. For patients scheduled for an invasive procedure, criteria included evidence of liver disease, history of malnutrition or malabsorption, and active bleeding (or evidence indicating it). Even with the generosity of the criteria, a substantial number of orders for prothrombin and partial thromboplastin times were probably unnecessary, predominantly those ordered as preoperative screenings. Preoperative orders for prothrombin and partial thromboplastin times are a fairly common practice in this country, a practice I believe is unwarranted.

This study was fairly time-consuming, thus we felt it would be more rewarding to focus the follow-up study on screening preoperative patients. A number of the busier surgeons had removed prothrombin and partial thromboplastin times from their standard orders; thus, there was some cost containment as a result of the study. The number of nonacquired coagulation problems that are asymptomatic are so small that most hospitals will find that there is a large potential for cost savings in this area. One study showed that 55% of the preoperative coagulation studies, including tests for prothrombin times, partial thromboplastin times, bleeding times, and platelet counts, were not indicated based on a review of 282 elective surgical cases.[24]

An additional worthwhile quality indicator would be a review of test orders for coagulation factors when the prothrombin and partial thromboplastin times are normal.

Platelet Counts Below 100×10^9/L

Was the patient adequately worked up to determine the cause of the low platelet count?[25] If platelet transfusions were required, was the treatment adequate?

Multiple Chemistry Profiles

From a clinical standpoint, few doubt the necessity of ordering chemistry profiles. The question is whether it is more cost-effective to order repeated chemistry profiles as opposed to individual tests. Some people argue that profiles should not be ordered at all for healthy asymptomatic patients before elective surgery (eg, knee surgery); they argue that the yield is extremely small and false positives may be the most frequent test result. Those arguing for routine chemistry profiles contend that they provide standard baseline values that might be useful for comparison with values generated later in the admission or those of a future hospital admission; they also point out that the profiles detect the occasional abnormal result, which can lead to a significant diagnosis of disease.

The quality indicator is repeated chemistry profiles for the same patient. Since normal results are based on a 95% gaussian distribution curve, the more tests in the profile and the more profiles ordered the more likely it is the profile will show an abnormality that may not be clinically important but could demand a follow-up, such as a costly workup. If borderline elevated test results are ignored, the abnormality turns out to be clinically important; a malpractice suit is risked: Why didn't you follow this up? How did you decide the abnormality was an acceptable variant and not worth the effort of follow-up? To further complicate this delicate issue, there is growing pressure from insurers not to reimburse for tests other than those directly related to the patient's symptoms.[26]

In a case-controlled analysis comparing duplicate with nonduplicate profiles, repeated tests were significantly more likely to have been ordered by a physician who had not ordered the patient's previous profile.[27] This is also true in the studies I have done. To prevent this, a single physician should be responsible for ordering all tests regardless of how many physicians are involved in the care of the patient.

When we decided to review multiple chemistry profiles at the Tucson Medical Center, we knew the issue would be controversial and spark substantial discussion. This study had two phases. The first phase looked at purged data, which included each patient's laboratory summary, printed out once all laboratory work was finished, and all their chemistry profiles. We sent letters to physicians who had ordered multiple chemistry profiles for a single patient, asking for a response if they had any questions. The letter reviewed the issues just discussed, including false positives and cost containment by ordering individual tests, and questioned the necessity of repeated chemistry profiles on consecutive days. We also summarized the data in a medical staff newsletter to make physicians aware of this monitor. The data were also discussed at specialty meetings.

Some physicians responded that multiple chemistry profiles were needed for patients undergoing parenteral nutrition or that additional chemistry profiles were ordered by other physicians. A substantial number of patients with multiple chemistry profiles showed only protein abnormalities; others had initial and follow-up chemistry profiles with normal results. As in the literature,[27] a number of the multiple chemistry profiles in our study were frequently ordered by different physicians for the same patient. A laboratory information system that detects repeated orders within a certain time could have a demand response before accepting the orders. For example, when a second chemistry profile is ordered, before proceeding with the order the nurse would be required to inform the physician that there are already chemistry profile results in the chart. Reminding a clinician that an order has been repeated and letting a clinician know that his or her orders are being reviewed regularly could lead to a change in ordering patterns. Hence, you have an ongoing quality indicator.

The second phase sent physicians a letter asking them to explain why they had ordered multiple chemistry profiles for the same patient (Figure 7.2). A positive statement (eg, "I feel the multiple chemistry profiles were indicated because") was used on the form to avoid putting the physicians on the defensive. If the physicians could not supply valid reasons for repeated chemistry profiles, they checked a statement on the form that said the multiple chemistry profiles were not indicated.

James Bond, MD
3102 E. Goldfinger
Tucson, AZ 85710

Dear Dr Bond:

Listed below are your cases with more than one chemistry profile on a single admission. This is one of the areas that the government and insurance companies are looking at. Please respond to this letter.

This is the second step in the audit process. We have previously reviewed data of selected cases in which there were multiple chemistry profiles and not asked for a response from the attending physician. In the previous study many of the profiles were ordered by multiple physicians or the physician was not aware that he ordered multiple profiles.

Thanking you in advance.

Respectfully,

Paul Bozzo, MD
Medical Director

_____ I agree these multiple chemistry profiles were not indicated.
_____ I feel the multiple chemistry profiles were indicated because __
_____
_____

Patient Name: John Doe
Chemistry Profiles: 11/15/89; 11/18/89

Figure 7.2   Letter asking physicians to explain their ordering of multiple chemistry profiles for the same patient.

Again, sometimes multiple chemistry profiles are ordered because patients are receiving parenteral nutrition, which requires looking at a large number of frequently changing parameters. However, the majority of patients should be followed up with individual test orders, which is more cost-effective. Even though some resistance to not ordering multiple chemistry profiles remained, the number of orders for multiple chemistry profiles in the second study declined from 19% to 10%. This is a fairly easy study to do and should be continued on an intermittent, spot-check basis.

Standard Test Orders

I reviewed standard test orders for hip and knee surgery requested by the busiest groups practicing at our hospital. I then summarized the data so each group could easily see how its standard orders compared with others'. The physician groups' orders were identified by numbers except for the reviewing physician's, who knew which orders were his or hers. After discussing the findings with a representative from each of the groups, I sent a letter based on the discussions (Figure 7.3). Included with the letter were prices for the following tests:

Partial thromboplastin time
Blood time
Electrocardiogram
Anteroposterior bilateral hip x-ray
Lateral view hip x-ray
Routine chest x-ray
Coagulation profile
Platelet count
Blood products: type and screen, type and crossmatch
Sedimentation rate
SMA-12
Complete blood count with differential
Electrolytes
Urinalysis
Urine culture and sensitivity

The letter was well received and induced significant cost savings almost immediately for the hospitals, third-party payers, or patients, depending on the type of reimbursement. Thus, this monitor helped create standards for preoperative laboratory tests for knee and hip surgery.

By conducting a study that debates standard test orders for particular diseases, you will find that physicians will probably be induced to look more closely at the appropriateness of test orders. In fact, the application of peer pressure without actually setting standards should result in a decreased number of laboratory tests ordered (and has in my experience). Challenging standard orders is a good place to start when establishing the appropriateness of testing. One hospital eliminated standard orders except for patients in intensive care, patients with hyperalimentation, and patients who undergo organ transplantation, which resulted in a substantial cutback in laboratory orders.[28]

A Medicare bulletin tells of a Florida medical center that no longer allows physicians to have standard test orders, with the exception of tests for patients in intensive care and tests from physicians with high use rates. The center cut standard orders in half. The center has just two sets of standard orders for the entire obstetrics specialty, one for normal vaginal deliveries and one for cesarean sections. Every standard order is reviewed by a cross-section of 15 specialists, who feel test ordering is now more appropriate. In addition, the laboratory and radiology department work loads have been considerably reduced. Eliminating standard test orders could result in significant savings, but even greater cost-effectiveness might be achieved by having a group of physicians agree on a set of guidelines for specific diseases or procedures. However, these guidelines must be flexible enough to adapt to new technology. One final problem with standard orders is the lack of effort involved in ordering the test since you merely initial a pretyped sheet, which could result in less attention paid to the results. The bottom line is that standard orders need to be watched closely for appropriateness.[29]

Daily Test Orders

All orders that call for daily testing should automatically be considered suspect. The tests may prove to be appropriate, but it is generally difficult to justify daily orders since the symptoms of the patient cannot be known ahead of time. To determine the appropriateness of daily testing, review the orders of physicians who frequently order tests in this manner.

Preoperative Electrolyte Testing

The literature shows a low prevalence of electrolyte disturbances in healthy individuals who are not taking medication; in fact, the prevalence is so low that the number of false-positive results are higher than the false-negative results.[30] Preoperative orders for electrolyte testing are common. It is worthwhile to establish how often electrolyte abnormalities occur in patients less than 40 years old at your institution who are not taking diuretics; with this information, you can determine how appropriate testing is at your hospital for patients that fall into that category.

Electrolyte Testing in Critical Care Units

Baigelman et al[31] looked at the frequency of orders for electrolyte testing in patients requiring critical care. With no specific criteria, they reviewed all sets of electrolyte tests for patients requiring critical care ordered more than once in a 24-hour period against the patients' charts and determined that 10% of the orders were unnecessary. This quality indicator could be even more focused by including in its review sets of electrolyte tests ordered more than once in a 24-hour period for *all* patients. Other studies include reviewing all sets of electrolyte tests ordered more than once in 24 hours for patients with minimal abnormalities and for patients with no therapeutic changes in that period. Another study could review all sets of electrolyte tests ordered more than once in 24 hours more than 24 hours in advance. You cannot validly predict the need for two sets of electrolyte tests for a 24-hour period 1 day in advance. When conducting these reviews, part of your monitor could focus on routine or standard orders for electrolyte tests rather than orders that are a response to the patient's condition.[12]

Response to Therapeutic Drug Levels

At the Tucson Medical Center a study was conducted to see if a physician's response to toxic levels of theophylline and digoxin in patients was appropriate.

Re: Standard test orders

Dear Dr Bond:

This follow-up on our recent discussion applies to standard orders for hip and knee surgery. I know you receive a lot of mail but I'd really appreciate it if you would look at this and get back to me by phone or mail.

Coagulation Studies: The coagulation profile at Tucson Medical Center is divided into two types: a bleeding coagulation profile if the patient is symptomatic, which includes a prothrombin time, partial thromboplastin time, fibrinogen level, thrombin time, and platelet count; and a nonbleeding profile that would normally be performed, which includes a prothrombin time, partial thromboplastin time, platelet count, and a template bleeding time. The nonbleeding profile contains the same tests that would be ordered individually in standard orders (see attached).

Because of problems that arise in patients taking anti-inflammatory medication, I contacted Doug Triplett, MD (Muncie Center for Medical Education, Indiana University School of Medicine), who is considered an authority on coagulation. He said that the prothrombin time and partial thromboplastin time would not be contributory unless there were symptoms related to bleeding disorders; the bleeding time and the platelet count could be the tests affected by anti-inflammatory medication.

Sedimentation Rate: None of the group representatives believed a preoperative test for the sedimentation rate was indicated for these patients.

SMA-12: Anesthesiologists as a group agree that a chemistry profile is not indicated prior to surgery unless a patient is symptomatic. The following tests are recommended by anesthesiologists before surgery:
Postmenarche women: hemoglobin, hematocrit, urinalysis
Premenarche women: urinalysis
Men <40 years old: urinalysis
Men ≥40 years old: urinalysis, hemoglobin, hematocrit

Chest X-rays: Studies have shown that routine chest x-rays are not worthwhile unless the patient has pulmonary symptoms. If you still believe that it is necessary to obtain a chest x-ray even though the patient has no pulmonary symptoms, it may be fruitful to ascertain if the patient has had a normal chest x-ray in the previous 6 months. If so, then there is even less support for obtaining another chest x-ray.

Electrolytes: Anesthesiologists tend to believe that testing for electrolytes is ordered too often. They recommend it only when the patient has an electrolyte disorder or is taking diuretic, antihypertensive, or other cardiac medications. *(continued following page.)*

Figure 7.3 Letter discussing standard test orders.

Urinalysis: Urinalysis is a standard test order, and cultures are done when indicated. With the exception of pregnant women, there is no need to do a urine culture if the urinalysis results are normal.

Blood Bank: At the Tucson Medical Center, we determined that a blood type and screen are sufficient; afterward, if atypical antibodies are found, only then do we proceed with a crossmatch.

EKGs: EKGs might be indicated in a patient over 50 years of age but certainly not in a healthy asymptomatic patient. They are not predictive without a treadmill.

Thus, some of the tests that might be considered standard may not be necessary. Insurers and HMOs are questioning standard test orders and the use of them. Please examine your group's standard test orders and tell me what you find.

Respectfully,

Paul Bozzo, MD
Medical Director

Enclosure

Figure 7.3 Letter discussing standard test orders (continued).

There were a few cases where there was no documentation of a response. You must be careful when judging responses as inappropriate, since patient response to most drugs is idiosyncratic: what is toxic for some patients may be necessary in other patients to achieve the desired therapeutic effect. Examine the clinical charts to ascertain if there were signs of toxicity in the patients who are considered toxic based on the drug levels found in the laboratory. If the patient can be classified as toxic, an appropriate response is to lower the prescribed dosage of the drug or cease therapy for a period. It is worthwhile to regularly assure ourselves that there are no problems in the therapeutic levels of drugs prescribed to patients. Such a study also keeps the physicians on their toes by requiring them to pay close attention to the drug levels they prescribe.

Response to Critical Results

At the Tucson Medical Center physicians were sometimes slow to respond to critical laboratory results, such as white blood cell counts greater than 15×10^9/L, so we reevaluated the level for critical results by consulting with clinicians. This action produced new critical result levels that were more appropriate to patients' needs, that is, the levels demanded immediate notification to the attending clinician so that he or she could respond appropriately and rapidly.

When following up a study on physician response, you should evaluate your critical results, especially those where physicians are slow to respond or do not respond at all. Clinician consensus is necessary in defining what exactly are critical result parameters. At the Tucson Medical Center we found a few critical results that did not receive immediate physician response although the situation demanded it. Fortunately, these were isolated occurrences.

In tracking physician response, you are looking for a trend in inappropriate response by a particular group of physicians or individual physicians. I initially conducted this study as a retrospective one; I now do prospective studies, using charts of hospitalized or recently discharged patients, while the events are still fresh in the minds of the clinicians.

Response to Hematuria

At the Tucson Medical Center we studied the clinical response to hematuria (defined as greater than four to five red blood cells per high-power field) not associated with manipulation of the genital urinary tract, such as surgical procedures or catheterizations. We also excluded midstream clean catch urine samples from menstruating females. We conducted this study several times and found very little improvement in the physician response. We did find that physicians were frequently aware of the abnormality but did not treat it unless hematuria was present and associated with symptoms at the follow-up office visit after discharge. The problem with appropriate response was primarily documentation. There was some improvement in the appropriateness of response, or at least documentation of response, immediately after the second study, because we called many of the physicians to inform them that their response to the findings of hematuria had been inappropriate, but as is the case for much follow-up action, as soon as the educational efforts ceased the response diminished. Still, no individual trends were noted; thus, group education efforts will continue and the study will have to be repeated.

Follow-up of Abnormal Test Results

Appropriate follow-up to abnormal test findings has long been a problem. Since the early 1960s, studies have indicated that 20% to 40% of abnormal results are typically not followed up.[32,33] At the Tucson Medical Center we have highlighted abnormal results as high or low; some computer printers are also capable of highlighting abnormal results in different colors or by placing them in different columns. Despite hopes these measures would alert physicians to the importance of abnormal findings, their inappropriate responses still remain a problem. Still, these measures should have a positive impact on physician awareness overall.

A recent study found the follow-up rate for abnormal test findings was only 53%. Even with automated reminders this response rate does not always improve.[32,33] Measuring the response to abnormal test results can be part of an ongoing quality assurance study, which does not necessarily have to be large in volume and can be relatively simple without detracting from its usefulness. Merely select a single parameter, such as the response to hematuria, and check 20 to 30 charts for documentation of some form of follow-up or at least acknowledgment of the laboratory abnormality. The ongoing intermittent tracking of abnormal results can in itself be effective follow-up action. Again, this must be combined with looking for trends by groups or individuals. In my experience the issue often is a lack of documentation of response to the abnormal test result, not a lack of physician awareness of the result.

A study that focused on abnormal calcium levels found that 14 of 53 calcium levels were abnormal on repeated testing but were not followed up. After analysis of the data, the authors concluded that "contrary to common opinion, when physicians ignore abnormal laboratory values they are making complex clinical judgments based on the degree of abnormality, the likelihood that further investigation will affect therapy and the cost of risk associated with further investigation."[34] The caveat to this article is that the study focused on test results that were repeated when the initial test was abnormal. In my review of this article, I found that other abnormalities were not noticed or were ignored. Twenty-six of 128 elevated calcium levels were abnormal but ignored; these were not focused on because they were not repeated.

Admitting Orders

You can use information from accounting to determine the appropriateness of testing. Pierre Keitges, MD (Chief of Pathology, Physician Reference Lab, Chicago, Ill), looks at the cost for all initial test orders for new admissions (oral communication, May 1989). If the cost exceeds a certain dollar value (chosen arbitrarily; Dr Keitges uses $200), he evaluates the orders to see if the cost is justified and contacts the physician for an explanation when the reason for the laboratory test is unclear or if the test should have been done prior to or after admission to the hospital. As long as the physician is asked to justify excessive costs in a nonaccusatory manner, this quality indicator can be effective because it has the potential to focus on physician test orders that are not appropriate.

Abnormal Liver Function Tests and Liver Scans

The literature suggests that liver scans done for liver metastasis when liver function tests are normal may not be appropriate. Hepatic metastasis in patients newly diagnosed as having colorectal carcinoma can almost always be predicted by elevation of liver function test results, including not only lactate dehydrogenase and alkaline phosphatase levels but also the carcinoembryonic antigen level. One study found that a preoperative liver scan added no additional data to predict early metastasis to the liver as long as the liver function test findings were normal.[35] Thus, it seems worthwhile to monitor the ordering of liver scans when liver function test findings are normal. This monitor is a multidisciplinary study, involving nuclear medicine, radiology, and pathology.

Optimal Timing for Measuring Drug Therapeutic Levels

Blood levels of drugs reach a steady state at various times (eg, 3 to 5 days for phenytoin) after change of dose or initiation of a regimen. In one study,[36] 56% of the drug level analyses were unjustified because the measurements were performed less than 3 days after a change in dose or initiation of a regimen. Hicks et al[36] found several patients who were toxic due to unwarranted dose change related to misleading prestudy serum levels. In a study conducted by Alan Barreuther, PhD (Pharmacy Department), and myself at the Tucson Medical Center, approximately one third of the tests ordered for blood levels of drugs were ordered with inappropriate timing. You can conduct a similar study by reviewing charts from patients whose therapeutic drug levels were tested—simply determine the time required to reach a steady state for each drug studied after a change in dose or initiation of a regimen. Before doing this study, however, you should try to first inform physicians of the time required for therapeutic drug levels to reach a steady state.

The following list is from a study designed by Alan Barreuther and myself. This study combined features from the above study on appropriate timing of orders for therapeutic drug levels with criteria that addressed the reasons for ordering tests for drug levels.

1. Check level after giving dose.
2. Check level for a newly admitted patient previously receiving treatment.
3. Check level for a patient with seizures.
4. Check level if there is a drug-drug interaction.
5. Check level after a dose or a route of administration change.
6. Check level if patient has signs and symptoms of toxicity.
7. Check level for no specific reason.[36-38]

All these reasons are justified except for number 7. Approximately 30% of the orders were classified as "no specific reason." We estimated our cost savings per year at $15,000, based on the number of tests ordered with inappropriate reasons or at an inappropriate time. You will realize the most savings by focusing your studies on the therapeutic drug levels ordered most frequently.

Blood Culture Results

The clinical indicator was no less than two and no more than three blood cultures in a 24-hour period. There should be no orders for a solitary blood culture, since one culture might miss an organism; the concentration of organisms in the blood fluctuates and frequently increases parallel to a rise in body temperature. For example, the organism associated with septicemia may be in very low concentration in the bloodstream and could be easily missed with one culture. When there is a need to rapidly initiate therapy, two cultures could be done using blood drawn from each arm. At the Tucson Medical Center we found almost no inappropriate orders; in the rare case there was one, we simply sent a brief educational note to the physician calling attention to the problem.

Carcinoembryonic Antigen Determinations

Carcinoembryonic antigen levels should not be measured in patients without evidence of cancer or documentation that cancer is suspected. Once the level is definitely elevated, continued testing for carcinoembryonic antigen levels is not indicated unless you are looking for therapeutic response.

Blood Use

The JCAHO criteria for accreditation include a requirement that medical staff look at the appropriateness of all blood component transfusions.[39] If after reviewing all transfusions for 6 months no problems are identified, a review of indications for transfusion on a spot-check basis would be adequate. The criteria should be specific regarding the review of the blood ordering practices of physicians, and there should be a plan for analyzing the data and for follow-up action when necessary. The JCAHO also requires analysis of confirmed transfusion reactions.

Although the transfusion review can be done retrospectively, it is best done concurrently because of the timeliness with which educational efforts can be applied. Some hospitals have used the prospective approach by having physicians complete questionnaires that list indications for transfusion at the time of the request.[40]

Below are criteria that David Goldman, MD, developed working with the transfusion committee at the Tucson Medical Center to serve as guidelines for blood use.

Red blood cells:
Acute blood loss greater than 15% of their total blood volume.
Hemoglobin level less than 80 g/L.
Chronic blood loss with a hemoglobin level less than 80 g/L (effort should be made to identify the cause and to apply specific therapy).
Hemoglobin level greater than 80 g/L but with cardiorespiratory obstruction or other symptoms related to the anemia.
Fresh frozen plasma:
Elevated prothrombin time. Some plans require a prothrombin time greater than 30 seconds if the patient is taking sodium warfarin (Coumadin), otherwise a prothrombin time greater than 15 seconds.
Abnormal partial thromboplastin time or specific coagulation factor assay. Some plans require a partial thromboplastin time greater than 50 seconds when associated with severe liver disease.[40]
Antithrombin III deficiency.
Patients with multiple coagulation defects, for example, liver damage.
Therapeutic plasma exchange.
Protein-losing enteropathy in infants.
Selected cases of immune deficiencies.
Reverse warfarin therapy.

Platelets:
A platelet count less than $20X10^9/L$ or a preoperative level less than $50X10^9/L$.
Functional defects (eg, due to aspirin).
Prophylaxis (cancer treatment).

The above guidelines represent the highest volume products used in routine blood banking. The following additional guidelines are for less frequently used products (although less frequently used, the development and publication of standard guidelines related to their use is worthwhile).[41]

Albumin solution:
Replace volume of removed plasma resulting from plasma exchange.
Patients undergoing cardiopulmonary bypass surgery.
Acute volume expansion associated with low serum albumin level (<25 g/L).
Third-degree burns.

Immune globulins:
Prophylaxis in patients with congenital hypogammaglobulinemia.
Invasive procedures in patients with immune thrombocytopenic purpura.
Chronic immune thrombocytopenic purpura in young children.

Rh immune globulins:
Rh negative woman giving birth to Rh positive infant.
Rh negative woman at 28 weeks' gestation with abortion, uterine hemorrhage, amniocentesis, abdominal trauma, or intrauterine transfusion.

Cryoprecipitate-antihemophilic factor:
Fibrinogen levels below 1 g/L with active bleeding.
Factor VIII deficiency unresponsive to other therapy.
Alternative to lyophilized factor VIII in von Willebrand's disease associated with bleeding or prophylaxis.

Factor VIII concentrate:
Hemorrhage in patients with known or suspected hemophilia A.
Prophylaxis in patients with known factor VIII deficiency prior to surgery or following trauma.

Prothrombin complex concentrates:
Treatment of hemorrhage in a patient with known or suspected hemophilia B.
Treatment of hemorrhage in a patient with hemophilia A with an acquired inhibitor.

Prophylaxis in patients with known factor IX deficiency.

Perform quality assurance studies on a number of the above quality indicators as well as whole blood and major components on a quarterly or semiannual basis to test for the appropriateness of testing for these factors. For the most part, there are very few instances where whole blood should be used, thus it would be simple to track whole blood transfusions on a weekly basis. Since most patients concerned would still be hospitalized, access to their charts would be easy.

The order form for blood bank products could be changed so the clinician must note the rationale for an order. This form could combine patient information such as laboratory results and nursing instruction. For example, when a transfusion is indicated, the following items might be recorded:

blood loss	estimated amount
anemia	hemoglobin level
	fibrinogen level
	albumin level
hemostasis	platelet count
	prothrombin time
	partial thromboplastin time

Nursing instructions sometimes include safeguards designed to prevent blood products from going to the wrong recipient, and to detect promptly any reaction to the transfusion. Signs of possible transfusion reaction and steps to take when one is suspected could be included in those safeguards. Two nurses or a nurse and a clerk could be required to assume joint responsibility for the correct identification of the transfusion unit and the recipient. This multidisciplinary (laboratory, nurse, clinician) quality indicator should have 100% compliance.

When there are problems in compliance they most often are related to the completion of paperwork. The paperwork must be completed and the protocol followed to avoid the serious consequences of transfusing mismatched blood products. These safeguards result in benefits, such as more appropriate use of blood products, less likelihood of a wrong recipient, and in the long run, less clerical work when reviewing the appropriateness of transfusion practice.

Type and Screen vs Type and Crossmatch

An area that can easily generate cost savings is reviewing type and crossmatching vs type and screening for blood products. If a substantial percent of blood is typed and crossmatched but not used then you have a problem that hopefully can be corrected easily with some educational efforts. For example, you could focus your review on tests ordered for nononcologic gynecologic cases where you would expect minimum blood usage; with few exceptions, orders for type and screen are more appropriate than a crossmatch for this type of surgical procedure.

You could also review the ratio of crossmatched to transfused blood orders for individual physicians, specifically looking for those who routinely have a high ratio. The exact ratio is not as important as patterns of use by groups or individuals. The ratio can be easily ascertained by reviewing computer-compiled data or keeping a log in the blood bank specifically for this topic. The data should be reviewed on an ongoing basis so that the pathologist can discuss the problems with any physicians whose orders for crossmatching are inappropriate before time is spent doing unnecessary crossmatching.

Testing for Ova and Parasites

Patients who develop diarrhea after more than 3 days in the hospital should not be tested for ova and parasites. A study conducted at the University of Pennsylvania over a 3-year period found no ova and parasites in 90 specimens from patients hospitalized for more than 3 days,[42] supporting strongly the belief that ova and parasites are not etiologically significant if the diarrhea developed during the hospitalization.

Glucose Tolerance Tests

Glucose tolerance tests are inappropriate if the patient is not having a normal or unstressed existence and has not had an adequate amount of carbohydrates (>200 g per day for 3 days) prior to the test.[43] It should be a rare to almost nonexistent order in most hospitals.

Incorrect Test Requests

Some orders, for example, sputum samples submitted for anaerobic culture, are obviously inappropriate. When such an order is submitted, inform the physician who placed the order of the test's inappropriateness. This audit is ongoing since any orders of this nature should immediately be brought to the attention of the section supervisor or pathologist, who documents them as quality indicators if the incorrect orders recur.

Thyroid Tests

What is the correct test required for a patient with suspected thyroid problems? A test for the thyroid-stimulating hormone is generally considered acceptable for hyperthyroidism; however, the use of a number of other tests for hypothyroidism is not as clear-cut. Finn et al[44] computerized data for ordering thyroid function tests on a problem-oriented test menu that included the following acceptable test combinations:

1. Hypothyroidism: test for thryoid-stimulating hormone with or without test for free thyroxine index or thyroxine.
2. Hyperthyroidism: any combination of tests for thyroxine, triiodothyronine, or free thyroxine index.
3. Thyroid function screen (detection of hypothyroidism or hyperthyroidism): test for thyroxine or free thyroxine index with or without test for thyroid-stimulating hormone.
4. Monitoring replacement therapy: any combination of tests for thyroxine, thyroid-stimulating hormone, and free thyroxine index.
5. Monitoring suppressive therapy: any combination of tests for thyroxine, triiodothyronine, thyroid-stimulating hormone, or free thyroxine index.

Finn et al[44] initially found that physicians wrote inappropriate orders for thyroid testing for 67 (37%) of 181 patients. After implementing the computer-based order menu, the percent decreased to 25%.

Wong[45] argues that the grouping of tests can encourage excessive ordering. Complete "thyroid panels," including testing for thyroxine, triiodothyronine, resin triiodothyronine uptake, and thyroid-stimulating hormone, accounted for

From: Director of Clinical Pathology
Subject: Use of Laboratory Tests

To: Dr X

John Doe may have excessive orders for the laboratory test listed below.
Please review this matter and provide a brief response.
   Test:
   Number per week:
   _____ Excessive testing
   _____ Appropriate because _____
Thank you for reviewing this matter and for providing a response. Please
return to James Bond, MD.

Figure 7.4   Letter regarding overordering of tests.

80% of thyroid function test orders. Some endocrinologists suggest the new, more
sensitive test for thyroid-stimulating hormone is sufficient for screening for
hyperthyroidism and hypothyroidism, and monitoring of therapy, yet most hospitals and private laboratories continue to offer thyroid panels.

To create a quality indicator for thyroid testing, guidelines for testing must be
formed by consensus of the leaders in your medical community and must be in
agreement with the literature. This could result in a significant cost savings at
many institutions.

Number of Tests

A threshold is chosen according to each individual test and whether the test
results are normal or abnormal. For example, the threshold for electrolyte testing
with normal results is one time per day; with an abnormality the threshold for
electrolyte testing is three times per day. The recommmended maximum number
of tests for electrolytes is three per week for normal results, whereas if abnormal
results are found, the recommendation is 14 per week. The same thresholds are
not applied to patients who undergo operations or patients in intensive care. For
patients in intensive care, the threshold is two per day if test results are normal
and three per day if abnormal. Thresholds are also not necessarily applicable to
surgical patients since their condition is less predictable. If the patient has
ketoacidosis or severe metabolic disorders then there is no threshold for electrolyte
testing.

Schifman[46] devised a system that uses a threshold number per unit of time for
tests to indicate whether the test might be appropriate. Clinicians were involved in
setting the thresholds. When the threshold is surpassed, a letter (Figure 7.4) is
sent to the attending physician, followed by verbal contact.

As a result of the thresholds, even though the guidelines are quite generous, Schifman[46] found a marked decrease in testing; the absolute number of some tests was cut in half. Manually entering all the data into a personal computer could be extremely time-consuming; however, a laboratory information system with threshold recognition included in the software could provide an ongoing quality indicator. Even without a computer a review could be done for certain tests on a spot-check basis.

Thresholds need to be set for a number of different tests. For example, in my experience if a magnesium level is normal there should be no more than one test for magnesium per day; if the level is abnormal there should be no more than two tests per day. If protein electrophoresis findings are normal, it need not be done more than once per admission; if the findings are abnormal, electrophoresis need not be done more than one time per week, since those findings are not likely to change quickly.

Computer-based programs similar to Dr Schifman's have set thresholds for the number of tests that are appropriate in a particular situation. These programs have been tried at the Hospital of the University of Pennsylvania, Johns Hopkins Hospital, and the New Mexico Medicaid Program and have involved laboratory tests, including therapeutic drug levels related to injectable drugs.[47-50] These programs have met with variable success. At both Johns Hopkins and the University of Pennsylvania there was no significant change in the ordering of multiple determinations, while at the University of New Mexico their use of injectable drugs dropped by 60%. However, these programs were installed in the late 1970s when physicians were less concerned about cost containment. Additionally, there was no individualized education used at Pennsylvania and Johns Hopkins, while there was at New Mexico. Thresholds are most effective when they draw attention to problems in test ordering and in an ongoing manner encourage practical solutions that improve patient care.

Urine Cultures

There should be a reason for ordering urine cultures related to laboratory data or clinical symptoms. If the urinalysis results are normal, a culture is generally not indicated. Some exceptions include the pregnant patient and the rare symptomatic patient with repeatedly normal urinalysis results. To correct inappropriate ordering of urine cultures, inform the physician that he or she is at variation with your guidelines so that the physician can respond appropriately. General educational efforts and staff newsletters are helpful. At the Tucson Medical Center we found that a substantial number of physicians who had apparently needlessly ordered urine cultures had additional data that were not on the inpatient chart, such as previous abnormal urinalysis results or symptoms related to the urinary tract, which if known would have justified the original request for the urine culture. Letters were sent to physicians who apparently had needlessly ordered cultures to find out if there was a reason for the culture that was not indicated on the chart. Follow-up included calling those physicians who did not respond to written requests for information.

Cerebral Spinal Fluid Cultures

At times cultures ordered for cerebral spinal fluid may be a knee-jerk reaction. However, Hayward et al[51] found there was an abnormal opening pressure, cell count, or protein level in 145 of 148 cases of chronic bacterial infection or malignant meningitis. Otherwise, when these parameters were normal no further testing was really needed, with the exception of immunocompromised patients, those with multiple sclerosis, or those with childhood bacterial meningitis. Despite these findings, many hospitals will find that the majority of orders for cerebral spinal fluid analysis are accompanied by orders for cerebral spinal fluid cultures. This is an easy study to perform and has obvious cost savings. One focus for this study could be patients undergoing myelograms. The majority of these patients have potential herniated discs, which would not warrant spinal fluid analysis.

Difficile Toxins

Assay for difficile toxins should only be ordered after a patient has diarrhea associated with the use of antibiotics or shows evidence of pseudomembranous colitis as determined by colonoscopy. When reviewing the orders for this audit, you need only determine if there are problems with appropriateness of the orders or problems with documentation. You do not have to review a large number of orders to discover a problem: if three of the first five show the absence of antibiotics use and no evidence of pseudomembranous colitis by colonoscopy in the patients, then corrective action should be instituted, since you already know you have a problem. If initially the orders appear to be appropriate, review at least 30 consecutive orders before drawing any conclusions.

Follow-up action should be educational. If a large number of clinicians need to be educated, a newsletter is indicated. Whether there are a large or small number of variants, there should be educational efforts directed at all clinicians at variance with this quality indicator. As a last resort, the medical director or another physician could check the chart before the ordered test is performed.

Miscellaneous Tests

Below are three tests for which quality indicators could be developed. Thresholds for these tests should be established by the consensus of clinicians with expertise in the area. Once guidelines with thresholds are developed they should be circulated so that all clinicians are aware of them. Of course, there will always be some unusual extenuating clinical situations that warrant exceptions to standards or guidelines; however, these exceptions are generally uncommon. Encouraging clinicians to develop consensus guidelines almost guarantees their acceptance and encourages an educational exchange of ideas among those participating in their development.

1. Quality indicators for a neonatal bilirubin determination. This monitor could also review guidelines for an acceptable frequency for testing.

2. Quality indicators for creatine phosphokinase determination. These indicators could be incorporated into guidelines for all patients who are admitted with a diagnosis of myocardial infarction. These guidelines include frequency of requested orders (eg, at admission and every 12 hours), the total number of negative tests required to clinically exclude myocardial infarction (this should be related by time to initial or additional clinical signs and symptoms), and the indications for MB fractions.
3. Quality indicators for lactic acid determination for patients with no evidence of acidosis (abnormal serum pH, serum PCO_2, or breathing pattern).

ECONOMIC GRAND ROUNDS

Economic grand rounds may follow a number of formats. It is most commonly done along the following lines: A clinical case is presented and orders are given by a discussant, the audience, or a panel of physicians. The cost of each order is then discussed, including whether there are less expensive options. For example, an expensive antibiotic may be no more effective than one that is less expensive; a full electrolyte panel may not be warranted if all that is needed is a potassium level; a creatine phosphokinase MB fraction may not be worthwhile if the total creatine phosphokinase level is quite low. The focus of these discussions is on quality care through appropriate and cost-efficient orders. Additionally, economic grand rounds can be educational, since frequently physicians are unaware of the discussed costs. Every order considered is given a price tag.

At some point in the discussions, the appropriateness of laboratory orders are inevitably discussed. Were these tests ordered correctly? Was the timing correct? Should additional tests have been ordered? Should these tests have been ordered on an outpatient basis? Although economic grand rounds is not generally presented as a quality assurance monitor to the regulators, it frequently affects the appropriateness of laboratory tests ordered. When documented correctly, including showing a causal relationship of economic rounds to clinical ordering patterns, it should be an acceptable quality assurance monitor. The laboratory and, more specifically, the medical director or a designated pathologist should participate in these discussions of diagnostic costs.

Economic grand rounds should be documented in a summary form, stating the nature of the discussion and number of attendees and expertise of the panel or moderator. In addition, aside from the economic grand rounds, the medical director or pathologist may choose to communicate costs to physicians by attaching a list of laboratory costs of high-volume tests to the front of the patient charts or sending itemized patient bills to the responsible attending physicians. As long as physicians are reminded of test costs, their awareness will have an impact on test ordering.

UNDERUSE

Underuse is every bit as important as overuse of the laboratory. We all have some anecdotal experience that demonstrates the importance of testing; for example, the autopsy diagnosis of pancreatitis undetected clinically. One study audited all charts that showed orders for urinalysis, urine culture, or sputum culture after an intensive educational program for the house staff that outlined explicit consensus criteria for test orders.[52] During an interim period and 9 months after the study, they audited all charts from patients in whom signs or symptoms included in the guidelines were present but for whom these tests were not ordered. There were two major findings. First, administrative intervention (the residents were required to indicate the reason for the test on the order form) improved test ordering beyond educational efforts alone. Second, tests that should have been ordered were of the same proportion statistically during the intervention period and 9 months after the intervention, which shows a long-term effect on ordering patterns of this effort.

This study[52] would have been a more valid indicator of underuse if it had studied underuse before the educational period. The study's criteria for underuse simply used the same guidelines for supporting the ordering of tests as were used for looking at the underuse of tests. This study demonstrates how easily guidelines used to study overuse can be used to study underuse. This study, in which physicians had to document a reason for the laboratory order, illustrates how important it is for clinicians to focus on their rationale for a test order.

OUTCOME-RELATED MONITORS

Outcome-related monitors are theoretically a good idea, but the outcome does not always reflect the necessity of the test. I remember a lecturer in medical school who talked about the art of medicine and the needs of patients. A key point in that lecture was that regardless of what steps are taken, a large number of patients will recover in any case.

Outcome is physical, pathological, and social.[53] The patient who enters the hospital unable to walk but walks out under his or her own power has a measurably physical outcome. Unfortunately, the patient who dies during hospitalization is the obvious, clear-cut example of a pathological outcome. Outcome includes clinical endpoints, such as the ability to function in everyday life (job performance and social function), patient perception of general health, and patient satisfaction with treatment. Outcome is *not* merely making the patient suitable for discharge from the hospital.[54] Outcome related to patient satisfaction could be defined through surveys filled out by the patient before, during, and after treatment. Unfortunately, many outcome studies are tied to length of hospital stay, which is a superficial way to look at outcome but for which data are easily generated. With time and growing sophistication of hospital information systems, we may be able to generate data for outcome that better relates to the total health picture of the patient.

Appropriate test orders help to correctly diagnose and follow up patients. Thus, they increase the efficiency of care and affect the outcome regardless of how you define it. The inappropriate test order, for example, one blood culture ordered instead of three, could miss the diagnosis, result in improper treatment, and lead to a longer length of stay or even serious complications, as well as delay the patient's discharge, all of which results in increased costs. In addition, all service-related monitors can be indirectly related to improved patient care, although it would be difficult to relate a specific turnaround time causally to a focused patient outcome.

Conclusion

There are different approaches to the assessment of appropriateness. In monitoring appropriateness the primary focus is ordering laboratory tests and responding to the results of those tests. The process is influenced by the environment, which includes consensus guidelines established by clinicians, organizational bylaws, and administrative guidelines; for example, some hospitals do not allow standard orders. The amount of support provided by clinical staff and the administration for activities, such as review of laboratory use and quality assurance follow-up action, is a key ingredient for a successful program. Follow-up action is only effective if the administration and the clinical staff support it, especially when the action taken may result in some adversity.

Appropriateness of testing is an important part of any quality assurance program. It is a sensitive issue since it involves physician behavior and cost containment. Cost containment continues to be an important issue because of pressure from the media and third-party payers to justify costs and improve the quality of care. Computers and clerical personnel will play more of a role as standards for laboratory testing become incorporated in the laboratory information system and tied to ordering of tests. Remuneration may be based on the performance of appropriate testing, as described in the standards.

The focus tends to be on excessive testing, but equally important and less frequently evaluated is the underuse of tests. Earlier I discussed how reviewing underuse could be done simultaneously with overuse because the same guidelines can be used. Simple, small focused studies may be the most effective in terms of time and cost. The ability to track data with a laboratory information system makes tracking appropriateness of testing a whole lot easier.

The effort spent reviewing the appropriateness of testing is only worthwhile if it results in improvements in patient care. Approaches to changing habits of overuse have included rationing tests, requiring the fulfillment of specific guidelines, denying reimbursement, changing of test order forms, economic grand rounds, staff presentations, and newsletters. Guidelines tied to reimbursement are inevitable if third-party payers continue to find unwarranted testing[6] and no steps are taken to effectively correct this.

Standards (guidelines) must be set for quality indicators related to appropriateness of testing; in the future, guidelines may be set for turnaround times for diagnostic tests since they can affect length of stay, which is one of the major contributors to hospital costs. Cost will be the prime incentive to develop these guidelines; nonetheless, I believe the guidelines are best established by local consensus opinion. At the same time, these guidelines should allow for some variations because there are many valid exceptions to the rule. Obviously, the challenge is to develop guidelines that improve the quality of care. A number of groups, including the American Hospital Association, the AMA, the American

Medical Review and Research Company, Blue Cross/Blue Shield, and the American College of Physicians, are up to the challenge and are currently trying to set guidelines for what is appropriate testing.[55] These guidelines should be considered when attempting to establish local guidelines.

For improved appropriateness of diagnostic testing to be successful, a commitment of resources to meaningful and ongoing continuing education is necessary, since improvement frequently requires behavioral change on the part of the physician. Education, feedback, and some form of reward for positive behavior are essential to improvement. The literature is replete with articles showing that once the educational efforts cease, any prior improvement is quickly lost.[41] The message is clear: continue in an *ongoing* fashion to educate regarding appropriateness of testing.

In the future, payment may be tied to desired outcome, which may discourage people from a career in medicine. Lawyers who lose cases are generally paid, regardless of outcome; unsuccessful politicians may lose their jobs; but reimbursement is not determined by individual situations. There are already enough pressures in the practice of medicine—we don't need the added pressure of guidelines set by outsiders. Use your own local consensus guidelines as your educational tool. Be an *educator*, not a disciplinarian.

REFERENCES

1. Speiker E. Duplicate chemistry profiles correlate with multiple physicians. *Arch Pathol Lab Med.* 1988;112:235-236.

2. Eddy DM. Clinical decision making from theory to practice. *JAMA.* 1990; 263:441-443.

3. *American Medical News.* June 23, 1989:15.

4. Dunham WG, Quinlan A, Krolikowski FJ, Reuter K. Quality assurance programs with today's demands. *Pathologists.* 1986;40:24-28.

5. Brook RH. Practice guidelines in practicing medicine: are they compatible? *JAMA.* 1989;262:3027-3030.

6. *American Medical News.* January 19, 1990:12.

7. Civetta JM, Hudson-Civetta JA. Maintaining quality of care while reducing charges in the ICU. *Ann Surg.* 1985;202:524-530.

8. *American Medical News.* January 12, 1990:25.

9. *CAP Today.* May 1989:1.

10. *New York Times.* October 18, 1987:6.

11. *Clinical Chemistry News.* 1989;12:1.

12. Eisenberg JM. Clinical economics: a guide to the economic analysis of clinical practices. *JAMA.* 1989;262;2879-2886.

13. *Business and Health.* November 1987:23.

14. *MLO.* December 1989:20.

15. Suchman AL, Griner PF. Diagnostic uses of the activated partial thromboplastin time and prothrombin time. In: Sox HC Jr, ed. *Common Diagnostic Tests Use and Interpretation.* Philadelphia, Pa: American Colleges of Physicians; 1987:155-173.

16. Kelly JT, Kellie SE. Appropriateness of medical care. *Arch Pathol Lab Med.* 1990;114:1119-1121.

17. *CAP Today.* June 1989:1.

18. McNeil BJ. Relationships of beliefs and behavior and test ordering. *Am J Med.* 1986;80:865-870.

19. Kosecoff J, Chassin MR, Fink A. Variations data for consensus building. *Business and Health.* 1986;3:18-22.

20. Billings J, Eddy D. Physician decision making limited by medical evidence. *Business and Health.* 1987;5:23-28.

21. American Medical Association, Department of Health Care Finance and Organization. *Cost Effectiveness Evaluation Network Implementation Guide for Economic Grand Rounds.* Chicago, Ill: American Medical Association; 1984:27.

22. Heath DA. The appropriateness of diagnostic services. *Health Trends.* 1982;18:62-66.

23. Shapiro MF, Greenfield S. The complete blood count and leukocyte differential count. In: Sox HC Jr, ed. *Common Diagnostic Tests Use and Interpretation.* Philadelphia, Pa: American College of Physicians; 1987:133-156.

24. Roher MJ, Michelotti MC, Nahrwald D. Prospective evaluation of the efficacy of pre-operative coagulative testing. *Ann Surg.* 1988;208:554-557.

25. Savage RA. Suggestions for quality assurance: routines in the clinical hematology laboratory. *Lab Med.* 1989;20:556-559.

26. Diamond I. The clinical purpose of laboratory testing. *Arch Pathol Lab Med.* 1988;112:377-378.

27. Valenstein P, Leiken A, Lehmann C. Test ordering by multiple physicians increased unnecessary laboratory examinations. *Arch Pathol Lab Med.* 1988;112:238-241.

28. *MLO.* October 1989:31.

29. *Medicare Bulletin.* December 1989:175.

30. Griner PF, Glaser RJ. Misuse of laboratory tests and diagnostic procedures. *N Engl J Med.* 1982;307:1336-1339.

31. Baigelman W, Bellin SJ, Cupples LA, Dombrowski D, Coldiron J. Overutilization of serum electrolyte determinations on critical care units. *Intensive Care Med.* 1985;11:304-308.

32. Mendleson M. Automated reminders do not always improve follow-up of abnormal lab results. *Comput Biol Med.* 1986;16:131-134.

33. McDonald CJ, Wilson GA, McCabe GP. Physician response and computer reminders. *JAMA*. 1980;244:1579-1581.

34. Link K, Centor R, Buchsbaum D, Witherspoon J. Why physicians don't pursue abnormal laboratory tests: an investigation of hypercalcemia and the follow-up of abnormal test results. *Hum Pathol*. 1984;15:75-78.

35. Mortenson LE, Engstrom PF, Anderson PN, eds. *Advances in Cancer Control: Health Care Financing and Research*. New York, NY: Alan R Liss Inc; 1986:191-197.

36. Wong PKH, Brown DL, Bachmann KA, Forney RB, Hicks CI, Schwartz JI. Optimal dosing of phenytoin: an evaluation of the timing and appropriateness of serum level monitoring. *Hosp Form*. 1989;24:219-223.

37. Wing DS, Duff HJ. The impact of a therapeutic drug monitoring program for phenytoin. *Ther Drug Monit*. 1989;11:32-37.

38. Levine M, McCollum R, Chang T, Orr J. Evaluation of serum phenytoin monitoring in an acute care setting. *Ther Drug Monit*. 1988;10:50-57.

39. *Accreditation Manual for Hospitals, Pathology and Medical Laboratory Services, 1991*. Chicago, Ill: Joint Commission on Accreditation of Healthcare Organizations; 1990:156.

40. Campbell JA. Appropriateness of blood product ordering: quality assurance techniques. *Lab Med*. 1989;20:15-18.

41. Silberstein LE, Kruskall MS, Stehling LC, et al. Strategies for the review of transfusion practices. *JAMA*. 1989;262:1993-1997.

42. Siegel DL, Edelstein PH, Nachamkin I. Inappropriate testing for diarrheal diseases in the hospital. *JAMA*. 1990;263:979-982.

43. Beeson PB, McDermott W. *Textbook of Medicine*. Philadelphia, Pa: WB Saunders Co; 1975:1604.

44. Finn AF, Valenstein PN, Burke MD. Alteration of physician orders by nonphysicians. *JAMA*. 1988;259:2549-2552.

45. Wong ET. Ordering of laboratory tests in a teaching hospital: can it be improved? *JAMA*. 1983;249:3076-3080.

46. Schifman R. Comprehensive and concurrent surveillance of test use. *Am J Clin Pathol*. 1989;92:539.

47. Eisenberg JM, Sankey WV. Cost containment and changing physicians' practice behavior. *JAMA*. 1981;246:2195-2201.

48. Eisenberg JM, Williams SV, Garner L. Computer-based audit to detect and correct overutilization of laboratory tests. *Med Care*. 1977;15:915-921.

49. Johns RJ, Blum BI. The use of clinical information systems to control costs as well as improve care. *Trans Am Clin Climatol Assoc*. 1978;90:140-152.

50. Brooks RH, Williams KN. Effect of medical care review on the use of injections: a study of the New Mexico Experimental Medical Care Review Organization. *Ann Intern Med*. 1976;85:509-515.

51. Hayward RA, Shapiro MF, Oye RK. Laboratory testing on cerebral spinal fluid. *Lancet.* 1987;1:1-4.

52. Kroenke K, Hanley JP, Copley JB. Improving house staff ordering of three common laboratory tests. *Med Care.* 1987;25:928-935.

53. Donabedian A. *Exploration in Quality Assessment and Monitoring, I: The Definition of Quality and Approaches to its Assessment.* Ann Arbor, Mich: Health Administrative Press; 1980:16-17.

54. Tarlov AR, Ware JE, Greenfield S, Nelson EC, Perrin E, Zubkoff M. The medical outcome study. *JAMA.* 1989;262:925-930.

55. Nash DB. Practice guidelines and outcomes: where are we headed? *Arch Pathol Lab Med.* 1990;114:1122-1125.

8. Selection of Audit Topics and Quality Indicators

THERE IS NO specific method to select topics for quality assurance, but the selection should be based on whether the problem is *clinically relevant*. If a laboratory conducts quality assurance studies that repeatedly find no problems, I immediately wonder if the laboratory is selecting "safe" topics, that is, topics that whitewash problems. Good studies, although not necessarily all of them, find areas where patient care can be improved.

A good place to start to select audit topics is directly in the laboratory. Talk to the supervisors of each section and ask them if there are any problems. If they say there are no problems, raise questions regarding high-volume tests and service-related issues, (eg, turnaround time), especially in areas such as intensive care and the emergency department. Find out if there have been complaints or incident reports from outside of the laboratory. Do these incident reports and complaints show a trend? Ask specific questions: How is the turnaround time for and the appropriateness of stat orders for electrolytes or CBCs? What is the turnaround time for the surgical reports? Are you satisfied with the the frozen section service? If a problem is found, take steps to correct it, but also document those steps as a quality assurance monitor.

Some laboratories have used quality circles successfully to select audit topics. Quality circles are small groups of people (five to eight people) from the same work area. Each group meets regularly to identify, as well as assess and solve, problems.[1] For example, the group might select stat orders as an audit topic. Each member of the group then lists as many specific problems related to stat orders as possible, which might include items such as delay in receiving specimens in the laboratory, question of validity of stat request, or unavailability of physician to receive stat results. These items are prioritized and specific monitors are then selected. The advantage of quality circles is that they involve a large number of people in the laboratory in quality assurance and encourage alternative viewpoints to those of management and pathologists. The disadvantage is that they require a substantial time commitment.

Questioning personnel outside the laboratory can also be helpful in selecting audit topics. Make rounds of the hospital and ask clerks and nurses how the laboratory is doing; do not limit your questions to people in charge of a section. Ask the same questions of physicians. The charge nurse may have a different view of the laboratory from that of the ward clerk or physician. As a result of these clinical ward rounds at the Tucson Medical Center, we discovered some problems with turnaround times as well as problems with phlebotomy that were monitored and resolved. We then surveyed the nursing supervisors regarding these areas; they really appreciated the opportunity for their input. **Good public relations can contribute to good quality assurance!**

Clinical chart reviews help in the selection of audit topics because they document laboratory data, such as appropriateness of testing and follow-up of abnormal results. A pathologist should participate in these reviews, because they can be a major source of quality assurance topics. In addition, the pathologist's participation demonstrates that the laboratory wants to improve patient care and welcomes comments toward that end.

The following are sources for quality assurance audit topics:

1. Incident reports
2. Infection rates, especially nosocomial infections
3. Questionnaires
4. Complaints, regardless of the source, including those from physicians, nurses, ward clerks, administrators, and patient surveys (recording the nature of incoming telephone calls can reveal trends not seen when reviewing written complaints)
5. Clinician chart review committees
6. Problems identified by laboratory personnel
7. The literature
8. Rounds: ask "how is the lab doing?"
9. Minutes from hospital committees. While reading all the minutes from every hospital committee would be tedious, there should be a procedure in place that communicates relevant problems that relate to the laboratory.
10. Regulations
11. Regulatory inspection results
12. Accounting
13. DRG data
14. Insurance claims
15. Quality circles
16. Consultant in quality assurance
17. Other laboratories. Review what has been done in quality assurance to see what would be applicable in your laboratory.

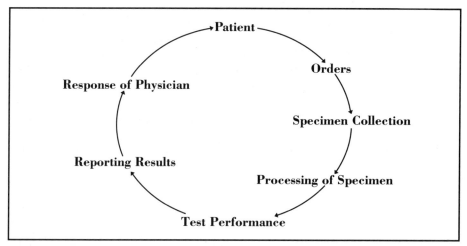

Figure 8.1 Components of the testing cycle.

18. CAP Q Probe program. The advantage of this program is that it allows you to compare your results with other laboratories', and the program is already defined and developed. Since this is not user-defined nor problem-oriented, it should be supplemental to your laboratory's personalized quality assurance program.

19. ASCP CheckPath programs. These programs are currently most useful for testing the individual pathologist's morphological diagnostic skills in surgical pathology, cytopathology, and hematology, but a clinical pathology section will begin in 1992.

Audit topics should be: (1) meaningful to the institution and clinically relevant (ie, problem-oriented and high-volume) so the study is more clinically significant; (2) relatively easy and economical to determine (ie, the cost of data collection is reasonable). This will be true of audits that stay focused on a particular problem.

SELECTION OF QUALITY INDICATORS

While quality indicators related to the appropriateness of testing were covered in the preceding chapter, quality indicators should also evaluate the total testing process from test selection to interpretation and application of test results.[2] They should examine all aspects of laboratory testing that affect patient care. Categorizing the testing under different components, as is illustrated in Figure 8.1, facilitates examination of each step of the testing process.

TEST REQUESTS

Timeliness

Are preoperative laboratory test orders for morning admission submitted on a timely basis? This study should be done in collaboration with nursing staff as a multidisciplinary audit, because the nursing service is involved in the ordering process and might be able to pinpoint timeliness problems pertaining to certain units. This audit should highlight physicians who do not send orders in with the patient or who do not submit orders in a timely fashion, which necessitates setting a standard by which you judge timeliness. The standard should be set by consensus, involving clinicians as well as the nursing service. Preoperative laboratory orders (for morning admission surgery) should ideally be available within one half hour of the time of arrival of the patient in the unit; a 1-hour wait would be unacceptable. (A similar monitor might focus on patients arriving at the intensive care unit without orders.)

Legibility

Are orders legible? A good standard for illegibility is more than one person having difficulty interpreting the orders due to illegible handwriting. Select a ward and look at all the orders the ward clerks have difficulty reading. Return every day for a week. The denominator is the number of orders written by a particular physician; the numerator is the number of illegible orders written by that particular physician. Some physicians' handwriting is consistently difficult to interpret. Other physicians' handwriting is related to the speed with which an order is written. What is an acceptable number of illegible orders? None.

Initially focus corrective action on physicians with frequent illegible orders. Do this until the problem is resolved. The first step to correct the problem involves informing the physician of the difficulty. If that fails, remedial handwriting courses should be tried. As a last resort, the physician should dictate orders, paying for their transcription.

Stat Orders

There are a number of indicators related to stat testing: Was the test ordered stat or was it modified by the unit clerk? Was it necessary to order a stat test? Was there reasonable turnaround time for the results? Was the ordering physician available to receive the results? Was there an appropriate response to results when indicated?

I have found that stat orders are a problem in most hospitals. In courses on quality assurance I have given to approximately 500 people from different institutions, almost 100% of the participants have said stat requests are a problem.

Stat orders should theoretically involve life-threatening situations for which results of the test are needed for therapeutic decisions that cannot be delayed until the time results from a routine order would be available. Stat tests are not cost-effective, since they are run individually rather than in batches, thus someone must be assigned to run stat tests or someone must stop what he or she is doing to perform the test. Additionally, separate controls must be run. It is reasonable to charge more for a stat order because of the cost incurred to perform the test on a stat basis; however, I have found that the extra charge involved doesn't tend to make physicians order fewer stat tests. Results from stat testing should have an immediate effect on patient care. Changing the behavior of physicians is difficult. Some physicians assume that stat orders are for their convenience.

We need to improve our overall turnaround time for stat orders, make the results more readily available (through monitors on the floors and in physician offices, and by use of the telephone to convey results), and resolve associated problems. One of the most effective tools is to have pathologists discuss with physicians the circumstances of and need for individual stat orders. Sometimes simply pointing out to physicians that their number of stat orders is much higher than their peers may effect a behavioral change: they do not want to stand out in peer review activitites that have consensus-based guidelines.

Many of the new software programs help track stat requests by physician, patient, unit, and test. Other useful factors include severity of disease and specialty of the ordering physician. All of these factors can be tracked manually, although it is very labor-intensive because tracking stat requests is a quality indicator that requires ongoing attention. Once physicians stop receiving calls regarding their rationale for stat orders, the number of stat requests often begins to increase.

Are physicians available to respond quickly to results received from tests requested on a stat basis? The definition of stat tests demands that physicians be available to apply the results to patient care immediately. Determining the timeliness of the physician response is best done as a prospective study, because the charts are available on the units and the circumstances related to the request are fresh in everyone's mind. Select 10 stat requests and review the charts. Check for validity of the order, the appropriateness of the order, and the response to the results. Not all results from stat orders require response, but they do require that the ordering physicians be available to respond to those results that theoretically are life-threatening. If the laboratory calls physicians directly to convey results for all stat requests, tracking is no problem: the time of the call simply needs to be included in the report or on a separate log. If personnel on the unit call the physician, nurses' notes or a log on the unit that makes note of the calls should be immediately available.

Accuracy

Do requisitions received in the laboratory accurately reflect physicians' orders on the patient charts? Review 5 to 10 charts once a month or quarter unless a substantial number of variants are found. If a number of variants are found they must be traced to the individual responsible for transcribing the orders. Use the specimen collection list or the actual requisitions for comparison with the orders in the patient's chart. You can simultaneously review legibility, appropriateness, and accuracy of the orders. At the same time, review the amount of time elapsed from the initiation of the orders to the identification of the orders on the specimen collection list in the office. Since this is part of turnaround time, it may be an important service-related issue. Thus, this one review can document many individual quality indicators at once.

Completeness

Are the orders complete, that is, do they provide all the information needed? For example, do they provide the time of the last dose for therapeutic drugs? Do they note that a patient was taking anticoagulation medication when coagulation tests were ordered? Obviously, the guidelines for orders vary according to the test. You might monitor a specific test, for example, a theophylline test. How many theophylline orders indicate the time of the last dose? If you are looking for peak levels, the time of the last dose and the exact time of the drawing are information that should be recorded along with the results of the test. All three parameters are necessary for valid interpretation of the test results, which is necessary for optimal care.

If a therapeutic drug level is drawn before peak serum levels, the clinician might be misled and prescribe an unnecessarily higher dose of the drug. It should be easy to monitor whether this information is available to make this judgment; however, the follow-up action may be more difficult to monitor. The only sure way to have 100% compliance is to refuse to test without all the necessary data. Given the potential adverse effects on patient care, such action would be reasonable.

SPECIMEN COLLECTION

These quality indicators apply whether the collection of samples is under the direct control of the laboratory or, for example, specimens are drawn by nurses or physicians.

Success Rate of Phlebotomy Drawings

How often are there unsuccessful attempts to obtain blood by the phlebotomist? This is measured easily on a spot-check basis or as part of an ongoing study combining other quality indicators, such as patient availability. After completing their assigned rounds, phlebotomists should indicate in a log what happened with each patient, using " + " for a successful draw, "N" for an unavailable patient, "U" for an unsuccessful draw, or "O" for other, which would include, for example, instances when the patient refuses to let the phlebotomist draw blood or when the situation requires a physician to draw blood from the femoral vein. There should be an area for clarification when necessary. If more than 5% are not acceptable, it is time to consider remedial action.[3]

Patient Availability

How often do phlebotomists arrive to draw samples in the nursing unit only to find the patient is in radiology or physical therapy? This is obviously not cost-effective if it occurs with any frequency. Corrective action must involve the nursing unit, generally focusing on more effective communication about patient availability.

How often are patients not available to have their blood drawn for an early-morning surgical admission program? This could result in incomplete laboratory results before the scheduled surgery, which is currently a common problem because of the popularity of, and cost-savings associated with, early-morning admission programs for same-day surgery. If laboratory results are regularly not available at the time of surgery, then effective corrective action should be taken. At the Tucson Medical Center we require all patients admitted in the early-morning admission program to have their laboratory work completed 24 to 48 hours before their scheduled surgery. If patients arrive late, try to detect trends related, for example, to a particular physician's office. Educational efforts directed at that office may be helpful, or all the physician's cases could be scheduled much later in the day.

Patient Identification

Patient identification is also important to specimen collection. How often does the inpatient have the correct identification, namely, an arm band? There should be a written protocol for identification of patients and all phlebotomists should be familiar with it.

Correct patient identification should be an ongoing monitor because of the potential fatal or significant consequences test results could have on an incorrect patient, such as a fatal hemolytic transfusion reaction. Compile a record of accuracy in patient identification, periodically summarizing the data and taking corrective action as needed. Problems in correct patient identification tend to occur intermittently, and often the problem is corrected by the existence of an ongoing study, since during the study phlebotomists are reminded of the importance of proper identification. The threshold for success should be 100%, because an exception could be disastrous. An ongoing monitor may be necessary to reach this threshold.

Patient Preparation

Was the patient's preparation for testing adequate? For example, did the patient fast when necessary according to test specifications? Some institutions routinely question the fasting status of patients. For a study, choose 30 fasting requests prospectively and have the phlebotomist question patients to see if they have eaten. If problems are found, then corrective action should be taken, which involves education not only of the phlebotomists but of the unit personnel, who should always make sure patients are fasting when the test guidelines demand it. This study can be done once a month or quarter as an ongoing part of a quality assurance program.

Another problem in specimen collection is the patient's diet for focused test groups, for example, carbohydrate loading for a glucose tolerance test. Glucose tolerance tests are done on ambulatory patients who should have had at least 150 g/d of glucose for 3 days prior to the test and are not under stress; it should be a seldom-used hospital test. Have a pathologist approve all glucose tolerance tests and look for trends in incorrectly ordered tests by individual physician (this could also be done for vanillylmandelic acid testing). Make sure guidelines for test ordering are readily available. If these problems persist, then speak more directly with nursing staff and clinicians. If this fails, then you could refuse to do testing for inadequately prepared patients.

Timing of Collection

How accurate were timed drawings? For example, was blood drawn for coagulation tests related to heparin therapy drawn at the prescribed time or close enough to the prescribed time to allow accurate interpretation of the results? The threshold might be plus or minus 15 minutes of the requested drawing time. Valid guidelines established using the literature need to be formulated, readily available, and communicated to involved personnel. If the threshold is not reached, scheduling changes or more personnel might resolve the problem.

How much time has elapsed between the time of drawing a specimen for testing of the therapeutic drug level and the actual time the patient was given medication? Valid interpretation of therapeutic drug levels requires knowing the time of the last dose as it related to the time the blood was drawn. Check the time with the patient if the patient is alert; otherwise, check with a nurse. Verify that the time elapsed is sufficient to give an accurate therapeutic drug level. The phlebotomist should document problems as a prospective study. Twenty to thirty orders for drug therapeutic levels should be enough to point out any problems worth pursuing.

Labeling

The threshold for accurate specimen labeling should be 100%. Specimens not drawn by phlebotomists (eg, drawn by the nursing staff) should not be accepted without accurate labeling. What do you do when you have received inaccurately labeled or unlabeled specimens? If you receive a specimen and the request slip is correct but the label on the blood tube is inaccurate, what is your course of action? Do you reject the specimen? Do you return the specimen to the head nurse and have it relabeled? Or if there was no label, do you return it to be labeled? Or do you hold the specimen and have someone from the ward come to the laboratory and certify what patient the specimen belongs to and what is the correct accompanying request slip? Try to avoid traumatizing the patient with an additional phlebotomy procedure if at all possible.

Test results that are incorrectly recorded for a patient due to mislabeled results have obvious therapeutic significance. For example, if a potassium test mistakenly indicates a patient has a low potassium level when in fact that patient has a high potassium level, treating this patient with potassium would have a negative impact on patient care. Thus, unlabeled or mislabeled specimens should not be accepted without positive identification. If only one unlabeled or mislabeled specimen is sent, then someone from the unit should be able to identify the specimen pretty easily. However, if more than one specimen is sent, then all the specimens should be redrawn. Only strict adherence to these rules combined with educational efforts aimed at the sources of the problem can resolve this problem.

If you categorize the number of unlabeled or mislabeled specimens by their source (eg, a particular nursing unit or a particular phlebotomist) and frequency, you can determine where corrective action is needed most. You may discover that specimens are sometimes incorrectly labeled but go undetected until you find that the test result does not match the clinical diagnosis, even after repeated testing. This is often the result of mixed up specimens, which in my experience is, fortunately, an infrequent occurrence. Generally, individual counseling is all that is needed for follow-up action. The labeling of specimens should also be checked at the time of specimen processing.

The label on each blood bank unit has a lot of information, including the name of the patient, medical record number, ABO type, and Rh factor of the unit to be transfused. This information should be spot-checked periodically; there should be complete compliance.

Quality assurance studies related to specimen collection are easier to conduct if they focus on individual sections, for example, microbiology, because such a focus limits the size of the study. An established protocol to identify a specimen should be strictly followed. No one should have to speculate on the identification of the specimen. Specimens drawn by phlebotomists should be periodically checked unnanounced by the phlebotomy supervisor to see that they are labeled accurately. In addition, technical sections could keep a record of inaccurately labeled specimens.

Are labels available on a timely basis? The specimen collection should not be held up because labels need to be printed. Labels should be available at all units for phlebotomy drawings not on the original collection list; no one should have to return to the laboratory to obtain labels. This quality indicator would demonstrate whether additional label printers are needed at each unit or in the laboratory. The follow-up action would be administrative in this case (as opposed to individual or group action).

Other Quality Indicators

Other quality indicators for specimen collection include verifying that the correct type of specimen was drawn, that an adequate amount of the specimen was drawn, and that the specimen was transported correctly. These indicators can be tracked by a software program, or data can be collected continually or intermittently by each section and then summarized to spot trends that need corrective action. A software program makes the data collection easier since the data base already contains some of the basic information you need for a quality assurance study, such as the date and time the specimen was drawn, the patient's name, the phlebotomist's name, and the test ordered.

Phlebotomy Observation

When conducting studies of specimen collection by observation, have more than one observer so you can eliminate observer bias. An observer asks questions such as: Did the phlebotomist identify the patient? Was the phlebotomist polite? Did

Laboratory Venipuncture Quality Assurance

Phlebotomist: _____ Observer: _____ Date _____

TYPE: Vacutainer Syringe Butterfly Blood Culture IP OP ER
                                                        Patients

CRITERIA: Did Phlebotomist . . . YES or NO	1	2	3	4
1. have all required supplies?				
2. check requisition?				
3. introduce self to patient?				
4. identify patient by armband?				
5. wear gloves?				
6. position arm properly?				
7. palpate vein before cleaning arm?				
8. prepare supplies at bedside?				
9. cleanse arm properly/maintain sterility?				
10. make no more than 2 attempts?				
11. change needle between attempts?				
12. insert needle smoothly and quickly?				
13. draw tubes in proper order?				
14. obtain sufficient sample?				
15. release tourniquet in a timely manner?				
16. apply gauze and pressurize site?				
17. label tubes immediately?				
18. check site before leaving room?				
19. apply Band-Aid?				

(continued following page.)

Figure 8.2 Laboratory venipuncture quality assurance check list.

20. dispose of needle properly?				
21. mix tubes as required?				
22. sign and time requisitions?				
23. raise bed rails if required?				
24. recheck patient ID?				
25. wash hands between patients?				

yes answers/# answers = score (1.0 = perfect score)

Figure 8.2 Laboratory venipuncture quality assurance check list (continued).

the phlebotomist use good technique in drawing the blood? (Note that while technique cannot be ascertained with patient questionnaires, some of the other quality indicators can.) Figure 8.2 shows the form used by Gail Straka at Chandler (Ariz) Regional Hospital (published with permission of Gail Straka, Laboratory Manager, Chandler Regional Hospital).

SPECIMEN PROCESSING

To process a specimen it is sometimes necessary to know how the specimen was collected; for example, catheterized urine specimens submitted for culture are interpreted differently from clean catch midstream specimens. Ideally, all urine cultures are planted or refrigerated within 2 hours of the time they are collected, which makes knowing when the specimen was collected necessary. The threshold for compliance should be 100%, and the best way to achieve this threshold is to refuse specimens that are received without a collection time. A related study would be to follow up rejected specimens. This study would determine if new specimens were submitted in place of the rejected specimens, which could be easily done by keeping a record of the patients, the dates, and the ordering physicians involved; the physicians should be called when no follow-up specimen is received within 24 hours. If a test is necessary, another specimen should always be submitted in place of the rejected one.

Centrifugation

Was the centrifugation adequate? Someone, such as a supervisor, could be assigned the role of verifying that specimens have been adequately centrifuged. For example, this person could check for platelets on serum samples that interfere with coagulation testing. Platelets should not be present if a coagulation specimen has been centrifuged adequately. Gross specimen abnormalities, such as hemolysis, should also be noted.

Logistically, a study of centrifugation is difficult to do because it requires either observation or someone to review a large number of specimens. This particular study is also applicable to outpatient situations, where specimens are centrifuged in an office or peripheral laboratory site.

Distribution

Was the time for intralaboratory distribution of the specimen to the proper sections acceptable? For example, cerebral spinal fluid examinations may be done partially in the chemistry, hematology, and microbiology sections, or a serum sample examination may be done partially in the chemistry and serology sections. (This is generally not a problem in smaller laboratories that have no true sections.) Spinal fluid examinations done in the emergency department frequently are ordered on a stat basis. Ideally, they should be distributed within 10 to 20 minutes. Routine examinations, such as a specimen split between the chemistry and serology sections, should be distributed before the testing is completed. A central processing area can help alleviate the distribution problem. In any case, distribution time is part of the turnaround time for tests, such as cerebrospinal fluid, synovial fluid, or other body cavity fluids. Since these are frequently ordered stat, this could be a major service issue in many laboratories.

At the Tucson Medical Center we studied the timing and routing of cerebral spinal fluid specimens to determine the most effective distribution. We used a routing slip for each specimen and found that laboratory sections delivered the specimen to the next section when it was convenient or when they finished their portion of the testing. Merely instituting a routing slip improved the distribution time. The routing slip included the specimen number, the patient's name, the time the section received the specimen, and the initials of the technician involved. Similar studies could be done for a number of different specimens, including body fluids (eg, synovial fluid) that have to be distributed to mulitiple sections. Again, the timing of the distribution is particularly important for specimens from time-sensitive areas, such as the emergency department.

TESTING PROCEDURES

Is the test performed frequently enough to satisfy the patient's needs? For example, gastrin testing and hepatitis profiles are performed twice a week by the laboratory; if physicians demand the results for these tests more often and a delay in getting them the results affects patient care, then a decision must be made regarding the frequency of testing: do you increase the frequency of the testing in the laboratory or do you send the tests to a reference laboratory that performs them more often? If there are physician complaints regarding turnaround time for specific tests, examine the laboratory's test performance schedule in relationship to the patient needs.

CONTAMINATED SPECIMENS (MICROBIOLOGY)

An ongoing record of the number of contaminated culture specimens and the unit that submitted them would be a useful quality indicator. If the laboratory handles a small number of orders, all contaminated specimens can be documented pretty easily. On the other hand, a laboratory that handles a large number of orders may find this collection of data overwhelming unless a computer program is available to facilitate the data collection; if not available, a regular spot check should suffice.

DELTA CHECK FOLLOW-UP

Many laboratory information systems or individual computer software programs have the ability to do a delta check, that is, a notation is made next to a test result that informs the technician that there has been a certain percentage change in test results from the previous results. For example, if a patient has a hemoglobin level of 140 g/L on Monday and a level of 60 g/L on Tuesday, a delta check is made. In such an instance, the patient identification should be verified and the test repeated. It should also be determined if this unusual change in results has correlating clinical effects. This can frequently only be verified by a review of the patient's clinical records, which is time-consuming, but done on a spot-check basis it might prove worthwhile.

REPEATED TESTING

Repeated testing needs to be considered carefully because of its expense. Why is the test being repeated? Why wasn't it done right the first time?[4] Keep a record of what test was done, who did the test, what time of day the test was done, and the equipment used for the test; the original test information may clarify why testing had to be redone, or it may pinpoint recurring problems in particular areas. You may find a repeated testing trend related to one technician, which should be further analyzed because of its potential for significant cost savings. Document briefly why each test was repeated. If the test was repeated due to a cumbersome methodology, try changing the methodology so there are fewer repeated tests; as a result, testing may become cheaper, more accurate, and faster. In the event testing becomes more costly due to a new methodology, overall cost savings may still be realized because the test does not have to be repeated.

TURNAROUND TIME

Turnaround time of test results is an important quality indicator, and some laboratories have an information system that allows them to track it. Some laboratory information systems track the turnaround time from the time the test order is received in the laboratory to the time results are released from the laboratory. The problem with this turnaround time is the difficulty in measuring the time between arrival of the test order in the laboratory and the recording of its arrival. An observer may be required to determine this. The real turnaround time is from the time the physician places the order to the time the test results are given to the ordering physician.

The time of the order can be tracked by the nursing service on the unit, which generally involves recording the time the unit clerk transfers the orders into the computer or onto a laboratory request slip. This still does not account for the time between the physicians' orders and the transfer by the unit clerk. In some institutions physicians can order directly into the hospital laboratory information system, which is capable of noting the time of that action. The real problem, however, is the final time, that is, the time the physician receives the results. This is almost impossible to track. At the Tucson Medical Center we generally use the time the result is charted on the floor or called to the floor, or the time the result is entered in the computer where physicians and nurses have computer access.

This real turnaround time is of particular importance for tests ordered stat from areas such as intensive care or the emergency department. For these areas in particular, turnaround time should be reviewed for all shifts, with specific attention on the weekend shifts.[5] One study has shown that the turnaround times for other orders are adversely affected when a large number of stat orders are placed with shifts having fewer personnel, for example, night, holiday, and weekend shifts.[6]

Since total turnaround time is complicated by interdepartmental involvement, a simpler approach is to first check your own backyard, namely, turnaround time in the laboratory. At the Tucson Medical Center we periodically study turnaround time in each of the laboratory sections by selecting a particular test and timing the period between the time the test is logged in and the time the results are logged out of the section. The difficult task is to define what an acceptable turnaround time is.

An acceptable turnaround time must take into consideration patient needs and laboratory resources. Trial and error helps find the time that will serve as a threshold for a particular test for a particular laboratory; an established mean turnaround time is a good threshold in most laboratories.[7] If turnaround times are exceptionally slow, analyze the process; for example, the chemistry analyzer may be too slow or may malfunction frequently. Stat orders may interfere with routine testing. Delays in specimen collection and transportation or an excess number of telephone calls tying up technical help can interfere with turnaround times. Thus, examine the process and figure out why there is a problem in turnaround time. Client dissatisfaction with turnaround times needs to be resolved in a timely manner, with effective communication of the actions taken to the dissatisfied client.

Obtain data on turnaround time for a particular test, analyze the process, and make the necessary corrections, then look again at your turnaround time. If there are no additional factors that you can change then you should have an acceptable range. Eliminate all outliers. For example, if your *intralaboratory* turnaround time for a particular test is 10 to 15 minutes 95% of the time, but is greater than 15 minutes the other 5% of the time, your turnaround time should be less than 15 minutes; however, there should be acceptable reasons for those times over 15 minutes. Turnaround time varies from institution to institution since each setting is unique. Repeat the same process looking at your overall turnaround time. Overall turnaround time is one of the more important quality assurance indicators used by clinicians and nurses, because for them turnaround time is more accurately measured from the initiation of the order to the reception of the result.

When setting standards for turnaround times, make sure expectations are reasonable. Many physicians expect a 30-minute turnaround time; however, they may be unaware of the time required for testing, specimen collection, and specimen preparation (which includes clotting and centrifugation). Outside of transportation time, time for paperwork, etc, these activities can take 30 minutes in and of themselves. Demands for faster turnaround times from outside the laboratory are not always realistic. A study of glucose and complete blood count testing, urinalyses, blood urea nitrogen tests, crossmatches, and prothrombin times found that the turnaround time for these orders improved in 54% of the laboratories surveyed, yet despite this the expectations of nurses and clinicians became even more demanding.[8] You must find a balance between acceptable laboratory performance and reasonable clinical expectations. A 100% threshold for turnaround times is desirable but generally not achievable. Turnaround goals must be based on a combination of practicality, appropriateness, and clinician expectation.[8] Reviewing quality assurance indicators, such as centrifugation and clotting times, with staff outside the laboratory often provides useful data that contribute to a better understanding of turnaround times. This sort of communication can be accomplished through newsletters, direct personal communication (especially for the nursing units), or discussions at departmental or general staff meetings.

Factors that affect turnaround time include the following:

1. Stat orders. The existence of a special laboratory for stat orders may shorten the turnaround time for stat orders, since equipment purchased for this area has features that aid stat testing, such as built-in controls in reagent test kits and less frequent need for standards and calibrations. Of course, the reagents and equipment may be more expensive. The technicians in this area do not have to do routine testing concurrently, which makes them more available. A separate stat area is a luxury that probably only a larger laboratory with a large number of stat orders can afford. Some words of caution: if you are thinking of establishing a stat laboratory, make sure that the stat orders are valid, as discussed earlier in this chapter.

2. Prioritization of tests according to their source of origin, for example, trauma, surgery, and intensive care units. The turnaround time for an order related to trauma or surgery is generally more important than the turnaround time for other sources. Thus, tests for these areas should be prioritized.

3. Phlebotomy schedules, for example, regular phlebotomy rounds to prevent stat orders. Scheduling phlebotomy rounds at set times is more efficient than going to the floors for individual stat test requests. If clinical personnel can expect a phlebotomist at set times, these rounds can substantially cut back stat requests. Additionally, bringing in groups of specimens at set times allows you to schedule batch testing more easily, which is more efficient than performing single tests. This increased efficiency is reflected in a shorter turnaround time overall. At the Tucson Medical Center we have phlebotomy rounds at 6 AM and every 4 hours thereafter; we plan to change the frequency to every 3 hours.

4. Ordering and reporting procedures. Orders not labeled "today" are often ordered for the following morning. By reversing the labeling, namely, all orders not labeled "tomorrow" are drawn on the next phlebotomy sweep and done that day, the turnaround time can be considerably shortened. Printing or charting times can be changed with the institution's needs in mind. The reporting procedure needs to improve physician access to results. Even if they are available in the laboratory information system, many physicians want a printed report. Ideally, physicians have access to results immediately in their offices.

5. Transportation/pneumatic tubes. Transportation of specimens to the laboratory can frequently be improved. Do phlebotomists wait until they have drawn all their specimens before they return to the laboratory? Are pneumatic tubes used, and if so, are they conveniently located for most efficient use, that is, do the areas with the largest number of specimens have the easiest access? The questions can be best answered by observing the phlebotomists and discussing these issues with them.

6. Processing of specimens (centralized or not). Centralized processing is theoretically faster because of dedicated personnel. The area can also be logistically central to the other sections, facilitating better distribution. Processing in the sections suffers from the fact that it is not always a priority because the person processing the specimen has other duties.

7. Staffing and equipment[9] are important for both turnaround time and cost containment. There is no set number of staff needed. The more automated the equipment, the more expensive the equipment, but the fewer the number of staff needed. The staff should be adequate, when combined with available equipment, for a reasonable turnaround time and quality results. Analysis of work load, for example, with guidelines from the CAP, or analysis of costs per test may be helpful. The bottom line is the ability to provide timely service, and turnaround time monitors contribute to this.

8. Bedside testing. Bedside testing provides the fastest turnaround time possible. However, there is presently a limited amount of testing that can be done at the bedside. With time, bedside testing will play a larger role in patient testing. Glucose testing, bleeding times, and pulse oximeters substituting for an arterial blood oxygen test are current examples of bedside testing. These tests are subject to the same quality assurance guidelines as testing in the main hospital laboratory. Thus, not only are there requirements for procedure manuals, quality control, proficiency testing, and documentation of training personnel, but guidelines should also be established for appropriateness of testing, including the frequency of testing.

9. Peripheral laboratories speed up turnaround time. Generally, the staff of peripheral laboratories is dedicated to performing tests for a limited area, for example, the emergency department or intensive care. The staff-to-test performed ratio is higher in the peripheral laboratory, and equipment is designed for stat orders. The problem is cost containment: it is more expensive to do testing in a peripheral laboratory. Cost must be weighed against service in deciding on the necessity of peripheral laboratories.

10. Physician ordering patterns. Physicians who order tests to be performed during peak testing hours experience slower turnaround times.

When looking at these factors ask yourself what you can afford to change in the process that will improve the turnaround time. Many of these factors are interrelated. If transportation time is slow, would a pneumatic tube be worthwhile? If the staff is smaller than desired, would automation of tests make the present staff level sufficient? If the volume of stat orders from one area is high, would bedside testing or a peripheral laboratory be a valid solution? Answering these questions may require making some difficult administrative decisions; for example, you must weigh buying new equipment, which is costly, against the benefits of improved efficiency, which would result in improved turnaround time.

Some studies on turnaround time should focus on key areas such as the emergency department, the intensive care unit, and surgery departments. Differentiate between stat, routine, and preoperative testing. Of particular concern is the turnaround time for stat crossmatches, specifically for trauma cases. After several studies at the Tucson Medical Center we established a standard turnaround time of 1 hour for stat crossmatch orders and achieved over 95% compliance.

The following are suggested quality indicators for studying turnaround time: for blood banks, routine crossmatches and stat orders; for hematology, urinalysis, complete blood count with differentials, and coagulation studies, especially prothrombin times and partial thromboplastin times; for chemistry, stat testing, especially for electrolytes, blood urea nitrogen, glucose, amylase, and arterial blood gases; and for microbiology, streptococcus screening.

Turnaround times for tests sent to reference laboratories should also be evaluated, one test at a time. Because esoteric tests are sent out, the time required for testing or the frequency with which these tests are performed could be substantially different from other tests. The turnaround time for tests sent to reference laboratories is measured from the time and date the specimen is first received in the laboratory until the results are received. As always, time spent looking for delays in turnaround time is well spent only if corrective action is taken when necessary.[5] For example, based on complaints at the Tucson Medical Center about slow turnaround times for a test we had been sending to a reference laboratory, we sent the reference laboratory our data and were able to get the test done more frequently.

REPORTING OF RESULTS

Critical Test Results

Were physicians notified immediately of critical test results? Before studying this quality indicator, make sure what you consider critical is valid. If you fail to notify physicians of critical results in a timely fashion there may be legal implications. A procedure should be in place that is followed closely when critical results are found; this procedure should include means to document that the physician was notified of the critical results on a timely basis.[10] The technician who completes the reports should initial each report and record the initials of the person who receives the report.

At the Tucson Medical Center we repeatedly studied how critical results were handled. At first we found that a certain percent of critical results were not being reported to the floor fast enough; however, because of the studies and corrective action problems disappeared over time. The only corrective action we used was individual counseling. This study can be done on an ongoing spot-check basis, selecting critical results from different sections. If the quality indicators are not studied periodically, the reporting may return to its previous level.

Charting

Once the reports arrive on the floor, are the results entered onto the patient charts within an acceptable time frame? This is especially important for results from preoperative testing, since some preoperative testing results, such as evidence of infection in an elective case, could result in cancellation of surgery. Consensus guidelines for when the patient should arrive for preoperative testing protect the laboratory and promote more effective care. It is frequently assumed that if the patient arrives in time to have blood drawn before surgery, those laboratory results will be charted before surgery. Surgery should not be started until those results are known. Thus, the patient who arrives late to have blood drawn could potentially have surgery delayed until the laboratory results are available. Another delay may occur because a physician will not accept results available on a computer monitor but wants a written report before proceeding with surgery. Delayed surgery leads to inefficient use of the operating room and staff.

Outpatient laboratory testing done 24 to 48 hours prior to surgery is more cost-efficient, because it allows not only surgery but also admission to the hospital to be canceled if the laboratory results indicate it. If a patient's surgery is canceled the morning of surgery, the hospital loses scheduling time and the cost of setting up an operating room for surgery. At the Tucson Medical Center we found a substantial number of patients had surgery cancelled because of laboratory results received only when the patient was in the operating room waiting for surgery. As a result of this, we have strongly encouraged that testing be performed 24 to 48 hours prior to admission. Most hospitals will accept testing done at any state-certified laboratory. Printers and telefax machines may facilitate reception of results from outside laboratories. What percentage of surgery is canceled at the last minute due to late reception of laboratory results? The threshold for this study should be 0%.

Are laboratory results charted in the correct place and sequence? This is generally not a major problem but is worth a spot check periodically. If results are charted in a chronological fashion, it should be consistent, that is, the oldest results are charted first or vice versa. The sequence is not important but consistency is, because a lack of consistency can appear to be a reflection of carelessness. Are old reports removed from the chart? This could be checked at the same time the charts are reviewed for chronological sequence.

Legibility

How legible is the telewriter message? Does your telewriter system identify problems with reception? The same criteria used earlier for legibility of orders would apply here: if two people have difficulty interpreting the message on the telewriter, it should be considered illegible.

Telephone Calls

Are clinicians calling the laboratory too often for results? Are they calling for results that are already available on the floor? Telephone calls interfere with the routine flow of the work load, which can cause delays in generating results, which in turn increases the number of telephone calls from dissatisfied staff.

I have periodically answered the telephones in the laboratory's front office without initially identifying myself. I recorded the nature of the calls and spoke with many clinicians and nurses, which in itself is good public relations and is sometimes effective corrective action. We discussed issues such as slower turnaround times for stat orders at peak laboratory work load hours and the need to try to work around those times, and actual times the results will be available on the wards, which eliminates the need to call for results. Frequently, the call came from the ward clerk; I then asked to talk to clinicians or nurses, who were generally pleased that the medical director was talking to them about problems.

The front office personnel believed my answering the telephones made a contribution, because there was a decrease in the number of phone calls afterward. Furthermore, it was a good morale booster for the front office staff. They were pleased that I took the time to "be in their shoes" and tried to resolve some of their problems. I even received a "thank you" note signed by everyone in the front office. I plan to go back periodically to answer telephones.

At the Tucson Medical Center we received two or three telephone calls a day from the total parenteral nutrition service. By meeting with the head of the service, we were able to devise a schedule that allowed the service to use the charted results, thus eliminating the need for the service to call us so often. Follow-up studies tallying the number of phone calls from parenteral services confirmed the effectiveness of this action. This change was easy to make, and the improved services benefitted patient care.

Physician Surveys

How well are you meeting the needs of the physicians who use the test results? Use surveys that ask physicians questions about the timeliness of reporting and the availability of test results. The survey should be short, simple, and to the point. I believe an effective survey has a response rate greater than 50%.

COMPUTER ERRORS

Are there errors in computer entry? At the Tucson Medical Center we reviewed computer data with our clerical staff, which focused their attention on decreasing the number of errors. The most common error was entering the wrong patient code number. Although the error rate was less than 1%, merely calling the clerical staff's attention to this resulted in an improvement. Newer laboratory information systems do not have this problem, because once the patient is admitted to the hospital the patient access number is automatically available to the laboratory. Nonetheless, there can still be clerical errors (eg, a laboratory result that does not match the patient condition) related to results given for the wrong patient; these may be detected by delta check or physician complaints. These errors should be tracked to see if there is a trend involving a particular clerk or technician.

USE OF TEST RESULTS

Critical Results

Does the physician respond appropriately to critical test results and in a timely fashion? Depending on the institutional policy, this quality indicator could also involve the nursing service; for example, if critical results are telephoned to the intensive care nurse, sometimes a nurse, without contacting the physician, will follow predetermined guidelines and treat a patient with a low potassium level by adding a predetermined amount of potassium chloride to the intravenous solution already in place. Again, before studying the response to critical results, you have to define critical. If from a review of the patient's chart you find that there is little evidence of response in a high percentage of particular critical test results, it may be that the clinician does not consider them critical. Critical results show problems that are potentially life-threatening; by their nature they demand a rapid response from the physician. The response may be in the form of a progress note, a notation in the nurse's notes, or a new order.

If critical results are called to the unit, an additional quality indicator could measure how long it takes for the results to be given to the physician from the unit. This would have to be tracked by the nursing unit, which would record the time the physician received the information. Some laboratories call the physician directly with critical results rather than calling the unit. At the Tucson Medical Center we call the units, because many of these critical results pertain to patients in the intensive care areas, where nurses may have to intervene before the physician contacts them. If they feel the patient's situation demands a response from a physician before the attending physician contacts them, they may call a house officer. You must establish your own standards, but I believe the attending physician—or a physician assigned to cover for him or her—should be available for consultation within 30 minutes to respond to critical results.

Therapeutic Drug Levels

What is the clinical response to toxic therapeutic drug levels? At the Tucson Medical Center we study annually the response for at least one drug on a spot-check basis. We have found appropriate responses with very few exceptions, most of which involve lack of documentation of a response. This study requires a review of not only the progress notes but also the orders, because merely reviewing the progress notes makes inappropriate responses appear to occur quite frequently. The only appropriate response to a high therapeutic drug level is to order a lower dosage of that drug or to document the idiosyncratic therapeutic needs of a patient for a drug level that would normally be considered toxic. Digoxin, theophylline, lithium, and phenytoin therapeutic drug levels would be potential monitors.[11]

Abnormal Results

Did the physician respond to all abnormal test results? This can be investigated by reviewing a sample of charts, looking at all laboratory data, or focusing on the physician's response to results from a specific test. Hematuria was the subject of a multiple hospital audit by the Professional Standards Review Organization for Southern Arizona in which the Tucson Medical Center participated. I reviewed the data for the local Professional Standards Review Organization and found that every institution had a substantial number of cases of hematuria that appeared to have been overlooked. This study was done retrospectively using patient charts; any patient who had procedures involving the bladder, such as catherization and/or surgery, was excluded. A number of patients in whom abnormal laboratory test results were found were followed up in the clinician's outside office, but that scheduled follow-up was not reflected in the hospital chart notes.

Studies in the literature show an alarming lack of documentation for response to abnormal test results. One study of a family practice setting found the documentation of follow-up to abnormal laboratory results occurred in only 53% of those results. Even automated reminders did not result in significant improvement.[12]

If you find a substantial number of abnormal results to which there is no response, consider the arrangement of the report. Is it well organized and easily understood? Are abnormalities adequately highlighted? Are clinicians aware of the problem? Again, an important part of follow-up action is finding out why problems occur.

Postdischarge Results

What is the physician response to laboratory results generated after the patient is discharged? These laboratory results are often important, but sometimes they are overlooked. The protocol for the communication of these results should be reviewed. Frequently they are sent to the medical records department, which incorporates the results into the patient's record. Theoretically, the discharge summary should not be made until the chart is complete, which means the inclusion of all outstanding laboratory data. If these results are merely entered onto the chart and the discharge summary has already been completed, the physician may have no reason to review the chart again. If the laboratory cannot ascertain which laboratory results are for discharged patients, have the medical records department send copies of all laboratory results received for discharged patients. After a reasonable period, for example, 2 months (this would allow for completion of mycology tests), ask the primary physician if the test results were received and when. If the answer is not uniformly "yes," review your protocol for effectiveness of communication of these results and ascertain if it needs to be changed or merely enforced. This is an important monitor and should be periodically spot-checked.

ANCILLARY OR PERIPHERAL TESTING

Bedside testing is on the increase; there are now few hospitals that do not perform glucose evaluation of finger stick specimens. Aside from glucose analyzers for glucose, there are stool guaiacs for detection of blood in the stool and chemical strips for urine analysis. If bedside testing is under the licensure of the main laboratory then the laboratory must assume responsibility for its quality assurance. Service issues, such as turnaround time, are of concern, as is accuracy. Establish a proficiency testing program for these peripheral laboratories and set guidelines for quality control against which the testing can be gauged. Using blood glucose testing as an example, calculate two standard deviations for the instruments used for bedside testing of blood glucose. Then gauge accuracy of the bedside equipment by using them to test blood already analyzed in the laboratory. Many laboratories require random split samples to compare results from the glucose analyzers with those found in the laboratory. In addition, some require a split sample for all results considered critical.

Often what is missing in these proficiency programs is a set course of follow-up action when problems in testing are found. If the tests cannot be done accurately, there should not be any peripheral testing. The requirements for peripheral testing must be as stringent as those in the laboratory, and as its use increases, we will have to keep in mind that other quality indicators and issues apply, such as appropriateness of testing.

MISCELLANEOUS STUDIES

Nursing Unit Rounds

Nursing units can be divided among pathologists, each of whose task is to talk to the head nurse and ward clerks to gauge user satisfaction. The pathologist should make clear in a friendly manner that because they are customers the laboratory has a genuine interest in their viewpoint. Questions should be asked positively, that is, ask how the laboratory is doing, not what the problems in the laboratory are. The high visibility of pathologists and the concern shown by them should improve the image of the laboratory.

Findings from the meetings between pathologists and nursing unit staff should be formally documented and brought up by the pathologists when they meet with their supervisors. Periodic meetings between pathologists and nursing staff will take place only with continued encouragement from the designated champion of quality assurance, that is, the quality assurance chairperson, the medical director, the laboratory manager, or a designated pathologist. It doesn't automatically happen! A tickler file would be a useful reminder that it is time for the nursing unit contact.

In one quarter at the Tucson Medical Center seven important problems were brought to our attention as a result of pathologists meeting with the nursing staff. In a different 6-month period, 27 problems were identified and resolved, including the timing of phlebotomy drawings for therapeutic drugs, turnaround times for stat orders, and communication with a particular phlebotomist. Implementing this quality indicator should lead to improved communication between nursing staff and the laboratory, resulting in fewer problems and quicker recognition and correction of problems.

Incident Reports

Reports regarding the laboratory's performance and problems the laboratory has that are beyond its control should be tabulated. A common incident report would probably pertain to mislabeled and unlabeled specimens submitted to the laboratory from the units. Another (hopefully rare) incident report might complain about specimens being submitted with needles still attached. Incident reports about the laboratory's performance pertain mostly to phlebotomy problems, which is not surprising since phlebotomy is a large part of the laboratory's work.

At the Tucson Medical Center incident reports are tabulated quarterly by one of the department supervisors who looks for trends and recommends corrective action when appropriate. The results are summarized and presented annually at the intralaboratory meeting. Incident reports directed at the laboratory frequently relate to turnaround time. Those originating from the laboratory most often focus on specimens that are unlabeled. (Incident reports for the histology section are tabulated separately because they involve anatomic pathology and originate primarily from the surgery department.)

As medical director, I meet semiannually with the heads of the histology, general surgery, ambulatory surgery, and labor and delivery departments to discuss problems focused in their areas. A large number of problems are related to adequate fixation of specimens and sufficient clinical information accompanying the specimens. These discussions center around preventing problems, including participation by the pathology department in their continuing education programs and changes in forms that facilitate their completion.

At the annual meeting, trends and corrective action are discussed, documentating that past corrective action was effective. An important part of following up incident reports is showing that there was a rapid response to problems (Figure 8.3). A key part of the rapid response is direct communication to the individual involved rather than a memo sent through the bureaucracy. If an incident report arrives dated weeks previously, call whoever sent the report and ask that person to call you, in addition to sending a memo, in the future. Doing this shows that you want to correct problems as soon as possible. An incident report that is recent is more easily investigated and more relevant to the involved individuals.

The key to successfully collecting incident report data is assigning one person, who is responsible for collecting and analyzing the data. Although a

```
┌─────────────────────────────────────────────────────────────────┐
│                                                                   │
│   Date: _____ Person Reporting Problem: _____     │
│   Patient Name: _____     │
│   Patient ID#: _____     │
│   Physician: _____     │
│   Test(s) Involved: _____     │
│   Date Drawn or Collected: _____     │
│   Problem: _____     │
│   _____        │
│                                                                   │
│   (The following applies only where accuracy of results is questioned.)│
│   Test Repeated on Original Specimen:      _____ Yes      _____ No │
│   If Yes, Date: _____ Result: _____     │
│   Comment: _____     │
│   _____        │
│                                                                   │
│   Was Specimen Recollected and Rerun:      _____ Yes      _____ No │
│   If Yes, Date: _____ Result: _____     │
│   Comment: _____     │
│   _____        │
│                                                                   │
│   Action Taken or Follow-up: _____     │
│   _____        │
│   Action Approved by: _____ Date: _____    │
│                                                                   │
└─────────────────────────────────────────────────────────────────┘
```

Figure 8.3   Form used to follow up incident reports related to specimen collection.

supervisor might be assigned this duty, anyone in the laboratory could do it. The advantage of assigning this duty to someone other than a supervisor is involvement of more people in the quality assurance program.

Many complaints are in the form of telephone calls or personal communication, not formal written complaints. Tracking complaints called in is often done by large commercial laboratories to spot problems that arise and to correct them to improve service. Tracking complaints could also be valuable in the hospital laboratory, especially if it includes calls made directly to pathologists, supervisors, and managers as well as those made to the front office. Compiled on a periodic basis it is an excellent problem-oriented monitor.

Patient Satisfaction Surveys

Patient satisfaction surveys should determine items such as: Were patients correctly identified, that is, did the phlebotomist verify the patient's name before drawing the blood? Was the conduct of the phlebotomists appropriate? Was an explanation of the protocol for tests, for example, midstream urine collections, given? The last item is generally the responsibility of the nursing service; the method of collection affects the validity of the laboratory results. Patient satisfac-

Date:
Section:
Monitor Initials:

Title: BSP Protective Gear

Criteria	Yes	No*	NA
1. Gloves are worn when touching blood, body fluids, mucous membranes, or nonintact skin.			
2. Gloves are worn for handling of items or surfaces soiled with blood or body fluids.			
3. Gloves are worn when contact with blood is possible (IV initiation, finger sticks, etc).			
4. Gloves are worn when policy or procedure requires them.			
5. Hands are washed immediately after gloves are removed.			
6. Gowns or aprons are worn when there is potential for blood and/or body fluids to splash on to the care giver.			
7. Masks, eyewear, and/or face shields are worn when policy or procedure require them.			
8. Protective facewear is worn when care is likely to generate droplets or splashing that could expose mucous membranes of care giver.			
9. Protective gear is available for use.			

Title of person being observed ____________

*Document noncompliant activity and follow-up action for each response in the "No" column on the audit. ____________

____

Figure 8.4 Body substance precaution survey regarding use of protective gear.

tion surveys are examined in more detail in the chapters on methodology (Chapter 4) and quality assurance in commercial laboratories (Chapter 12).

Body Substance Precaution

A quarterly unannounced survey of body substance precaution is required by regulatory agencies. The body substance precaution survey forms shown in Figures 8.4 to 8.7 were devised by the infection control department at the Tucson Medical Center for the entire hospital and then revised by me to focus on areas applicable to the laboratory. In the laboratory we evaluate quarterly 10 persons on each shift in each of the following categories: handwashing, protective gear, sharp object disposal, and infectious waste disposal. This is an ongoing monitor with a threshold of 100% compliance.

```
┌─────────────────────────────────────────────────────────────────────┐
│                                                                       │
│   Date:                                                               │
│   Section:                                                            │
│   Monitor Initials:                                                   │
│   Title: BSP Handwashing Compliance                                   │
│   Criteria                                          Yes   No*   NA     │
│   1. Washes hands after emptying wastes and or                        │
│      containers.                                                      │
│   2. Resources available for washing hands (soap,                     │
│      paper, towels, and sinks are all convenient).                    │
│                                                                       │
│   Title of person being observed _____                    │
│   *Document noncompliant activity and follow-up action for each response │
│   in the "No" column on the audit. _____     │
│                                                                       │
└─────────────────────────────────────────────────────────────────────┘
```

Figure 8.5 Body substance precaution survey regarding handwashing compliance.

Adverse Reactions to Transfusion

The following items could be monitored in relation to transfusion reactions:

1. Was there positive identification of the patient and of the transfused unit of whole blood or components?
2. Were the patients' vital signs (temperature, pulse, and respirations) recorded before the transfusion and available as a guideline?
3. Were the clinical signs and symptoms of the patient recorded? Nurses generally sign this record, but some hospitals require a physician's signature.
4. Was the transfusion stopped immediately and protocol followed? The transfusion form may detail this protocol. Protocol should be reviewed locally but could include starting intravenous saline and notifying a physician if the temperature elevation is greater than 2°C.
5. Was the post-transfusion reaction workup completed by the laboratory in a timely and correct manner?
6. Were the pathologist's comments valid and complete? This should be fairly straightforward and reflect the laboratory data. The comments should explain the origin of the transfusion reaction. The comments could also address the above items.

Use of Blood and Blood Products

The standard protocol following transfusion of blood and blood products should include, among other things, baseline pretransfusion vital signs and vital signs following transfusion. Even though the nursing staff is responsible for tracking vital signs, the laboratory is held responsible for it by the regulatory agencies. Additionally, a protocol for the correct identification of blood and blood products prior to transfusion should be developed, followed, and documented. The patholo-

Title: BSP Sharp Object Disposal

Criteria	Yes	No*	NA
1. All used needles/syringes contaminated with blood/body fluids are placed uncapped in the box for sharp objects immediately after use.			
2. Used needles/syringes that are recapped are done so with a recapping device or with a one-hand technique.			
3. All sharp objects from patient procedure trays are placed in the box for sharp objects immediately after the procedure is completed.			
4. Disposal boxes for sharp objects are not overfilled and are properly disposed of when full.			

Title of person being observed _____

*Document noncompliant activity and follow-up action for each response in the "No" column on the audit. _____

Figure 8.6   Body substance precaution survey regarding sharp object disposal.

gist in charge of the blood bank and the blood bank supervisor should take the lead in developing this protocol. Monitors should be done to assure that the protocol guidelines are understood and followed. It is obvious that these guidelines contribute to improved patient care.

SURVEYS

Tests are designed to meet the needs of customers (patients and physicians) who use results from the testing. The availability, scope, quality of results, and service aspects of testing should meet their needs. Surveys (questionnaires) that monitor these points provide insight into problems that can immediately be solved or be the subject of a more focused monitor. Surveys are covered in more detail in the chapter on methodology (Chapter 4), and an example of a survey is given in the chapter on quality assurance in commercial laboratories (Chapter 12). A survey should be short and to the point, and if well designed, should generate a large percent of respondents[13] who will provide information on whether these needs are being met.

Q PROBES

Q Probes is a program sponsored by the CAP and "developed by the Quality Assurance Service Committee to assist pathologists in the newly mandated hospital-wide quality assurance endeavor."[14] The advantages of this program

```
┌─────────────────────────────────────────────────────────────────┐
│                                                                   │
│   Date:                                                           │
│   Section:                                                        │
│   Monitor Initials:                                              │
│   Title: BSP Infectious Waste Disposal                          │
│   Criteria                                        Yes  No*  NA   │
│   1. Appropriate equipment/resources are available for           │
│      use for container or infectious wastes disposal             │
│      (autoclave bag).                                            │
│   2. Equipment and supplies (bleach and spray bottle)            │
│      are available for use on blood and body fluid spills.       │
│                                                                   │
│   Title of person being observed _____        │
│   *Document noncompliant activity and follow-up action for each response │
│   in the "No" column on the audit. _____  │
│                                                                   │
└─────────────────────────────────────────────────────────────────┘
```

Figure 8.7 Body substance precaution survey regarding infectious waste disposal.

include established quality assurance indicators and a nationwide data base allowing you to compare your results with a large number of hospitals. For example, the Q Probe on surgical pathology frozen sections received data from 380 laboratories and 1,394 pathologists on 993,751 surgical pathology cases, generating results on 79,647 frozen sections from 52,464 patients.[15]

The Q Probes are available in three programs: anatomic pathology, clinical pathology, or combined anatomic and clinical pathology. *The Q Probes were not designed to replace your quality assurance program, but to supplement it.* Q Probes available include[16]:

1. Blood utilization
2. Surgical pathology frozen section consultants
3. Reporting error
4. Fine needle aspiration cytohistologic correlation (FNAC)
5. Clinical laboratory turnaround time
6. Nosocomial infection rate
7. Test utilization
8. Cervicovaginal cytology evaluation
9. Complications of phlebotomy
10. Hematology utilization
11. Comparison of antimicrobial susceptibility patterns
12. Appropriateness of autologous transfusions
13. Laboratory quality assurance program
14. Lung fine needle aspiration cytohistologic correlation
15. Autopsy report adequacy, timeliness, and rate
16. Colorectal carcinoma surgical pathology report adequacy

CONCLUSION

Audit topics can be found everywhere in the laboratory. Take the time to listen. Take the time to look. Prioritize topics according to potential or perceived problems related to high-volume tests. This chapter has suggested a large number of quality indicators that could apply to your institution. To study all these indicators would be excessive. There are more than enough topics to satisfy the regulatory agents, and if selected properly these studies should reveal data that result in real improvements for the laboratory.

REFERENCES

1. Tilley KL. Putting quality circles to work in chemistry. *MLO.* 1987;19:41-49.

2. Hilborne LH. The total testing process and laboratory turnaround time: application in anatomic and clinical pathology. *ASCP Check Sample.* 1990; 28(1).

3. Schifman R. Comprehensive and concurrent surveillance of test use. *Am J Clin Pathol.* 1989;92:539.

4. Gambino R. Beyond quality control. *Lab Rep.* 1990;4:25-28.

5. Hallam K. Turnaround time: speeding up but is it enough? *MLO.* 1988; 20:28-34.

6. Hilborne LH, Oye RK, McCardle JE, Repinski JA, Rodgerson DO. Evaluation of STATs and routine turnaround time as a component of laboratory quality assurance. *Am J Clin Pathol.* 1989;91:331-335.

7. Valenstein N, Emancipator K. Sensitivity, specificity, and reproducibility of four measures of laboratory turnaround time. *Am J Clin Pathol.* 1989; 91:452-457.

8. Hilborne LH, Oye RK, McCardle JE, Repinski JA, Rodgerson DO. Use of specimen turnaround time as a component of laboratory quality. *Am J Clin Pathol.* 1989;92:613-618.

9. *CAP Today.* April 1990:8.

10. Griffith JL. How to diffuse legal dynamite in the lab. *MLO.* 1986;18:31-34.

11. Brodie MJ, McIntosh ME, Hallworth M. Therapeutic drug monitoring: the need for an audit. *Scott Med J.* 1985;30:75-82.

12. Mendelson M. Automated reminders do not always improve follow-up of abnormal laboratory results. *Comput Biol Med.* 1986;16:131-134.

13. Ogram D. Surveys: assessing the effectiveness of a service. *Can J Technol.* 1987;49:59-60.

14. *CAP Today.* November 1988:12.

15. *CAP Today.* September 1989:18.

16. Advertisment brochure. Chicago, Ill: College of American Pathologists; 1990.

9. The Quality Assurance Program You Have but Did Not Document

How OFTEN DO you receive a complaint from an irate physician, nurse, or ward clerk? You listen and make changes that hopefully will resolve the problem permanently. You have just done what a quality assurance study purports to do, but without documentation you cannot receive the credit that is yours from the regulatory agencies. It does not take much effort to document complaints and corrective action if you have a simple, uncomplicated form on which to fill out this information. These data can be summarized quarterly, from which trends can be spotted and the appropriate parties can be notified for corrective action. The following is an example of a guideline you could use for a simple uncomplicated quality assurance study.

Objective: Resolve complaints.

Incident: This is the data base. One or two sentences can summarize the complaint. For example, Dr James Bond called and said the vitamin B_{12} levels were frequently too low.

Data: What examination of the problem showed. The low vitamin B_{12} levels made up a small proportion of the results; the majority of results were in the normal range. Most of the tests were ordered by hematologists for patients who were anemic, so a certain number of results should be expected to be abnormal. Include concrete data. For example, in the last 10 testing runs for vitamin B_{12}, of 34 patients tested 20 had abnormal findings, 18 of which were from anemic patients.

Follow-up: After showing the data to the physician who made the initial complaint, the physician believed that the low values for vitamin B_{12} were legitimate. The complaint about the low values turned out to be an isolated incident and did not warrant a more extensive study at the time. Furthermore, one of the two patients who were not anemic but were treated with vitamin B_{12} had a resultant increased reticulocyte count.

There are thousands of different problems that are solved but never documented. One complaint might come from the emergency department regarding slow turnaround times for testing of digoxin levels. A study finds that the method and instrumentation are slow for the testing. As a result of changing the testing method, the turnaround time decreases. (To verify that the turnaround has indeed decreased, a follow-up study should be performed.)

Another problem might be urine specimens for culture that sit too long before being plated. If this problem occurs with any frequency, a policy should be instituted that instructs the patient to inform the nurse as soon as a sample is ready. This is a multidisciplinary quality assurance study — involving the laboratory as well as the nursing service and sometimes the transportation service — that can be easily documented. Merely record the time the urine sample is obtained from the patient and the time the culture is planted. If the time elapsed before the culture is planted is over 4 hours, the specimen is not valid and should not be accepted for culture. If this continues to occur with some frequency, document the occurrences and institute corrective action. A more formal study may be necessary, with other nursing and transportation services included.

Every complaint is a potential audit: there are objectives, data, analyses, and resolutions. Document all complaints or select a few for documentation. If the complaint recurs, spend time developing quality indicators for a formal audit. The resolution of these complaints relates to patient care in some way, so when you document the complaint, make a note of what this relationship is. In addition, documentation of the complaint can result in a more thorough resolution of the problem than merely discussing it with the person who submitted the complaint: debating and documenting an issue has more of an impact on the problem than a brief conversation. Once documentation is available, talk to the person who initially complained and show him or her the summary in writing. This shows the laboratory's interest in thoroughly investigating and resolving problems that affect the quality of care.

You are often improving quality in your laboratory by solving problems. With documentation you can take credit for these improvements; documentation also helps you organize a more permanent solution. Once a problem has been resolved, inform whoever initiated the complaint; such communication demonstrates the laboratory's commitment to quality results and service.

10. Risk Management and Quality Assurance

HISTORICALLY, RISK MANAGEMENT programs were developed to help limit losses, more specifically, to limit the liability of an institution and its employees. Risk management initially covered workmen's compensation, product liability, and casualty loss. With the rising cost of malpractice, its emphasis has shifted to clinical care as it relates to potential litigation, that is, risk management is now concerned with preventing malpractice claims.

There is a natural link between risk management and quality assurance. Quality assurance focuses on optimal care and measures performance to improve patient care; risk management is concerned with patient safety, medical record documentation, utilization review, quality control, infection control, privileges/credentials, patient satisfaction with care, and specific problems as they arise (complaints and incident reports). Quality assurance measures, evaluates, and resolves problems, which meshes with the preventive goals of risk management. Theoretically, as quality improves, risk diminishes since there are fewer problems to investigate.

Most risk management programs evaluate incident reports; they evaluate a specific problem as it occurs. Risk management programs might also suggest quality assurance indicators that detect trends related to high risk. For example, the body substance precautions discussed in Chapter 8 were partly developed in response to the increased liability related to AIDS. In this vein, risk management could be helpful to the laboratory in minimizing problems and in keeping lines of communication open regarding incident reports and complaints. Risk management can make sure that these problems are not only effectively resolved, but that they are also reviewed with an eye toward preventing their recurrence. Many of the generic areas that concern risk management dovetail with those of laboratory quality assurance. Since risk management is concerned with liability, it is useful for the quality assurance team in the laboratory to focus on the major categories of wrongful conduct that particularly concern the laboratory.

INTENTIONAL ACTS

An intentional act is a premeditated one.[1] If I aim and hit you with my fist, I have committed an intentional act. In the case of liability, an intentional act must show "an intent, either actual or constructive, to produce such harm, without just or lawful excuse or justifiable cause or occasion."[2] In other words, "I did it, I meant to do it, I have no excuse." Furthermore, there must be injury to the plaintiff as a result.[3]

Falsifying records, frequently referred to in the vernacular as "dry laboratory results," is an intentional act. Results are sometimes—hopefully rarely—reported by pathologists despite their knowledge that the results are false. This is an intentional act of wrongdoing. The pathologist who makes a diagnosis of atypical leiomyoma for which no slide or paraffin block exists that confirms the diagnosis is, in the eyes of an outside observer, intentionally falsifying records. A simple mix-up might, in review, appear intentional. A patient who has a critical and questionable diagnosis based on laboratory results, despite the laboratory having no record of receiving a specimen, would probably believe the laboratory falsified the record, even though the problem may be a computer mix-up. At times, the results are assigned to the wrong patient! Documentation is important, because, depending on the circumstances, lack of it could be considered intentional wrongdoing or negligence.

STRICT LIABILITY

"A manufacturer is strictly liable in tort when an article he places on the market, knowing that it is to be used without inspection for defect, proves to have a defect that causes injury to a human being. That is the doctrine of strict tort liability as expressed by the court which first applied the doctrine."[4]

This is not an area of importance for most laboratories, except for those few that continue to make their own media for microbiology.

NEGLIGENCE

This category makes up the bulk of a laboratory's risk management problems. Negligence is defined as a failure to do what prudence dictates. Paraphrasing this definition as it applies to the laboratory, negligence is a breach of duty resulting in injury with approximate cause, that is, there must be a link between cause and injury. Proving negligence involves substantiating that guidelines were breached leading to damages.[5] Failure to follow procedure could be viewed as negligence, which is particularly relevant to mismanaged cases. Running a red light and hitting a pedestrian without intending to hit that person would be an example of negligence.

The following is from the Arizona laws of malpractice:

"A physician is liable and must respond in damages for injuries or death sustained by a patient as the result of the physician's professional negligence in the diagnosis or treatment of the patient. Negligence of a physician is the doing of some act which is contrary to the standards of good medical practice or the failure to do some act which is required by those standards in the professional advice, supervision, medical care and treatment of the patient by the physician. If you find that defendants, or any of them, did some act which is contrary to the standards of good medical practice or failed to do some act which is required by the standards of good medical practice, which proximately caused injury to plaintiff, then you must find for the plaintiff."[6]

Wrongful conduct specifically includes the following (see also Chapters 7 and 8):

1. Improper consent. This applies particularly to bone marrow aspirations, autopsies, and fine needle aspirations. For true consent, the patients must have a clear idea of what they are agreeing to have done. Testing for human immunodeficiency virus without consent is also a sticky issue for the laboratory. I have found that physicians sometimes resent such guidelines because they believe they should have these test results without consent, claiming it serves to protect the personnel caring for patients who are at risk for AIDS. This is a false sense of security, however, since the detection rate is not 100%. Thus, universal precautions should apply to all patients.
2. Venipuncture.
   a. Damage to the patient from improper procedure.
   b. Patients falling or otherwise injuring themselves due to lightheadedness after the procedure. For example, suppose patients become lightheaded after blood is taken, and fall and injure themselves when they stand up.
   c. Mislabeling the specimen.
   d. Drawing the wrong specimen.
   e. Loss of the specimen.
3. Timeliness of tests.
   a. Turnaround time. This is a frequent inquiry. Lawyers believe that having the results sooner could have improved the care of their patient, so they examine the turnaround times for critical tests. According to one expert:
      "Although most quality assurance programs are able to identify problems resulting from errors of care, much less has been done to date to resolve errors related to omission, particularly errors of delay in diagnosis. While the malpractice literature attests to the frequency and often catastrophic severity of such problems, delays in diagnosis present difficult problems of detection and solution."[7]
   b. Communication of results. One concern is the communication of test results completed after the patient is discharged from the hospital; or in an

outpatient facility, test results that take more than 48 hours (eg, fungal cultures).
   c. Delay or failure to report critical results.
4. Miscellaneous
   a. Mislabeled specimens.
   b. Incorrect results. This could result in an admission to the hospital or performance of invasive procedures with the inherent risks attached. Elevated creatine phosphokinase-MB levels, low platelet counts, erroneous crossmatches, or mislabeled units of blood are risks that fall under this category.
   c. Lost specimen.
   d. Laboratory safety.
   e. Erroneous tissue diagnosis.
   f. Miscommunication of results to physicians.
   g. Unnecessary testing resulting in added costs.
   h. Lapses in communication such as a missing clinical history on a surgical specimen submitted to pathology.
   i. Improper quality control.

NECESSARY VS UNNECESSARY TESTING

Although appropriateness of testing is covered in a previous chapter (Chapter 7), it is worthwhile to cover the subject from the viewpoint of risk management or jurisprudence. Third-party payers and regulatory agencies are asking: What is necessary testing? What is unnecessary testing? What is cost-efficient testing? There are no definitive answers to these questions. Some hospitals are not being paid when testing is deemed unnecessary by reviewers working for the government or industry using their own guidelines. Cost of the test and potential benefit and damage to the patient are factors in these guidelines. Hospitals face liability for omitting a test but at the same time face the financial constraints of limited payments from third-party payers for services rendered.

If a physician is not cost-effective in ordering diagnostic tests, a hospital, because of limited payment for care, may be forced to determine whether it can afford to keep that physician on the staff; without staff privileges a physician has difficulty maintaining a medical practice. For physicians to protect themselves from liability and because of the real harm lack of testing could have on the individual, physicians often cannot afford to be cost-effective in test ordering.[8] For example, physicians may lose a malpractice suit because they omitted a test that seemed to have little statistical relevance to the situation, yet with hindsight would have been extremely useful. Is it warranted that in each similar situation physicians should obtain the additional diagnostic test? If the test is positive only once every 2000 times, then in my view the benefits do not outweigh the costs unless the disease detected is extremely devastating and expensive to treat. Risk vs benefit is a complicated question, with a great deal of literature devoted to it without an answer. Each situation must be analyzed, looking at any unusual circumstances that would allow deviation from local standards. These issues are frequently left up to society (and sometimes to juries) to answer.

The elements of negligence include duty, breach of duty, proximate cause, and damage with link between the proximate cause and the damage. As it relates to appropriateness of testing, duty represents consensus guidelines. A peer group decides that a particular test is worthwhile when certain guidelines are met. Even a test with 98% specificity will yield 2 false positives for every 100 tests. The gaussian distribution curve for defining most tests will yield only 95.45% true positives with 4.55% false positives. As you decrease the sensitivity of the test or specificity of the test, the number of false positives and false negatives are significant in analyzing the cost. Neuhauser and Lewicki[9] showed that a sixth guaiac test (compared with five stool guaiac tests for blood) to detect an additional bowel cancer costs $47 million over the period required to detect additional colon cancer.

The bottom line is that testing is appropriate when it is within the consensus opinion of the medical community. Nonetheless, that testing must be consistent with practice guidelines in other parts of the country, not just with local medical standards. In developing these guidelines for testing, costs, age, and benefit and damage to the patient must all be weighed.

RISK MANAGEMENT AND THE LABORATORY

People concerned with risk management should be contacted whenever complaints or incidents with potential liability arise. The laboratory's role is to cooperate fully in determining if any liability exists. Anything other than an isolated problem should be monitored with quality assurance indicators to see if there is a trend that requires follow-up action. The more important quality indicators the laboratory should review are the clinically relevant problems with the highest potential risk.

PEER REVIEW AND PROTECTION FROM THE LAW

Check with your local state laws regarding committee protection, immunity of committee members, discoverability, and admission. Generally, when carrying out a peer review process you are working for the hospital and are covered by the hospital insurance plan. The relevant laws are not federal but state.

SUMMARY

This chapter has shown how important risk management is to quality assurance. Additionally, this chapter has shown which functions of the laboratory pertain most closely to risk management. As mentioned earlier, quality indicators related to these areas are covered more specifically in Chapters 7 and 8. In short, risk management shares the following goals with quality assurance: the identification, evaluation, and resolution of problems.

REFERENCES

1. *Webster's New Collegiate Dictionary.* Springfield, Mass: G & C Merriam Co; 1976.
2. 74 Am Jur 2d, § 18.
3. 74 Am Jur 2d, § 26.
4. Williamson JW. *Assessing and Improving Health Care Outcomes: The Health Accounting Approach to Quality Assurance.* Cambridge, Mass: Ballinger; 1978.
5. Quinlan A, Krolikowski FJ, Dunham WG, Reuter K. Risk management enchances quality care and protection from liability. *Pathologists.* 1986; 40:29-32.
6. Stefan R Jr, ed. *The Arizona Law of Medical Malpractice.* Phoenix, Ariz: Medilex Co; 1988:157.
7. 63 Am Jur 2d, § 528.
8. Wilcox DP. Medicine and the law. *Tex Med.* 1985;81:49-51.
9. Neuhauser D, Lewicki A. National health insurance and the sixth stool guaiac. *Policy Analysis.* 1976:2:175-196.

11. Dealing With the Inspection

THE TWO KEY ingredients to a successful inspection are organization and content. If you have prepared everything necessary (content) for the inspection but the paperwork is not easily found or it is presented in a disorganized fashion, a closer inspection may take place because the inspectors believe that something so disorganized is likely flawed. The reverse may be true also: if a quality assurance program is well organized the inspectors may feel it does not need in-depth inspection. Faulty thinking? Yes, but a well-organized program can help smooth over some of the rough edges in content.

Develop a well-organized, neat notebook of quality assurance activities for each year. I suggest the following organization:

1. Quality assurance plan, including an accurate calendar of quality assurance activities. Also include a schematic depicting communication of results from the monitors.
2. Minutes of quarterly or semiannual meetings with the individual sections of the laboratory.
3. Summary reports that include a topic, purpose for doing the monitor (objective), criteria, summary of findings (data), conclusion, follow-up (with specific dates), effect on patient care, dates that reports were presented, any significant action taken, and the relationship of the monitored activity to patient care.

A more detailed report that includes all the original data should be easily accessible to the inspector.

About 1 month before the inspection, review your quality assurance program. The following should be stressed:

1. The action taken should be specific and aim at resolving the problem. Do not leave open loops. Ask why the problem occurred. Try to eliminate the reason for the problem.
2. Show evidence that results of the study were communicated to involved individuals and include dates of all committee presentations. The continuing education program for the laboratory should incorporate quality assurance topics, and this activity should be documented.
3. Appropriateness of testing must be addressed by quality indicators, with evidence of interaction with the test-ordering clinicians.
4. There must be evidence of safety procedure monitors, including body substance compliance.
5. There must be a record of the date of all follow-up action taken on quality indicators where necessary.

Both the quality assurance chairperson and the medical director should be knowledgeable of quality assurance activities in the laboratory. Both should be available to the inspector to offer assistance and answer questions during the inspection. Provide a comfortable environment where the inspector can review the quality assurance material.

Look on the inspection as a learning opportunity, a chance to share ideas on quality assurance. Ask the inspector to recommend quality indicators different from yours. Ask how you can improve your presentation. The inspection should not be an arena for argument but an informative event for both the inspector and the laboratory.

12. Quality Assurance in a Commercial Laboratory

THE COMMERCIAL (INDEPENDENT) laboratory (ie, a laboratory outside the hospital; or if inside, it is managed independently even if integrated into the hospital's laboratory) exists in a highly competitive environment. Cost containment, quality, and service are vital to its survival. Handling every complaint is a priority.

Because quality and service are so important, commercial laboratories should use some form of quality assurance to fine-tune their business. A key issue is the documentation of this quality assurance. Documentation is necessary and helpful because it can reveal trends, the knowledge of which leads to more permanent solutions to the problems that affect the bottom line of the commercial laboratory. With this documentation, a commercial laboratory can move from putting out fires (solving problems) to preventing them (avoiding problems).

In the commercial setting, quality is defined as specifications or guidelines that satisfy or exceed the customers' needs. Customers include not only the physician and patient but also third-party payers and self-insured organizations. The sections below outline a quality assurance program for commercial laboratories.

QUALITY ASSURANCE PLAN

The plan should include the same elements as discussed earlier (see Chapter 3). However, appropriateness of testing is difficult to incorporate into such a plan because the independent laboratory does not have ready access to physician records. Newsletters to clients or potential clients on the appropriate use of testing could be circulated, but it would be hard to judge the effectiveness of this activity. Indirectly, a decrease in the volume of orders for a specific test addressed in the newsletter may indicate a positive response. However, there are so many different patient attributes that it is flawed to use changes in volume of test ordering as indicators of a newsletter's effectiveness. And lacking a patient's history, a quality assurance plan for the appropriateness of testing in a commercial laboratory may not produce valid data. Some third-party payers, such as HMOs, request specific information to conduct utilization reviews of participating physicians. These third-party payers may want detailed data on laboratory tests ordered according to physician, diagnosis, and patient as a requirement for using a particular laboratory. Despite these complications, quality assurance activity documentation is still worthwhile. Ultimately, the objectives of the quality assurance plan—whether for hospital or commercial laboratory—are to have a plan that will detect and correct problems, thus making a contribution to improved patient care.

COMPLAINTS AND INCIDENT REPORTS

The who, what, when, and where for each complaint must be gathered to measure trends. Figures 12.1 and 12.2 are examples of a problem log and an incident report summary, respectively.

Details of each complaint or incident report should be summarized quarterly from the completed incident reports (see Figure 12.2), and discussed at a weekly supervisors' meeting to assure that problems that potentially affect patient care or business are handled effectively and in a timely fashion. I believe it is a good idea to have the medical director initial the reports as documentation of review.

In the quarterly summary look for trends in problems related to groups or individuals. The findings from each complaint category are reviewed with the appropriate supervisor. For example, under the technical category the findings are summarized according to the individual technologists involved with the incident and reviewed with their supervisors. Look at the process first and the individual second. If several individuals are having problems, the focus should be on the process; however, if only one technologist is having problems, obviously the focus should be on the individual.

Choose the appropriate corrective action, the results of which are included in the quarterly report. Also cite any anticipated follow-up studies. Each quarterly report includes the absolute number of problems in each category from the previous report (see example above). Between quarterly reports, a weekly review of the incident reports assures that problems are being resolved in an ongoing fashion. These problems should be resolved before the weekly meeting; however, a quarterly summary is needed for an overview of laboratory problems.

Various factors may have an effect on the results. For example, the volume of business for a quarter, computer downtime, major instrumentation problems, or employee shortages could skew the results. In addition, the emphasis placed on writing incident reports needs to be taken into consideration. Incident or problem reports take time. Unless employees are encouraged to write these they will not be

Problem Log

Date: _____ Person Reporting Problem: _____

Patient Name: _____

Patient ID #: _____

Physician: _____

Test(s) Involved: _____

Date Drawn or Collected: _____

Problem: _____
_____

When Applicable:

Test Repeated on Original Specimen: _____ Yes   _____ No

If Yes, Date: _____ Result: _____

Comment: _____
_____

Was Specimen Recollected and Rerun: _____ Yes   _____ No

If Yes, Date: _____ Result: _____

Comment: _____
_____

Action Taken or Follow-up: _____
_____

Action Approved By: _____ Date: _____

Figure 12.1   Form used to record problems.

done or simply be done so infrequently that they are not representative of problems. The summarizing of complaints and incident reports is an ongoing quality assurance study that helps to satisfy customers by promoting overall quality service and advancing the reputation of the laboratory.

An alternative scheme to review problems is to look at client service and processing logs; for example, you may find that a particular office calls in for results more than others. This could necessitate a change in delivery time or a different printing time of the report. In processing you may find that a particular office is submitting a number of hemolyzed specimens, which would indicate a potential problem with specimen handling. Sending someone to that office to examine the problem in detail and to conduct an in-service educational talk on processing serves both the client and the laboratory. I review problems on a weekly basis and write up a solution in a quality assurance book (see Figure 12.3). The documentation only takes a few minutes, yet it results in a valued quality assurance monitor and contributes to the quality of the laboratory's services.

Quartery Quality Assurance Summary Report
Incident Reports for the Fourth Quarter

Reason: To assess problems to determine trends needing correction.

Criteria: All incident reports are evaluated and categorized under Technical, Phlebotomy/Prep, Physician Communication, Courier, Billing, and Reference Labs.

Summary of Findings: There were 67 incident reports:

Area	First Quarter	Second Quarter	Third Quarter	Fourth Quarter
Technical	7	5	5	7
Phlebotomy/Prep	22	25	31	30
Reference Lab	6	8	6	2
Courier	6	6	1	10
Physician Communication	6	10	4	4
Miscellaneous	0	0	2	14

Conclusion: No significant trends.

Follow-up Action: Individuals involved with each incident report are counseled and the quarterly summary results communicated to the entire staff.

Figure 12.2 Incident report summary.

PATIENT SURVEY ON PHLEBOTOMY PROCEDURES

We periodically ask patients to fill out a survey at the TMCHE laboratory (Figure 12.4). The patients are asked to mail in their responses, although a number of patients prefer to complete it at the time of their visit. The survey is prestamped and folds so the laboratory's address appears on the front. As surveys are distributed, the location of the drawing station is marked in the corner. The phlebotomist initials the lower right hand corner of the form and gives it to the patient. Again, the findings from these surveys are collected and problems noted. We encourage patients to respond and have a response rate of approximately 90%.

Objective:	Survey patient satisfaction with the phlebotomy service.
Data:	Results of the survey. At our laboratory we involve all drawing stations. We do these surveys for 1 to 2 weeks at a time quarterly or semiannually. We distribute 250 to 500 surveys each time.
Action Taken:	Again, trends in problems should be noted, and the corrective action taken should be recorded in the summary report. Look at the process and determine why the problem occurred. If necessary, design a specific quality indicator to look at a particular issue, and give a date for the follow-up monitor of that quality indicator. These surveys make patients aware of your concern for

March 7, 1991 Quality Assurance Study

Problem:	Trend noted involving Drs A, B, and C's offices: specimens submitted with patient's requisition number filled out but name of patient not written on the specimen container.
Action Taken:	Protocol to be redistributed; service representatives to visit their offices to discuss the importance of this issue.
Follow-up:	Continue to review processing logs for this trend.

Figure 12.3 Write-up of problem and planned course of action to solve it.

how they are treated, and they make the phlebotomists more aware of patients' feelings. The phlebotomist is also reminded of the laboratory's concern for quality patient care.

Surveys need to be conducted regularly because of the high rate of turnover of personnel in phlebotomy and the ever-changing patient population. Surveys are a good public relations strategy, allowing the laboratory to learn how it is perceived by its customers; the very fact that a survey is being done should reflect well on the laboratory's reputation. And the laboratory's reputation increases even more in customers' eyes if it responds rapidly to correct their complaints. Additionally, a positive patient response is a good morale boost for the phlebotomists.

Physician Office Survey

Positive feedback from surveys of physician offices is a good morale booster for laboratory personnel, since positive customer feedback typically results in positive feedback from management. If a low rating occurs with any frequency it should be quickly followed up with corrective action that ideally eliminates the problem permanently. Figure 12.5 is representative of the survey we use for physician offices. The data are numerical, which means they can easily be input into a computer program or calculated manually. All surveys have the specific physician office typed on the back, and any question that receives a "poor" or "fair" (1 or 2) response is automatically followed up for remedial action. When the problem is resolved, we inform the office that initiated the complaint, which demonstrates how seriously we take complaints and how committed we are to quality service.

Turnaround Time

Turnaround time for test results is a critical service issue in the commercial laboratory, but unlike the hospital laboratory most results are not expected until the following day. Additionally, since patients for whom tests are done in the commercial laboratory are generally not as ill as hospitalized patients, stat orders occur less frequently and are less of a problem in the commercial laboratory. Nonetheless, it remains an issue worth reviewing periodically.

1. Was the phlebotomist/receptionist courteous?
   Comment:
2. How long did you wait to have your blood drawn?
   Comment:
3. Was the phlebotomist skillful and knowledgeable?
   Comment:
4. Were your questions answered satisfactorily?
   Comment:

[name of] Laboratory prides itself on quality service, therefore, we are interested in your opinion. Thank you for taking a moment to fill out and return this questionnaire.

Sincerely,

| [name of] | [name of] |
| Client Services Manager | Medical Director |

Figure 12.4 Patient survey regarding phlebotomy procedures.

At our laboratory we found it rewarding to record the turnaround times for tests sent out to reference laboratories. We found that there are different testing schedules for reference laboratories and that some reference laboratory pickup times result in an additional 24-hour delay. These findings were noted in the course of a turnaround time study for specific test results. We recorded the turnaround times for 10 to 20 units sent out for some of the most frequently ordered tests, which was sufficient to detect trends in turnaround time. As a result of this monitor, the reference laboratory instituted a different testing schedule, which corrected the problem.

STAT ORDERS

The independent laboratory should review its turnaround times for stat orders, no matter how few, because these orders are often the ones that customers recall when asked to evaluate a laboratory's service. The independent laboratory must set its own thresholds for turnaround times for stat orders. The data should include the time the order is received (frequently by telephone), the time the courier service is notified of a pickup (or the time the patient arrives if the patient comes to one of your drawing stations), the time the specimen is picked up by the courier, the time the specimen is processed, the time the specimen is received in the technical area, and the time the results are telephoned (if someone other than the technician conveys the results, then record the time the specimen is given to the client services to make the call and the actual time of the call). By looking at these [name of] Laboratory is proud to provide laboratory services for your practice. We are continually looking for ways to improve our service to you. Please share this questionnaire with your staff. When complete, please place it in the attached envelope for courier pickup.

1	2	3	4	5	N/A
POOR	FAIR	GOOD	VERY GOOD	EXCELLENT	NONAPPLICABLE

Please rate the following according to the above scale.

Courier Service:
_____ Prompt
_____ Friendly
_____ Professional

Phlebotomists:
_____ Friendly
_____ Professional
_____ Patient satisfaction

_____ Telephone etiquette of staff

_____ Turnaround time for routine testing

_____ Turnaround time for stat testing

_____ Quality of laboratory results

_____ Responsiveness of technical staff

_____ Responsiveness of pathology staff

Efficiency of client services department:
_____ Specific Name
_____ Specific Name

Effectiveness of service representatives:
_____ Specific Name
_____ Specific Name
_____ Satisfaction with frequency of visits of service representatives

Billing service:
_____ Accuracy
_____ Responsiveness

Your suggestions and comments are important to us, so please feel free to list them on the back of this form. We appreciate your time and effort in completing this questionnaire.

Name of person completing questionnaire: _____

Figure 12.5 Physician office survey.

different times as a unit existing problems can be analyzed, and thresholds for the turnaround times for each of these areas can be established. Additional variations include whether the specimen is drawn at the main laboratory, eliminating the role of the courier; the distance to a drawing station or physician's office if couriers are involved; and the time required to run the individual test.

In our commercial laboratory, electrolyte testing and complete blood counts are the most frequently ordered stat tests; for all drawing stations within 2 miles of the main laboratory where the test is run, our threshold is a turnaround time of 1 hour for electrolyte tests and complete blood counts. Analysis of the different units of time involved, as described in the preceding paragraph, has allowed us to make some changes. For example, we discovered that too much time elapsed between courier delivery and specimen processing. As a result of this, the courier must now give the specimen directly to someone in the processing area. Stat specimens are also labeled with a large circular red sticker to alert all involved that it is a stat order; this label accompanies the specimen throughout the processing and technical areas. We have also set a threshold of 30 minutes for the courier service to make deliveries within a set radius of the laboratory; if this is fulfilled for a given time, that service receives a bonus.

Stat service is remembered by the client, because generally the client and the patient are waiting for the result so that therapeutic decisions can be made. Stat orders are a highly visible part of the independent laboratory's service; good turnaround times for stat orders are perceived as a sign of quality by clients.

Billing

At TMCHE laboratory, several patient files are reviewed each month to check the accuracy of billing. The patient's test results are pulled to see if the tests done match the billing; we look for both tests that are billed but not performed and tests performed but not billed. If there are problems, we first look for a processing error rather than blame an individual. We also track incoming calls related to billing each month, placing them in several categories and analyzing these categories. We noted that there were a large number of calls related to misinformation on insurance coverage. As a result of this, every drawing station now has a copying machine so that a copy of the patient's insurance card goes to the billing department.

Communication

Quality assurance involves everyone, which means that everyone in the laboratory needs to be aware of the findings and action taken on behalf of a quality assurance study. Specifics, such as individual names, do not have to be brought up, but people should know why changes are made or why corrective action is taken. Ideally, the discussion itself is part of the corrective action. Again, wherever possible, action taken should be educational not punitive.

SUMMARY

A private laboratory will find that implementing quality assurance helps to fine-tune its business. Many of the same quality assurance monitors (eg, accuracy of reports, adequacy of specimens) from the chapter on audit topics (Chapter 8) can be done in the private laboratory. The studies mentioned in this chapter should be ongoing as part of a commercial laboratory's quality assurance program. The immediate findings should be discussed at weekly staff meetings and action decided on to correct any problems. Emphasis should be on the process and not the individual. Laboratories should also encourage a team concept combined with individual pride in the job. Commercial laboratories should keep in mind the following simple guidelines for their quality assurance program:

Involve everyone.
Measure everyone's satisfaction.
Make the study ongoing.
Review and communicate.
Take care of all problems no matter how small.
Measure, measure, measure.
Keep the study simple and focused.
Document or you have no quality assurance.
Do something. Now.

13. The Computer and Quality Assurance

HOSPITAL INFORMATION SYSTEMS are designed to enhance management of operations. The data generated by these systems are used to initiate easier, faster, more accurate, and more cost-effective quality assurance studies. Ideally, the laboratory computer system interfaces with the hospital information system, since many of the laboratory quality assurance studies involve multiple disciplines and are oriented to service or appropriateness of service issues. For example, a laboratory system should be able to provide information related to patients, such as medical history, progress notes, resultant orders, and physician response to test results. Such a system requires artificial intelligence with electronic charts, which would facilitate gathering information necessary for quality assurance monitors.

Edward H. Shortliffe, Chief of Medicine at Stanford University, says:

"I suspect that the most useful artificial intelligence systems will be fiscally motivated, for example, systems that help assure efficient use of the laboratory in managed care systems or programs that optimize (diagnosis related group) assignments."[1]

The ideal hospital information system selects a field and generates related data, for example, DRG data regarding laboratory tests. You may want to examine laboratory data related to diagnoses of high frequency; or you may want to compare laboratory charges by physicians for a specific disease. The hospital information system can provide you with information about the severity of disease so you have a more valid comparison. These studies are easily done using a state-of-the-art information system but are extremely difficult without one. Some systems have the computer generate some data but require additional data to be entered manually. Obviously, the sophistication of your system dictates the extent to which you can use the computer software to fulfill your quality assurance needs.

ADMISSION ORDERS

Have the system automatically print out information related to admission laboratory charges over a certain dollar amount (I suggest $200) for the medical director on a regular or intermittent basis as a method of looking for potential problems. Should these patients have been worked up more as an outpatient? Are these appropriate orders for an inpatient setting? This is an easy ongoing study when done with the laboratory information system.

DRG DATA

Use DRG data to identify high-volume laboratory users. Graphics can be used to plot total laboratory charges or laboratory charges by disease for each physician. A further breakdown can plot the different types of tests ordered and point out any unwanted patterns. Look for repeated orders despite normal results. As a follow-up, consensus guidelines can be set for testing for each disease based on the comparative data gained from the DRGs.

FINANCIAL DATA

Select a couple of cases each month to see if the bill generated by the hospital matches the laboratory data. Do not compare what has already been sent to financial services, compare laboratory results, that is, tests performed, with the charges generated. You might find some tests were cancelled and not performed, but the charges were not removed from the computer; or you might find some tests were added after the specimen was received from the floor, but the charges were not entered.

LABORATORY TURNAROUND TIME

Enter the time the order is placed, the time the specimen is drawn, the time the specimen arrives in the laboratory, and the time results are generated into the laboratory information system. The last time corresponds to the time the test results are available to the physician (if clinicians have access to a monitor; otherwise, someone must inform you of the time the information is available on the floor). With this information available in the laboratory information system, these quality indicators can be studied easily on a case-by-case basis (or a more general overview), and problems can be spotted. Sometimes merely abstracting the information and discussing it with those involved will temporarily improve services; if this is the case, the study needs to be done periodically. Of course, specific corrective action improves services more permanently.

NUMBER OF TESTS

As was discussed in the chapter on appropriateness of testing (Chapter 7), guidelines can be set for the acceptable frequency of ordering additional tests in response to normal test results and abnormal test results, paticularly for higher volume tests. For example, a patient with a normal complete blood count should not need a repeated test for several days; however, a review of repeated tests for complete blood counts within 3 days shows how often patients with initial normal test results undergo potentially unnecessary repeated testing. The computer can track adherence to these guidelines by individual physician.

STAT ORDERS

Stat orders are easily tracked with the aid of a computer. The unit of origin of the stat order, the time of day of the order, the primary diagnosis of the patient, and the name of the ordering physician are all factors that should be readily available. To record this information manually would be prohibitively time-consuming. Ideally, circumstances of each stat order should be investigated, although the computer cannot do that; however, the computer-generated data can highlight trends that can then be investigated in a more detailed manner.

CRITICAL RESULTS

Ideally, a software package demands a response for all critical results, requiring that the critical results are communicated to the attending physician or someone at a responsible level, such as the charge nurse on a unit, before the computer will allow you to go to the next test. Without a computer, technologists must sign their name when they communicate the results, which means that all the work sheets have to be looked at manually to verify that the critical results have been communicated to the appropriate person. I know how frustrating and time-consuming it is to scan the work sheets when clinicians claim they were not called. A laboratory information system should have a space in the report for the technologist's initials and the initials of the party called, as well as the time this occurred, near the critical results information, or the system should at least have the ability to pull this information up on the monitor if it is not part of the printed report.

CASCADE ORDERING OF TESTS

The computer allows you to establish guidelines for cascade ordering of tests that are automatically available to the staff when a specific test order is initiated (eg, a thyroid-stimulating hormone test if there is a low thyroxine level). In the future, electronic charts and artificial intelligence will play a greater role in medicine. For example, with the electronic chart progress notes can be checked for key orders or phrases when therapeutic drug levels are in the toxic range. Artificial intelligence will allow you to review guidelines for test selection based on parameters which consider the history and physical. It could also question an order's value, such as a second order for a chemistry profile when the first one was done 24 hours earlier with normal results. In the future, guidelines for test requests may also be available in the hospital information system and demand a response when requests are outside these guidelines. Diagnostic testing may be one of the first areas to be extensively involved with these guidelines.

HEMATOLOGY

The computer could be used to generate data for complete blood count, erythrocyte sedimentation rate, and the leukocyte differential count as each relates to frequency of testing, ordering physician, and turnaround time. The computer could also be used to focus on areas where the turnaround time is more critical (eg, the emergency department).

CHEMISTRY

The computer could demand pathologist approval whenever glucose tolerance tests are requested on an inpatient basis, because this test is more appropriately done on an outpatient basis. The glucose tolerance test frequently is not appropriate in the hospital setting because diet and stress can invalidate the results. Likewise lipid studies for cardiac heart disease risk evaluation are best done in an outpatient setting since the hospital environment affects the results.

QUALITY CONTROL

Demand response for the Westgard rules can make a contribution to improved accuracy and precision in the clinical laboratory. With a demand response in place the technician must make changes that yield results within the recommended quality control guidelines before proceeding with patient test samples.

INTERFACE WITH PHARMACY

If the laboratory information system interfaces with the hospital information system, pharmacy orders can be reviewed to see which patients are taking drugs whose therapeutic levels are measured in the laboratory, how long they have been taking the drugs (to determine if they have reached a steady state), and whether a dosage change has been initiated to compensate for elevated therapeutic levels. If the drug dose has not been changed, then the chart should be examined closely for a rationale for keeping the patient's drug level above the *usual* recommended therapeutic range. A laboratory information system makes it easy to screen the change in response to dosage in the majority of cases without leaving the computer monitor.

MICROBIOLOGY

Studies tracking use of antibiotic sensitivities on cultures compared with actual antibiotics ordered can be facilitated by a computer. If the patient responds clinically to treatment that does not agree with culture-associated antibiotic sensitivities then there is no need to always adhere to the culture-related sensitivities. However, it is more likely that drug resistance indicated on the culture will reflect drug resistance in the patient. If the laboratory's computer system interfaces with the pharmacy's system, you can easily find patients who are taking a drug despite a culture showing their resistance to that drug, and check the charts to verify the validity of the order.

Create a computer program to track normal urinalysis findings. A large number of urine cultures associated with normal urinalysis findings is a potential problem. No concrete conclusions can be drawn from the initial computer-generated data: closer examination of the findings is necessary, particularly since some of the workup may have been done outside of the hospital. There may have been symptoms that warranted performing the culture even with normal urinalysis results. Urine cultures are indicated in pregnant women even when there are no abnormal urinalysis findings. Guidelines need to be developed against which the computer system can generate data.

PHLEBOTOMY

Information on duplicate testing—that is, tests that are ordered separately but included in profiles ordered simultaneously—and repeated testing within a particular time period can be part of the laboratory system's software. As part of this system, certain personnel—whether clerks, nurses, or physicians—on a demand response basis could be asked if the test should still be ordered.

SEROLOGY

Use the computer to track serologic tests that yield valid results only when they are performed in duplicate. Most serologic viral studies indicate acute disease only when there is a two-tube dilution change in titer of the antibody directed against that virus. This cannot be judged with a single test. The computer can identify trends in single test orders of this nature by physicians. Realistically, these serologic tests are ordered with such infrequency that very few trends will be found, but if even a few physicians with such test ordering patterns are found and education results in better test selection, patient care will improve.

CYTOLOGY

Using the computer to identify cases that need to be rescreened based on historical data on file, such as previous abnormal Pap smear or postmenopausal bleeding, contributes to quality assurance (see Chapter 6 on cytology).

A monthly printout by individual physician of the percent of Pap smears that have endocervical cells compared with the percent with endocervical cells for the entire physician population is worthwhile. In my experience, the ensuing discussions of these types of data have produced an increase in the percent of specimens with endocervical cells, in some cases almost doubling the percent.

A laboratory information system that automatically tracks related cytologic specimens and previous biopsy specimens facilitates review of these specimens together. For example, if the results of the cytologic specimen do not match the results of the cervical biopsy specimen, the results from the cytologic specimen should be reviewed for accuracy. If the cytologic specimen was overcalled, for example, the cytology report indicated severe dysplasia whereas the review indicated mild dysplasia, the physician can be assured that a biopsy specimen showing mild dysplasia accurately reflected the disease. If the cytologic specimen is accurate and the surgical biopsy specimen shows a lesser degree of dysplasia, then in all probability the biopsy missed the pathologic area.

ANATOMIC PATHOLOGY

Software programs in anatomic pathology can provide a monthly printout on work load, turnaround time, and removal of normal tissue. If a surgeon consistently removes an excess amount of normal tissue or tissue with minimal disease that is coded as a variant of normal tissue, this trend should be tracked and referred to the appropriate committee.

SUMMARY

This chapter has focused on how the computer can be integrated into quality assurance. Not all the quality assurance indicators that can be studied more expeditiously with the computer have been included in this chapter because they encompass most of the examples in this book; instead, a few examples more readily available through many of the laboratory information systems have been highlighted. With the advent of artificial intelligence and the electronic chart the number will increase. Studies will be easier, faster, and more accurate.

The computer provides easy access to information that is useful in detecting trends and improving the quality of the laboratory's operation. Quality assurance requires ceaseless measurement. Computer software programs can do the measuring, and they are often most helpful when collecting data in areas where manual gathering of data with any frequency would be almost impossible.

Hospital-wide information systems that interface with the laboratory's information system have an increased importance in quality assurance. In the future, software programs will be designed to deal with specific quality assurance issues, yet should be flexible enough to fulfill individual laboratory's needs.

REFERENCE

1. *American Medical News.* January 12, 1990:3.

APPENDIX
CAP and JCAHO
Standards

This appendix contains selected regulatory guidelines that should be kept in mind as you create quality assurance monitors for your laboratory.

CAP STANDARD I[1]:
DIRECTOR AND PERSONNEL REQUIREMENT

Standard

The pathology service shall be directed by a physician or doctoral scientist qualified to assume professional, scientific, consultative, organizational, administrative, and educational responsibilities for the service. Generally, it is medically preferable that the director be a board certified pathologist. The director shall have sufficient authority to implement and maintain the Standards.

When a non-pathologist physician or doctoral scientist serves as director, such individual must be qualified by virtue of documented training, expertise, and experience in the areas of analytical testing offered by the laboratory. Where the functions of the laboratory so require, the services of a qualified consulting pathologist shall be retained. In all facilities where anatomic pathology services are provided, a pathologist shall perform such services.

Special function laboratories shall be directed by either a physician who is qualified to assume professional responsibility for the special function laboratory or a qualified doctoral scientist with documented training, expertise, and experience in the appropriate specific clinical discipline and area of testing.

The location, organization, or ownership of the laboratory shall not alter the requirements of this Standard, its interpretation, or its application.

Interpretation

To fulfill the duties and responsibilities as director of the pathology or medical laboratory service effectively, the director should possess a broad knowledge of clinical medicine, basic medical sciences, clinical laboratory sciences, and operations. The director should have the appropriate training and background to handle the following responsibilities:

1. The director judges the medical significance of laboratory data and communicates the interpretations of the data and related correlations to physicians.[2]
2. The director can perform anatomic pathology procedures.
3. The director provides consultation to physicians regarding the medical significance of laboratory findings.
4. The director serves as an active member of the medical staff for those facilities served.
5. The director interacts effectively with representatives of accrediting and regulatory agencies, administrative officials, the medical community, and the patient population.[2]
6. The director defines, implements, and monitors standards of performance

related to quality control, quality assurance, cost-effectiveness of the pathology service, and other ancillary laboratory testing programs.[2]

7. The director monitors all work performed in the laboratory to determine that medically reliable data are generated. The director correlates laboratory data for diagnosis and patient management.
8. The director ensures that the laboratory participates in monitoring and evaluation of quality and appropriateness of services rendered, within the context of the institution's quality assurance program, regardless of testing site(s).[3]
9. The medical director ensures that there are sufficient qualified personnel with adequate documented training experience to supervise and perform the work of the pathology laboratory.
10. The medical director sets goals and develops and allocates resources appropriate to the medical environment.[2]
11. The director effectively and efficiently administers the pathology service, including budget planning and control, with responsible financial management.[2]
12. The director provides educational direction for the medical and laboratory staff, and participates in educational programs of the institution.[2]
13. The director plans and directs research and development appropriate to the facility.[2]
14. The director selects all referral laboratories, that is, all referred specimens are sent to a laboratory that is accredited by the CAP, licensed under the Clinical Laboratories Improvement Act of 1967, or licensed by the state or federal government.
15. The director promotes a safe laboratory environment.

The medical director should ensure that appropriateness of testing, appropriate allocation of resources, correlation of laboratory data, and cost-effectiveness, in particular, are focused on in the quality assurance plan.

CAP STANDARD III[1]: QUALITY ASSURANCE

Standard

There shall be an ongoing quality assurance program designed to monitor and evaluate objectively and systematically the quality and appropriateness of the care and treatment provided to patients by the pathology service, to pursue opportunities to the patients by the pathology service, and to identify and resolve problems.

Interpretation

The pathology service should have a systematic process to monitor and evaluate the quality and appropriateness of the service's contribution to patient care and to identify and resolve problems. There should be a written description of the program that, where applicable, is integrated with the institution's quality assurance program. The director of the laboratory is responsible for assuring that such a program is implemented and that the pathology service participates in the institutional quality assurance programs that deal with patient care.

The effectiveness of the laboratory's monitoring, evaluation, and problem-solving activities must be evaluated periodically as defined by the institution's quality assurance program (where applicable).

Quality assurance applies equally to anatomic pathology, surgical pathology, autopsy pathology, and cytopathology. A written program of quality assurance surveillance designed to evaluate the accuracy of diagnoses provided may include, but is not limited to, the use of intradepartmental and extradepartmental consultation, circulation of diagnostic material (random or by case type), archival case review, correlation of histologic and cytologic material, and the periodic review of completed diagnostic reports. Program will depend on such variables as the size of the departmental staff and volume and type of diagnostic material processed.

CAP STANDARD IV[1]: QUALITY CONTROL

Standard

Each pathology service shall have a quality control system that demonstrates the reliability and medical usefulness of laboratory data.

Interpretation

A laboratory quality control system contains the following components: (1) The selection of test methods appropriate to the medical requirements of the patients served; (2) An internal quality control program that monitors accuracy and precision of laboratory performance on a daily basis. Such a program should be clearly defined in writing, provide established limits of control, prescribe appropriate actions required before acceptance or rejection of batches or analytic "runs," and be documented with evidence of understanding and implementation by the laboratory personnel; (3) An interlaboratory comparison system (proficiency testing) designed to compare laboratory performance with other laboratories; (4) An instrument maintenance program that monitors and demonstrates the proper calibration and function of equipment and instruments; (5) Appropriate feedback mechanisms to assure clinical usefulness and relevance of laboratory data; (6) An educational program for the entire laboratory staff designed to maintain or improve the quality of personnel performance; (7) An external audit or accreditation process; (8) Appropriate documentation for the foregoing.

Procedures manuals should follow a standard format and indicate sources, dates of adoption, and evidence of periodic review as described in the National Committee for Clinical Laboratory Standards' (NCCLS) *Clinical Laboratory Procedure Manuals Approved Guidelines* (Volume 4, 1984).[4]

Methods and instruments should be validated when introduced and when reintroduced following correction of an "out of control" situation. A complete quality control program should include regular preventive maintenance and appropriate function checks.

Written instructions should be available that provide, in detail, the methods for procuring, transporting, and processing appropriate specimens. There shall be a written description of the system for the timely reporting of patient data to the physician and of the safeguards taken to ensure that such data is correct.

Programs for surveillance and control of incoming material should ensure that all reagents, specimens, and materials used in the analytic process have the properties necessary for reliable performance.

The pathology service should participate regularly in the College of American Pathologists' Interlaboratory Comparison (Surveys) Program based on the type of testing the laboratory regularly provides.

If any survey results are unsatisfactory according to the criteria established by the Surveys program, the cause of the unsatisfactory result should be investigated and the problem resolved. The findings of the investigation and the corrective measures instituted should be recorded, dated, and signed by the responsible technologist or supervisor and by the director of laboratories.

THE JCAHO REGULATION MECHANISMS

The JCAHO regulation mechanisms are somewhat similar to those of the CAP but they bear repeating.[3] What I believe are the key regulatory statements applicable to quality assurance appear below; the asterisked items are particularly important in the accreditation decision process.

PA.1.2.6 A pathologist has an active role in the in-service educational programs of the pathology service and the hospital and participates in medical staff functions as required.

*PA.1.2.7 Within the hospital's overall quality assurance program, the director of the pathology and medical laboratory services assures that the department/service participates in the monitoring and evaluation of the quality and appropriateness of services provided.

PA.1.4.2 Continuing education programs are based at least in part on the findings of the monitoring and evaluation of quality of laboratory services provided and on the principles of laboratory safety.

PA.2.1 Provision is made, either on the premises or in a reference laboratory, for the prompt performance of adequate examinations in the fields of anatomic pathology, hematology, chemistry, microbiology, clinical microscopy, parasitology, immunohematology, serology, virology, and, as it relates to the pathology and medical laboratory services, nuclear medicine. [Note how comprehensive this statement is and that promptness is important.]

*PA.2.3.4 Special precautions, including compliance with pertinent requirements of the "Infection Control" and the "Plant, Technology, and Safety Management" chapters of this *Manual*, are taken to avoid unnecessary physical, chemical and biological hazards in the pathology and medical laboratory services.

PA.3.1.2 Requests for examinations of surgical specimens contain a concise statement of the reason for the examination.

PA.3.3 Communication systems within the pathology and medical laboratory services and between it and other departments/services efficiently accomplish both the urgent and the regular transfer of information.

PA.3.3.3 Criteria are established for the immediate notification of the practitioner responsible for the care of the patient when critical limits of specified test results are exceeded.

PA.3.4 There is assurance of the direct transfer of information between the pathologist performing an operating-room consultation, with or without a "frozen section," and the operating surgeon.

PA.3.4.1 When it is necessary to perform such a consultation at a laboratory located outside the hospital, care is taken not to subject the patient to any undue hazards, such as excessive general anesthesia, while awaiting the results of the tissue examination.

PA.3.4.2 When operating-room consultations by a pathologist are not available within the facility, the medical staff establishes criteria for circumstances under which it is preferable to transfer the patient to a hospital where such service is provided.

PA.4.1.1 The director of the pathology and medical laboratory services is responsible for all hospital laboratory reports.

PA.4.2 The pathologist is responsible for the preparation of a descriptive diagnostic report of gross specimens received and autopsies performed.

PA.4.2.1 Diagnosis made from surgical specimens and necropsies are expressed in acceptable terminology of a recognized disease indexed for retrieval.

PA.4.2.2 The degree of detail recorded in the microscopic evaluation is the responsibility of the examining pathologist, but in all cases when a microscopic evaluation is performed, any diagnosis rendered on the tissue is based on those findings.

PA.4.3.1 The hospital assures that the reports are filed promptly in the patient's medical record.

*PA.5 Quality control systems and measures of the pathology and medical laboratory services are designed to assure the medical reliability of laboratory data.

*PA.5.2 There is a documented quality control program in effect for each section of the pathology and medical laboratory services.

*PA.5.3.4 Daily surveillance of results by the director or appropriate supervisor.

PA.5.3.4.1 Surveillance includes results of tests ordered and reported through the transmission of information between the laboratory and nurses' stations (including direct computer feed), as well as tests performed on an emergency basis outside of regularly scheduled laboratory staffing periods.

*PA.5.3.5 Documentation of remedial action taken for detected deficiencies/defects identified through quality control measures or authorized inspections.

*PA.5.3.16 Review of the performance of personnel on all laboratory work shifts on a regular basis by the pathologist or appropriate laboratory supervisor.

PA.6.1.1.3 Medical staff, in consultation with the pathologist, decides the exceptions to sending specimens removed during a surgical procedure to the laboratory.

PA.6.3.1 Clinical laboratory services required by the medical staff are available at all times from sources internal or external to the hospital.

PA.6.3.2.1 In establishing the necessity for and extent of routine admission laboratory studies, cost-benefit factors are considered.

PA.6.3.3 The director of the pathology and medical laboratory services defines for the medical staff the guidelines for requesting and receiving test results on an emergency or stat basis.

PA.7 As part of the hospital's quality assurance program, the quality and appropriateness of pathology and medical laboratory services are monitored and evaluated in accordance with standard QA.3 and Required Characteristics QA.3.1 through QA.3.2.8 in the "Quality Assurance" chapter [*JCAHO Manual*].

*PA.7.1 The physician director of the pathology and medical laboratory department/service is responsible for implementing the monitoring and evaluation process.

PA.7.1.1 The department/service collaborates with the medical staff in
PA.7.1.1.1 the identification of the important aspects of care for the department/service;
PA.7.1.1.2 the identification of the indicators used to monitor and evaluate the quality and appropriateness of the important aspects of care; and
PA.7.1.1.3 the evaluation of the quality and appropriateness of care.

*PA.7.2. When an outside source(s) provides pathology and medical laboratory services, or when there is no designated pathology and medical laboratory department/service, the medical staff is responsible for implementing the monitoring and evaluation process.

*QA.3.1. There is a planned, systematic, and ongoing process for monitoring, evaluating, and improving the quality and appropriateness of care provided to patients.

QA.3.1.1. This process is designed to effectively utilize quality assurance resources to
QA.3.1.1.1 identify and take opportunities to make important improvements in patient care; and
QA.3.1.1.2 identify and correct problems that have the greatest (or an important) effect on patient care.

QA.3.1.2 The monitoring process is designed to identify
QA.3.1.2.1 patterns or trends in care that warrant evaluation; and/or
QA.3.1.2.2 important single clinical events in the process or outcome of care that also warrant evaluation.

QA.3.1.3 The evaluation is designed to
QA.3.1.3.1 determine the presence or absence of an opportunity to improve, or a problem in the quality and/or appropriateness of care; and
QA.3.1.3.2 determine how to improve care or correct the problem.

*QA.3.2 The monitoring and evaluation process has the characteristics described in Required Characteristics QA.3.2.1 through QA.3.2.8.

*QA.3.2.1 Those aspects of care that are most important to the health and safety of the patients served are identified.
QA.3.2.1.1 These important aspects of care are those that
QA.3.2.1.1.1 occur frequently or affect large numbers of patients;
QA.3.2.1.1.2 place patients at risk of serious consequences or deprivation of substantial benefit when
QA.3.2.1.1.2.1 the care is not provided correctly; or
QA.3.2.1.1.2.2 the care is not provided when indicated; or
QA.3.2.1.1.2.3 the care is provided when not indicated; and/or
QA.3.2.1.1.3 tend to produce problems for patients or staff.

*QA.3.2.2 Indicators are identified to monitor the quality and appropriateness of important aspects of care.
QA.3.2.2.1 The indicators are related to the quality and/or appropriateness of care and may include clinical criteria (sometimes called "standards, guidelines or parameters of care or practice").
QA.3.2.2.1.1 These indicators are
QA.3.2.2.1.1.1 objective;
QA.3.2.2.1.1.2 measurable; and
QA.3.2.2.1.1.3 based on current knowledge and clinical experience.
QA.3.2.2.1.2 These indicators reflect structures of care (for example, resources), processes of care (for example, procedures, techniques), or outcomes of care (for example, complication rates).

*QA.3.2.3 Data are collected for each indicator.
QA.3.2.3.1 The frequency of data collection for each indicator and the sampling of events or activities are related to
QA.3.2.3.1.1 the frequency of the event or activity monitored;
QA.3.2.3.1.2 the significance of the event or activity monitored; and
QA.3.2.3.1.3 the extent to which the important aspect of care monitored by the indicator has been demonstrated to be problem-free.

*QA.3.2.4 The data collected for each indicator are organized so that situations in which an evaluation of the quality of appropriateness of care is indicated are readily identified.
QA.3.2.4.1 Such evaluations are prompted by
QA.3.2.4.1.1 important single clinical events; and

QA.3.2.4.1.2 patterns of care or outcomes that are at variance with predetermined levels of care or outcomes (sometimes called "thresholds for evaluation").

QA.3.2.5 When initiated, the evaluation of an important aspect of care

*QA.3.2.5.1 includes analysis of trends and patterns in the data collected on the indicators;

*QA.3.2.5.2 includes review by peers when analysis of the care provided by a practitioner is undertaken; and

*QA.3.2.5.3 identifies opportunities to improve, or problems in, the quality and/or appropriateness of care.

*QA.3.2.6 When an important opportunity to improve, or problem in, the quality and/or appropriateness of care is identified,

*QA.3.2.6.1 action is taken to improve the care or to correct the problem; and

*QA.3.2.6.2 the effectiveness of the action taken is assessed through continued monitoring of the care.

QA.3.2.7 The findings, conclusions, recommendations, actions taken, and results of the actions taken are

*QA.3.2.7.1 documented; and

*QA.3.2.7.2 reported through established channels.

*QA.3.2.8 As part of the annual appraisal of the hospital's quality assurance program, the effectiveness of the monitoring and evaluation process is assessed.

REFERENCES

1. *Standards for Laboratory Accreditation.* Skokie, Ill: College of American Pathologists; 1988. (Reprinted with permission from the College of American Pathologists, Northfield, Ill.)

2. Criteria for the clinical laboratory director. *College of American Pathologists Policies and Guidelines Manual.* Skokie, Ill: College of American Pathologists; 1987. Appendix O.

3. Pathology and medical laboratory services. *Accreditation Manual for Hospitals, 1991.* Oak Brook Terrace, Ill: Joint Commission on Accreditation of Healthcare Organizations; 1990:141–163, 219–221. (© 1990 by the Joint Commission on Accreditation of Healthcare Organizations, Oak Brook Terrace, Ill. Reprinted with permission.)

4. Bender JL, Bettner B, Blank CH, Hassemer D, Moran JJ, Stevens JE. *Clinical Laboratory Procedure Manuals.* Villanova, Pa: National Committee for Clinical Laboratory Standards; 1984;4.

Index

Numbers in **boldface** refer to pages on which figures appear.

L

Labeling specimens, 38, 118
Laboratory manager, 6
Leadership skills, styles, 6–7
Legibility, 114, 129
Letter
  on multiple chemistry profile orders,
    89
  on overordering of tests, **101**
  regarding inadequate information, **40**
  for standard test orders, **92–93**
Leukocyte differential count, 84–86
Liability, 143
Liver testing, 95

M

Medical director, 1–5
Medical knowledge, 81–82
Medical technology, 82–84
Medisgroups, 82
Meetings
  minutes of, 9
  staff, 2
Methodology, 18–32
Microbiology, 122–123, 163
Microscopic findings, 46
  sampling errors, 41
Misdiagnosis, 42–43, **43**, 70
Mislabeling, 38
Monitoring, 11, 14
  activity calendar, 1–3, 7, **12**
  approaches to, 21
  frozen sections, 41–44
  JCAHO 10-step process for, **17**
  leukocyte counts, 86
  outcome-related, 21, 28–29, 105–106
Mortality rates, 59–60
Mortality review report, 63–65

N

Negligence, 143–145
Newsletters, 2

Nursing unit rounds, 132–133

O

Objectives, 10
  general vs specific, 25
  overall, 10, 13
  primary, 10
  technical vs artistic, 25
Objectivity, 19
Observations, 21–22
Ongoing audits, 24–25
Outcome-related monitors, 21, 28–29,
    105–106
Ova testing, 99–100

P

Parasite testing, 99–100
Patient
  availability, 116–117
  care, 28–29
  characteristics, 82
  focus, 25–26
  identification, 117
  name, 69
  preparation, 117–118
  satisfaction surveys, 134–135, 153–
    154, **155**
Peer review, 47–48, 83, 146
Periodic review, 3–4, 7
Periodic summary report, 56, **56**
Peripheral testing, 132
Pharmacy interface, 162
Phlebotomy, 163
  drawings, 116
  observations, 119, 121
  patient survey on, 153–154, **155**
  quality assurance check list for, **120–
    121**
Physician
  proficiency, 81
  values, 81
  office survey, 129, 154, **156**

Platelet counts, 87, 98
Postdischarge results, 131–132
Practice, group vs solo, 36
Presentations, committee, conference, 53–54
Problem log, **152**
Procedures, appropriateness of, 56–57
Process review, 21
Proficiency testing, 55–56
Prospective audits, 20, 42
Prothrombin time, 87, 99
    complex concentrates, 98

Q

Q Probes, 43, 137–138
Quality assurance
    in anatomic pathology, 33–67
    CAP standard for, 168–169
    chairperson's role, 3, **3**, 6-8
    in commercial lab, 150–158
    implementation of, 2–3, **3**
    and laboratory manager, 6
    medical director's role in, 1–5
    parts of, 10–13
    plan, 9–17, 150–151
    sample, 13–16
Quality control, 162
    CAP standard for, 169–170
    for histopathology, 46–47, **47**
Quality indicators, 2, 19, 20, 29
    abnormal test results and, 94–95
    blood tests and, 87, 96–99
    carcinoembryonic antigen determinations and, 97
    cerebral spinal fluid cultures and, 103
    chemistry profiles and, 87–89
    critical results and, 93–94
    daily test orders and, 91
    difficile toxins and, 103
    glucose tolerance tests and, 100
    hematuria response and, 94–95
    incorrect test requests and, 100
    leukocyte differential count and, 84–86

measuring drug therapeutic levels and, 96
miscellaneous tests and, 103–104,
number of tests and, 101–102, **101**
ova and parasite testing and, 99–100
preoperative electrolyte testing and, 91
prothrombin, partial thromboplastin times and, 87
response to therapeutic drug levels and, 91, 93
selection of, 113
standard test orders and, 90–91
thyroid tests and, 100–101
urine cultures and, 102
Questionnaires, 22–23

R

Random sampling, 23, 24–25
Realistic criteria, 27–28
Red blood cells, 97
Reporting results, 127–129
Request slip, 68–69
Rescreening, 70–72, **71–72**
Response
    to critical results, 93–94
    to hematuria, 94–95
    to therapeutic drug levels, 91, 93
Responsibility, 11, 13
Retrospective audits, 20
Review
    number of cases, 50–52, **52**
    outcome, 21
    periodic, 3–4
    process, 21
    structural, 21
    timing of, 52
Rh immune globulins, 98
Risk management, 142–147
Risk rescreening factors, **71**

S

Safe topics, 11, 13